School's Out

School's Out

Gay and Lesbian Teachers in the Classroom

Catherine Connell

UNIVERSITY OF CALIFORNIA PRESS

University of California Press, one of the most distinguished university presses in the United States, enriches
lives around the world by advancing scholarship in the
humanities, social sciences, and natural sciences. Its
activities are supported by the UC Press Foundation and
by philanthropic contributions from individuals and
institutions. For more information, visit www.ucpress.edu.

University of California Press
Oakland, California

© 2015 by The Regents of the University of California

Library of Congress Cataloging-in-Publication Data

Connell, Catherine, 1980–.
    School's out : gay and lesbian teachers in the
classroom / Catherine Connell.
        p. cm.
    Includes bibliographical references and index.
    ISBN 978-0-520-27822-6 (cloth : alk. paper)
    ISBN 978-0-520-27823-3 (pbk. : alk. paper)
    ISBN 978-0-520-95980-4 (ebook)
    1. Homosexuality and education.   2. Sexual
minorities—Education.   3. Gender identity.   I. Title.
    LC192.6.C68   2015
    371.1008664—dc23   2014014443

Manufactured in the United States of America

24 23 22 21 20 19 18 17 16 15
10 9 8 7 6 5 4 3 2 1

In keeping with a commitment to support environmen-
tally responsible and sustainable printing practices, UC
Press has printed this book on Natures Natural, a fiber
that contains 30% post-consumer waste and meets the
minimum requirements of ANSI/NISO Z39.48–1992 (R 1997)
(*Permanence of Paper*).

For Emily

CONTENTS

TABLES

ACKNOWLEDGMENTS

I am so grateful to the teachers, administrators, and advocates who opened their hearts, their homes, and their classrooms to me. Their willingness to examine and reveal their experiences and deepest held beliefs made this book possible. I was also incredibly fortunate to have Christine Williams as a mentor from the original stirrings of this project to the final edits; her endless energy, attention, and care for this project were vital to this book's production.

At the University of Texas, Javier Auyero, Ben Carrington, Dana Cloud, Sinikka Elliot, Gloria Gonzalez-Lopez, Sharmila Rudrappa, Deb Umberson, Michael Young, and Wei-Hsin Yu provided crucial feedback and support. My senior colleagues at Boston University, including Nancy Ammerman, Emily Barman, Julian Go, Nazli Kibria, and Laurel Smith-Doerr, were helpful for navigating the process of translating my dissertation research into a book project. Especially important at BU were my colleagues in the Junior Faculty Working Group—Nicole Aschoff, Ruha Benjamin, Japonica Brown-Saracino, Ashley

Mears, and Sigrun Olafsdottir—along with our colleagues from Harvard, Tufts, and Northeastern—Bart Bonikowski, Ryan Cetner, and Liza Weinstein. The BU Gender and Sexualities Studies group also pushed me to incorporate theoretical insights from across disciplines, and I am thankful for their inspiration. Thanks also to the members of BU's Turtulia, a cross-disciplinary junior faculty working group, for giving feedback on an early draft of chapter 4. I am grateful to my ambitious and brilliant students in the Fall 2013 Sexualities Seminar, whose incisive—and often tough!—critiques of sociology pushed me to make this book better. Thank you to all of my students over the years, who helped me clarify my contribution and provided additional insight.

The research for this book was generously supported by a number of fellowships and awards, including the Martin P. Levine Memorial Dissertation Scholarship from the American Sociological Association's Section on Sexualities, the UT Austin Women's and Gender Studies Dissertation Award, and the Stanford Lyman Memorial Scholarship from the Mid-South Sociological Association. I am grateful to have had the opportunity to attend the National Sexuality Resource Center's Summer Institute in 2008. There, I spent three weeks working with and learning from sexualities scholars from across the country and across disciplines. In particular, Jessica Fields provided discerning and insightful feedback on my fellowship applications during that time that helped me secure the above awards.

I would also like to thank Naomi Schneider and Christopher Lura for their editorial guidance throughout the book revision process. Thank you to Jessica Fields, Jennifer Pierce, and Christine Williams for reading and providing substantive feedback on the entire manuscript—their comments improved the book beyond measure. The detailed and brilliant editorial suggestions of Rebecca Steinetz were priceless. Portions of chapter 4 of this book appear in the journal *Sexuality Research and Social Policy* (vol. 9, no. 2: 169–77). I thank the editor and anonymous reviewers of *SRSP* for their critique. An abbreviated version of this book's argument appears in the chapter "Reconsidering the Workplace Closet: The Experiences of Gay and Lesbian Teachers," in *Sexual Orientation at Work: Contemporary Issues and Perceptions,* edited by Fiona Colgan and Nick Rumens, who were also helpful in their feedback.

Thank you to Elizabeth Marcellino-Boisvert and the group for supporting me through the emotional highs and lows of writing this book. Thanks also to Emily Belanger for the encouragement and enthusiasm over many an appetizer. Thank you to the Fuel America coffee shop and staff for allowing me to write much of this book while lingering over coffee and sandwiches! Stacy Wagner and Stephanie Kinnear, Lisa Storer, Courtney Cogburn, Caitlin Vanderbilt, and the Queertastiks family, especially Joanna and Toshia (and Ziv!) Caravita, Erika Nuñez, and Sonya Sowerby, I thank for their friendship, support, and much-needed moments of levity throughout the process! Stacy and Steph, thanks especially for hosting me for a month during my research trip to California and for always being supportive— and emphatically cheesy—over the past decade. Sarah Murray, Corinne Reczek, Megan Reid, and Angela Stroud—I could not have written this without your guidance and support. Corinne, Megan, and Angela were my graduate school comrades, my first writing group, and will always be my sociological home base. Corinne and Sarah worked alongside me in the Cambridge Public Library almost every day for an entire summer and put in still *more* hours processing the experience with me most evenings. Megan kept me grounded, encouraged, and taken care of throughout the entire experience. Finally, thanks to my family and especially, my sister Emily, who inspired this project and inspires me every day to be a better teacher, scholar, educator, activist, and all-around person.

CHAPTER ONE

Pride and Professionalism

The Dilemmas of Gay and Lesbian Teachers

At seven o'clock on a June morning in 2008, I gathered with a group of Los Angeles–area public school teachers and students to march in the West Hollywood LGBT Pride Parade.[1] While conducting research for this book, I had met the members of an advocacy group for teachers and administrators in LA public schools, and they had invited me to join them in marching with several local high school Gay Straight Alliance (GSA) members and their advisers. I arrived at our designated parade lineup position to find a small group of students and teachers milling around, eating doughnuts and chatting in the early morning sun. As more of our marchers arrived, a GSA adviser brought over poster board and markers and set us to work making signs for the march. Students and teachers worked side by side, writing slogans such as "Rainbow Pride," "I Teach Justice," and "Support Gay Teachers & Students." Two students from a high school in Watts, a low-income Los Angeles neighborhood, were attending Pride festivities for the first time and proudly posed for a picture with their spray-painted "Gays in the Hood" poster.

After a couple of hours of restless waiting, the march finally began. Everyone seemed a little nervous, and we smiled tentatively at each other as we lined up to march. But when we rounded the first corner and came into view of the waiting crowd, we were hit with a roar of applause and whistles. Spectators jumped off the curb to hug and high-five us, shouting, "We love gay teachers!" and "Thank you for the hard work you are doing!" As we marched on, this enthusiastic response changed the teachers and students around me. Their nervousness dissipated, and they took longer strides, held their heads high, and waved their signs in the air with beaming smiles.

A few exuberant miles later, we finished the parade route. June, a white lesbian high school teacher who had marched, marveled, "Wasn't that incredible? I feel so proud of the work I'm doing now."[2] She clasped my shoulder and pointed to a group of students crying and hugging a few feet away. "These kids," she declared, with emotion in her voice, "they are from Crenshaw [another low-income Los Angeles neighborhood], and they've never been to a Pride parade before. They've never seen any kind of support for gay people before. They told me they are just overwhelmed by the impact of so much support, and I gotta say—I am, too! Today I am so proud. Proud to be a gay teacher." As I drove away a few minutes later, I realized that I, too, had been affected by the emotional charge of the experience. I had marched in Pride parades before, but I'd never felt the magnitude of crowd enthusiasm that our group had garnered. The adrenaline, emotion, and feeling that I was part of something important stayed with me through the day.

A few days after the march, I went to see June at work. Her exuberance and pride in being an openly lesbian teacher seemed to have faded since the heady experience of the march. Instead, she was preoccupied with a recent classroom incident. During a discussion of *The Adventures of Huckleberry Finn,* a student had snickered loudly, "Huck Finn was a fucking faggot!" June's co-teacher, who was leading the lesson, had ignored the crack and continued teaching, even though June was convinced she had heard it. June was conflicted about her own response. She explained, "If [my students] know I'm gay and I'm sitting here and allowing someone to [ignore gay slurs]? Silence is complicity, and I'm not going to allow that to happen ... in the future, anyway. And I think that as I become more comfortable and confident in my role as a 'gay teacher' here that I will be more demonstrative about it. But then again, at what cost?" Later in our conversation, however, June shifted direction and rejected the label of "gay teacher," saying that she wanted students and coworkers to think of her as a "teacher who happens to be gay." "I'm not a 'gay teacher,'" she reiterated, shaking her head, "I'm a teacher who is gay." Despite her pride in the "gay teacher" label at the parade, June was now markedly more uneasy and distanced herself from the term.

June's conflicting statements suggest ambivalence about commingling sexual and professional identities. There was clearly something about the label "gay teacher" that made her proud and uncomfortable at the same time. At the Pride parade, she embraced the label because she saw herself as a role model to the students there, particularly to those from low-income, mostly Black and Latino neighborhoods. In school, she asserted distance from the label, insisting that her professional identity was separate from and more of a priority than her sexual identity. In this study of gay and lesbian teachers, I argue that the tension June experienced is driven by a fundamental incompatibility between the demands of contemporary LGBT politics, which center on the ethos of gay pride, and the norms of teaching professionalism, which expect teachers (gay and lesbian teachers in particular) to be cautious and self-disciplining about their personal—and sexual—lives. To be a professional in today's teaching context entails constant self-monitoring for any possible breach of propriety. For historical reasons that I will explain in the next chapter, any mention of homosexuality is especially suspect. Meanwhile, since the 1960s, the prevailing politics of gay pride have increasingly demanded that its constituents be "out and proud" in all contexts. Gay and lesbian teachers like June are as subject to this expectation as anyone else. Indeed, they face added pressure from those who argue that out teachers are important role models for LGBT and questioning students. The resulting clash between pride and professionalism significantly influences how they experience their workplaces, communities, and identities.

We are in a pivotal moment in the history of gay rights. Same-sex desire, once the "love that dare not speak its name," is increasingly accepted, celebrated, even considered mundane in many parts of the United States and, indeed, the world.[3] Yet antigay discrimination and harassment, running the gamut from subtle insults to lethal violence, persist, even in this new "gay-friendly" era. Social scientists and the general public alike are scratching their heads at this paradox. Are we really, as some would say, becoming "postgay"? If so, what does that mean? This book offers much-needed answers to such questions. Analyzing the experiences of gay and lesbian teachers, who work in one of the remaining strongholds of explicit homophobia, makes it clear that the exuberance of the postgay claim is premature.[4] But the problem goes farther than that. It turns out that the "postgay" ideology, which celebrates the assimilation and normalization of LGBTs, can be just as harmful to gay and lesbian teachers as the antigay culture of the schools where they work. Teachers are doubly constrained, on the one hand by the norms of teaching professionalism and on the other by the identity demands of the gay rights movement. This should be a warning to those of us who want to pursue sexual justice in workplaces and schools.

The clashing expectations of pride and professionalism force gay and lesbian teachers into a no-win struggle between their political and professional obligations. Some teachers respond to these clashing expectations by attempting to maintain a strict distinction between their identities as teachers and as gay or lesbian adults, in effect splitting into different selves whose emergence depends on their proximity to the classroom. Others try to knit together these identities into a cohesive whole. Neither strategy fully resolves the fundamental pride/professionalism dialectic, with the result that some quit teaching altogether. This book traces each of these paths and their consequences, as I argue that teachers will not be able to reconcile their political and professional selves until we systematically challenge the ideology that upholds the tensions between pride and professionalism.

While all gay and lesbian teachers must contend with this ideological conflict, its effect on their teaching experiences varies. In this book, I focus on these variations, with a particular emphasis on how attention to place, race, and gender performance helps us understand them. To do so, I draw on in-depth interviews and observations of a range of gay and lesbian teachers in California and Texas, states similar in size and demographics but starkly different with regard to gay-friendly law and policy. By considering the stories of teachers in different legal climates and school environments, with different relationships to race and gender privilege, this book sheds light not only on consistent experiences with the ideological tensions of pride and professionalism but also on important differences that demonstrate how sexuality intersects with other dimensions of privilege and oppression.

SEXUALITY AND POWER

A sociological perspective on sexuality is crucial to understanding the experience of gay and lesbian teachers. While sexuality is often treated as a biological given, sociologists tend to approach it as a socially constructed phenomenon. From this perspective, sexuality is not merely a natural drive or orientation but a cultural artifact that reflects the social conditions of any given historical moment. Early sociologists of sexuality drew on labeling theory to make sense of sexual identity. In "The Homosexual Role," for example, Mary McIntosh argued that the label of "homosexual" did not capture meaningful distinctions in sexual behavior but rather was a selectively applied mechanism of social control.[5] The study of sexuality has drawn heavily on the metaphor of sexual scripts, which, like theater or film scripts, tell (social) actors what they should say, do, and even feel when it comes to sex. John Gagnon and William Simon, the architects of sexual scripting theory, have gone so far as to argue that no one act or desire is inherently sexual: rather, acts and desires come to be defined as such through the process of sexual scripting, which defines not only what sex *is* but also what it *should* be.[6]

Gay and lesbian teachers are subject to two contrasting scripts—one sexual, the other occupational. Contemporary scripts for gay and lesbian identity center sexual identity as the most important and essential component of the self. According to this script, gays and lesbians are supposed to feel united with all other LGBT individuals under the banner of gay pride. Coming out, which itself follows scripted conventions, is paramount.[7] The guiding script for teachers, as I will show, comes into direct contradiction with this. Teachers are expected to perform a sexually neutral and gender-normative self in the classroom—and beyond. How teachers juggle these contradictory scripts is the subject of this book.

While labeling and scripting theories were instrumental in establishing the social construction of sex, they are often inadequate for explaining how and why certain labels or scripts come to hold greater cultural sway than others.[8] Since the 1990s, the infusion of queer theory into the sociology of sexuality has helped to explain the emergence and relative intractability of certain scripts.[9] First, queer theory's claim that sexual distinctions lie at the heart of modern systems of power helps to account for the emergence of sexual scripts, which are instruments of power that organize and regulate sexual behavior and sort us into hierarchies. Gayle Rubin argues that these hierarchies are organized into a charmed circle of "good" sex (for example, married, monogamous, procreative, vanilla) and the outer limits of "bad" sex (for example, homosexual, casual, commercial, kinky).[10] Second, the emphasis on *discourse* in queer theory, particularly in the work of Michel Foucault, helps to explain the diffusion of sexual scripts, including the validation of some and the marginalization of others. Like McIntosh, Foucault challenged prevailing ideas about the essential nature of sex and sexuality. In particular, he rejected the *repressive hypothesis*,[11] or the belief that sex is a natural and driving human force that must be repressed and controlled for the good of society. Instead, he argued that in the transition from premodern societies to modernity people gave increasing power to sex, first through religious and later through scientific and medical discourse. A discourse is a formalized way of understanding a particular phenomenon or behavior that circulates and comes to be taken for granted as "truth." Religious, medical, and scientific discourses transformed sexual behaviors like sodomy from mere acts to markers of identity, that is, markers of a person's essential self. Religious practices like confession, followed later by the scientific study of sex, transformed it from something we do to *who we are*.

Foucault and subsequent queer theorists like Eve Sedgwick noticed that discursive formations tend to develop binaries.[12] Binary logics—either/or understandings of the world—eliminate nuance and uncertainty. They also create power distinctions, where one side of a binary is deemed right/good/healthy, the other wrong/bad/sick. Sexual discourses created such binaries for sexual behavior, the most significant of which was the binary distinction between heterosexual and homosexual. For queer theorists, what is especially pernicious about these sexual binaries is how they control and limit people. What's worse, they are enforced not only externally but internally: we use them to interpret ourselves and then behave accordingly. The ability to regulate from within as well as without is what makes discourse such a potent—and dangerous—instrument of power. A significant task of queer theory, then, has been to deconstruct discourses as mediums of power and control.

The application of queer theory in sociology has shifted how we study and understand sexuality. Sociologists of sexuality who draw on queer theory denaturalize sexual binaries by focusing on the fluidity, ambiguity, and contradictions of people's lived experiences of sex and sexuality.[13] Queer theory also helps us understand the limits of sexual identity politics as a social movement frame. For example, Steven Epstein has used queer theory to critique the contemporary rights-based model of LGBT organizing, which defines its members as a distinct class or quasi-ethnic constituency.[14] This organizing strategy, while effective, reinforces the very homo/hetero binary that created sexual inequalities in the first place. It also creates pressures to pledge allegiance to one's sexual identity over other identities, such as those of race, class, or gender.

In this book, I draw on these insights to make sense of the polarizing influences of teaching professionalism and gay pride. Teaching professionalism demands a classroom presentation of sexual neutrality, which I will argue is actually not neutral at all but rather a sexually *normative* presentation of self. At the same time, gay pride demands an "out and proud" ethos that is at odds with the realities of most gay and lesbian teachers. Ultimately, this binary opposition—you can be professional or proud—not only hinders the careers of gay and lesbian teachers but masks the messier nature of their actual lives. Further, it hinders teaching and learning about sexuality in the context of schools and obscures the operation of sexuality in this and other professional spaces.

GENDERED SEXUALITIES

While this book focuses on sexual identity, gender is intimately interwoven with the experience of sexuality. Where popular narratives base gender in the bedrock of birth-assigned sex, sociologists usually think of gender as a thoroughly social accomplishment.[15] First articulated by Candace West and Don Zimmerman, "doing gender" refers to the way gender is both created and heavily policed in everyday interactions, and views gender as a highly routinized accomplishment rather than a biological essence.[16] Through the interactive process, we learn what is expected of us as men and women, and we modify our bodies, speech, comportment, and self-concept accordingly. Those who attempt to transgress the boundaries established through interaction are held accountable. For example, if a man fails to do masculinity appropriately for any given social situation, he may be socially sanctioned with hostile stares, laughter, or aggression.

Doing gender has remained the most popular explanation of gender in contemporary sociology since it emerged three decades ago, but more recent reexaminations suggest some limitations. Barbara Risman argues that the theory's near ubiquity in the sociological literature has diluted its initial value as an explicitly feminist theory of gender.[17] Further, although West and Zimmerman's original formulation offered the promise of transforming gender, the theory has, in practice, been used almost exclusively to demonstrate the intractability of the gender order and gender inequality.[18] As a result, some feminist sociologists have proposed new conceptual frameworks intended to capture more precisely possible challenges to that gender order, including the concepts of undoing and redoing gender. Barbara Risman and Francine Deutsch both suggest the term *undoing gender* to refer to moments when the mechanisms that sustain the doing gender order are challenged. Through the continued undoing of gender, some argue, we can do away with binary gender divisions entirely.[19] Others add that the visibility and persistence of transgender, intersex, and genderqueer people and politics will ultimately undo gender by challenging the institutional and interactional mechanisms that maintain gender (and sex) as binary.[20] In response, West and Zimmerman question whether gender can ever truly be undone.[21] They argue that the accountability structures that uphold gender distinctions might be *redone* to support a more egalitarian version of gender but that gender will never disappear entirely.

Along with theories of doing, undoing, and redoing gender, sociologists of gender draw on Judith Butler's theory of gender performativity. Like West and Zimmerman's doing gender, Butler's gender performativity deconstructs the assumed coherence between sex, gender, and sexuality. Butler argues that each of these is constructed on "stylized acts"; she holds that there is no ontological reality to sex or gender, only "styles of the flesh."[22] Whereas the theory of doing gender focuses on the production of *accountability structures*, gender performativity theory emphasizes the production of *discourse*. Despite these fine-grained differences, the two theories ultimately make similar arguments from different disciplinary positions and with different analytical foci.

My analysis applies the insights of doing, undoing, and redoing gender theories, as well as gender performativity theory, to the experiences of gay and lesbian teachers. They each emphasize the omnipresence of gendered expectations; even when individuals transgress gender norms, they do so within the context of those very norms, putting themselves at the risk of being found wanting. This is not to say that gender is necessarily performed with conscious purpose; indeed, as I will show, gender transgression can feel as natural and innate to one person as gender conformity does to another. Rather, I mean to emphasize that gay and lesbian teachers must contend with these accountability structures when making decisions about revealing their sexual identity in the workplace. The teachers I interviewed were often keen observers of their own gendered embodiments and considered how things like voice register, mannerisms, clothing, and hairstyle signaled either conformity or resistance to the gender order. In keeping with emerging theories of undoing and redoing gender, I pay particular attention to how gay and lesbian teachers' experiences are marked both by moments of gender binary retrenchment and by moments that challenge that binary.

Performing gender and performing sexuality are closely intertwined processes. Homosexuality and gender non-normativity were discursively linked in the medical and scientific "discovery" of homosexuality, so much so that early theories of homosexuality argued that gender confusion, not sexual desire, drove individuals to homosexual behavior. In this model, homosexuals were "inverts" whose gender confusion could be corrected through medical and psychiatric intervention.[23] A legacy of this history is the continued conflation of gender performance and sexual identity. To do gender correctly is to perform not only ideal masculinity or femininity but also heterosexuality. When people do gender "incorrectly," the common response is still to label them gay or lesbian, regardless of their sexual identity, behavior, or desire. The experience of being a gay or lesbian teacher, then, is mitigated by the process of doing gender, which affects their control over disclosing or not disclosing their sexual identity to administrators, fellow teachers, students, and parents. Teachers who do not want to disclose their sexual identity but perform gender in a way that suggests homosexuality find themselves in a *glass closet*, where they are inadvertently exposed as gay or lesbian.[24] Conversely, gay and lesbian teachers who do gender normatively are presumed heterosexual until proven otherwise. While this gives them more control over sexual identity disclosure, it also means that if they want to be openly gay or lesbian they must continually come out and contend with any attendant surprise, skepticism, and discomfort. Throughout the book, I pay particular attention to how this interplay between sexuality and gender organizes the day-to-day experiences of gay and lesbian teachers.

THE INTERSECTION OF SEXUALITY, GENDER, RACE, AND CLASS

As I have argued above, it is virtually impossible to understand the social construction of sexuality without considering the social construction of gender, but one cannot adequately theorize either without also attending to the social construction of race and class. Not only are sexualities gendered and genders sexualized, but each is also raced and classed. The interactive effects of race, class, gender, and sexuality are the focus of intersectionality theory.[25] Women of color feminists developed intersectionality in response to feminism's overemphasis on gender (to the exclusion of race and class) and disproportionate focus on issues important to white middle-class women.[26] As a model of conceptualizing identity and inequality, intersectionality does more than just tack race, class, and sexuality onto theories of gender inequality: it focuses explicitly on the intersections of these inequalities and how those intersections produce distinct social experiences.[27]

Intersectional approaches hold that race, class, gender, sexuality, and all other systems of inequality are indivisible from each other. Patricia Hill Collins argues that, in fact, each system of oppression relies on the others to maintain itself.[28] Collins moves away from additive or multiplicative ways of conceptualizing inequality to theorize inequalities as mutually dependent axes within a matrix of domination. This model rejects "either/ or" and substitutes a "both/and" conceptual stance rooted in the acknowledgment that "all groups possess varying amounts of penalty and privilege in one historically created system."[29] Context and multiple perspectives become key to understanding how various groups can simultaneously oppress and be oppressed. In this way, intersectionality theory helps answer the question of why oppressed groups are often complicit in—and even perpetuate—the oppression of other groups.[30]

Even before intersectionality was codified into a theoretical perspective, bisexual and lesbian women of color, including Cherríe Moraga and Gloria Anzaldúa, identified a relationship between gender, race and homophobia and critiqued the emerging disciplines of women's studies and gay and lesbian studies for neglecting to attend to race and racism in their scholarship.[31] Their work brought much-needed attention to the ways in which bisexual and lesbian women of color must contend with both racism in LGBT communities and homophobia in communities of color. When Collins later helped articulate the formal theory of intersectionality, she too addressed how sexuality interacts with raced and gendered hierarchies, discussing the hypersexualization of Black women's bodies and the racialized politics of prostitution, pornography, and rape.[32] Later intersectional contributions to the study of sexuality further demonstrate how race, class, and gender shape sexual desire, communities, and identities.[33]

What Roderick Ferguson terms "queer of color critique" provides another key theoretical tool for investigating race, gender, and sexuality simultaneously.[34] Ferguson and others powerfully demonstrate how discourses of racial and sexual deviance are intertwined and how race was central to the production of the homosexual as a category.[35] Linkages between the discourses of racial and sexual deviance in the United States reinforced the emerging Black/white and homosexual/heterosexual binaries that have had such punitive consequences for queers, people of color, and especially queer people of color. Social science itself is implicated in this history: Ferguson explains how the liberalism and historical materialism that underlie canonical sociological thought contributed to the privileging of whiteness and heterosexuality and the abjection of queer people of color.[36] It is important to note that these philosophical underpinnings don't just do symbolic violence to queers of color; they also inform the political environment that authorizes literal violence against them.[37] The insights of women of color feminism and queer of color critique are essential to decolonizing sociological theory so it can be used for dismantling inequalities, not buttressing them.

Intersectional studies of schools have emphasized how schools create and sustain hierarchies of race, class, gender, and sexuality. For example, Ann Ferguson's ethnography of a Bay Area elementary school revealed how routine disciplinary practices and daily interactions between teachers and students construct Black masculinity as inherently criminal and endangered, thereby setting up Black boys for failure.[38] Similarly, Julie Bettie's high school ethnography shows how schools use race and class to sort girls into different tracks—and, in the process, very different futures.[39] Such studies also pay attention to how students creatively resist these institutional forces: for example, Lance McCready demonstrates how Black gay and gender-nonconforming students reappropriate school spaces (such as African dance classes and GSAs) to remake them in their own image.[40] An intersectional analysis of schools helps us understand the institutional and individual dynamics that socially construct race, class, gender, and sexuality as meaningful categories.

Intersectionality and queer of color critique are key theoretical tools for understanding the experiences and perspectives of gay and lesbian teachers. The tensions between pride and professionalism are racialized in a number of ways. For example, I found that coming out and the performance of sexual identity are different experiences for white teachers and teachers of color, who face unique challenges as multiply marginalized teachers. Intersectionality theory and queer of color critique provide analytical frameworks for seeing how these marginalities interact in their everyday lives. Throughout the book, I consider how race shapes the history of teaching professionalism, the experience of coming out, and the everyday performance of gay and lesbian identity.

Further, many teachers I interviewed taught in schools made up largely of students of color; their narratives about role modeling were often predicated on a belief that these students wouldn't otherwise see positive role models, as June's comments about the students from Crenshaw illustrated. In chapter 6, I draw on intersectionality and queer of color critique to understand how assumptions about homophobia are embedded in raced and classed hierarchies that structure how both white teachers and teachers of color think about and experience homophobia. Specifically, many white teachers use race as a predictor of homophobia, in the process constructing a homophobic Other out of the poor Black and Latino families that make up their school communities. Teachers of color also assume that Black and Latino people are more homophobic, but they have different narratives about the meaning and consequences of race and homophobia. The politics of respectability that have developed as a strategy of survival in communities of color inflect their expectations of homophobia within such communities.[41] The differences between how white teachers and teachers of color participate in racialized discourses of homophobia are instructive for understanding how racial formations shape the experience of queer sexuality.

SCHOOLS AS WORKPLACES

A key claim of this book is that gay and lesbian teachers must contend with a fundamental incompatibility between the professional demands of teaching and the political demands of contemporary gay and lesbian citizenship. To understand how this tension emerged, I turn to sociological theories of work and professionalism. Historically (with some notable exceptions), organizational theory has given short shrift to the ways organizations both influence and are influenced by gender, sexuality, and race.[42] The predominant assumption of much of the field has been that organizations and occupations are race-, class-, gender-, and sexually neutral entities. Inequalities in organizations are often attributed to individual acts of discrimination and harassment, as opposed to the constitutive elements of organizational logic. Joan Acker's groundbreaking theory of gendered organizations challenged the assumption that organizations are gender neutral.[43] Rather, she showed how the basic elements of organizational structure, like job descriptions and spatial organization, are already imbued with gendered assumptions about the ideal worker that disadvantage women. What's more, she later clarified, work is not just gendered but also raced and classed.[44] Acker has called this the outcome of "inequality regimes," the "interrelated practices, processes, actions and meanings that result in and maintain class, gender, and racial inequalities within particular organizations."[45] While the concept of inequality regimes focuses largely on race, class, and gender, Acker also acknowledges sexuality as a significant contributor to organizational inequalities.

Historically, there were few sociological considerations of how sexuality shapes organizations and vice versa,[46] but this has slowly begun to change.[47] Much of the contemporary scholarship on sex work, for example, explores how employment conditions and organizational contexts (for example, the gendered organization of strip clubs) inform the sexual and gender identities of both sex workers and their customers.[48] Similarly, the sociological study of sexual harassment documents the organizational and occupational variations on where symbolic boundaries are drawn between sexual harassment and "harmless" flirting or fun.[49]

Of particular interest for this book is the sociological literature on LGBT sexualities and work. LGBT employees experience workplace discrimination and harassment in a variety of workplace contexts.[50] Even explicitly LGBT organizations, including activist and advocacy nonprofits, reproduce heteronormative hierarchies internally, despite their intentions to disrupt them elsewhere.[51] To understand how and why the professional expectations for teachers are incompatible with non-normative sexuality, I draw on previous research about the professional lives of gay, lesbian, and bisexual employees. In their now classic study, James Woods and Jay Lucas find that gay professionals experience a pressure to "play it straight" to fit in and succeed in the corporate world.[52] Since their 1993 research, the "gay-friendly" workplace has emerged as an increasingly prominent model of corporate organization. Theoretically, the pressure to play it straight should be significantly diminished in the gay-friendly workplace, where gay, lesbian, and bisexual workers are not just tolerated but welcomed. Christine Williams, Patricia Giuffre, and Kirsten Dellinger find that instead another pressure has developed.[53] Today's gay, lesbian, and bisexual employees are expected either to downplay their sexuality, as Woods and Lucas's research subjects did, *or* to conform to narrow stereotypes of gay, lesbian, and bisexual appearance and behavior. They are thus forced to choose between acceptance and visibility, rather than achieving true parity with their heterosexual colleagues.

Nick Rumens and Deborah Kerfoot revisited the question of gay men's professional identity formations in this new, gay-friendly era.[54] They found that the ethos of gay-friendliness has allowed openly gay men to feel like valued workplace contributors but that, at the same time, the normatively masculine standards of professional conduct, dress, and comportment continue to clash with the styles their research participants use to express and display their gay identities. Thus they are thwarted in their attempts to identify themselves simultaneously as professional and openly gay. I find that a similar tension exists for gay and lesbian teachers, but unlike Rumens and Kerfoot's research participants, the gay and lesbian employees in my study work in a largely gay-*hostile* work context.[55] Studying gay and lesbian teachers complements the existing work on contemporary LGBT workplace experiences by revealing how the acceptance/visibility binary plays out under less friendly working conditions. Further, it extends Woods and Lucas's contributions, as well as Rumens and Kerfoot's, by considering how both gay *and* lesbian teachers negotiate their sexual and professional identities.

Schools as workplaces are unique in that school employment invites a public moral vigilance uncalled for by many other kinds of work. Public opinion idealizes schools as asexual spaces that shield children from the immoral influences of the adult world.[56] Yet sociological examinations reveal that schools are actually steeped in sexuality. In their now classic study, Barrie Thorne and Zella Luria find that institutionalized gender practices in elementary schools inculcate children into an understanding of "'the sexual' [as] prescriptively heterosexual and male homophobic," which in turn influences their sexual understandings and practices later in life.[57] As such, schools are an important venue for messages about appropriate and inappropriate sexuality.

This education in gender and sexual normativity appears to extend into high school. In an ethnography of adolescent masculinity, C.J. Pascoe finds that sexuality is not missing from high school interactions and rituals; rather, it is omnipresent, in discourses, rituals, and interactions that are rife with homophobia and heterosexism.[58] Similarly, in her analysis of class subjectivity among girls, Bettie finds that sexuality is a key symbolic marker of the divisions between working and middle class, arguing that working-class girls use rituals of "heterosexual romance and girl culture" as a reparative strategy against class injury.[59] Jessica Fields's work on sexuality education explores what she calls the *evaded curriculum* of sex ed, the omission of which is just as instructive as what is actually said and done. The evaded curriculum includes gender inequality and homophobia; its erasure legitimates the sexism and heterosexism experienced by students. As these and other studies show, sex is not absent from schools but rather is an important part of their *hidden curriculum* or unspoken socializing objectives.[60] Schools teach children not just language, math, and sciences but the "right" and "wrong" ways to do gender and sexuality.[61] As such, they reproduce the taken-for-granted notions of sexuality that maintain systems of inequality.

Most of the available research focused specifically on the experiences of gay and lesbian teachers comes from education scholarship. The psychological toll of managing one's sexual identity is a predominant theme. The literature suggests that a common strategy for the "negotiation of self" is to compartmentalize roles and identities.[62] As a profession, teaching is characterized by a strict delineation of the "public-private, inside-outside, natural-unnatural, personal-professional, [and] neutral-political";[63] maintaining these divisions with regard to their sexual identities is a powerful expectation for gay and lesbian teachers. Navigating their positions in the educational system thus entails strenuous emotional labor.[64]

Teachers manage this process by dividing their public and private selves, which enables them to survive the forces that set up "gay and lesbian" and "teacher" as incompatible. Sherry Woods and Karen Harbeck describe a bifurcation of experience among lesbian teachers who feel compelled to split their sexual and teacher identities.[65] Didi Khayatt's study of eighteen lesbian-identified teachers in Canada and Ronni Sanlo's study of sixteen gay- and lesbian-identified teachers in Florida confirm this fragmentation.[66] In all three studies, this identity split had a deleterious impact on teachers' lives and career satisfaction. This book reveals a similar pattern among teachers who try to split their sexual and professional selves, but I find that such splitting is actually one of three strategies for managing the contemporary tensions of being a gay or lesbian teacher. In exploring all three of these strategies, I consider the structural, cultural, and embodied factors that affect which strategies teachers employ, as well as how norms of teaching professionalism and the politics of gay pride shape their visibility as gays and lesbians in schools.

The teachers in these earlier studies used impression management strategies to survive the stigma of being a gay or lesbian teacher.[67] In particular, "passing" strategies, which depend on a desexualized presentation of self, helped them avoid drawing attention to their sexual identities. Kate Evans and Janna Jackson both found that gay, lesbian, and bisexual teachers carefully consider the *appearance rules* of hetero/homosexuality and sometimes make conscious decisions to avoid "acting gay" or otherwise signaling potential gender nonconformity.[68] In an autoethnographic account of his experiences as a gay male teacher, Eric Rofes reports similar pressures to enact normative masculinity.[69] I show, however, that gay and lesbian teachers do not all have equal access to these passing strategies. This, in turn, affects the ability to survive in homophobic school environments.

I analyze the experiences of gay and lesbian teachers from a distinctly sociological viewpoint, arguing that their perspectives provide unique insight into the heterosexual norms embedded in schools. First, their distance from heterosexuality gives them insight into the heterosexism of everyday school life, which often prohibits them from talking about romantic partners, displaying family pictures in their classrooms, and seeing themselves reflected in curricula. Exploring that distance provides an opportunity to uncover the taken-for-granted classroom privileges organized by sexual identity. I find these moments especially revelatory for deconstructing the prevailing discourse of schools as sexually neutral institutions.

Second, because they have to make conscious decisions about negotiating their sexual and professional identities, gay and lesbian teachers are more attuned to the role of personal identity in shaping pedagogical practice. As they actively manage two identities socially constructed as conflicting, they offer exceptional insight into more general processes of identity negotiation engaged in by workers on the job. Their experiences thus extend our understanding of how organizations affect the individual enactment of identity.

Finally, teachers offer a perspective on heterosexism in schools that has been missing from the sociological literature. Most of the education literature on teachers is limited to the professional and pedagogical consequences of their experiences. Most of the sociological theory on schools has focused on students. This book, in contrast, sheds new light on how schools as institutions construct sexuality. As such, it offers fresh insights into the interrelated dynamics of gender, sexuality, employment, and schools.

THE POLITICS OF GAY AND LESBIAN CITIZENSHIP

Along with the sociology of workplaces, the sociology of social movements is a crucial context for understanding the experience of being a gay or lesbian teacher. Social movement scholars note that the collective shift from shame to pride is the cornerstone of identity politics for social movements against stigmatization.[70] In the history of homosexuality, the concept of gay pride made this shift explicit. The homophile slogan "Gay is Good" laid the foundation for this concept, which was cemented, in the United States, by the Stonewall Riots of 1969.[71] One year after patrons of the Stonewall Inn resisted a police raid on the known gay bar, activists organized marches to commemorate the event. These marches, initially referred to as liberation or freedom marches, eventually became our contemporary Gay Pride marches, parades, and festivals.

Around the same time, coming out of the closet became the primary tool of political action for the emerging gay pride movement. Activists discouraged gays and lesbians from living "in the closet," or keeping their sexual identities concealed from family, coworkers, friends, and the general public. Accepting life in the closet signaled complicity with the idea that homosexuality was shameful. Conversely, coming out of the closet was the ultimate expression of pride. The significance of the act of coming out reached primary and secondary school teachers in 1978, when the Briggs Initiative, or Proposition 6, threatened to ban gay and lesbian teachers from working in California public schools. Along with a coalition of other activists, Harvey Milk, the first openly gay elected government official, organized the "No on 6 Campaign" to defeat the measure.[72] The slogan of the campaign, "Come Out! Come Out! Wherever You Are!" urged people to come out and show California voters that gays and lesbians were among their friends, families, and coworkers. The events surrounding the Briggs Initiative simultaneously reminded gay and lesbian teachers of their vulnerability and encouraged them to come out.

Today, "gay pride" stands as the defining ethos of LGBT identity. The philosophy of gay pride assumes that sexuality not only *is* but also *should be* the primary source of identification, community, and self-esteem. The corollary concept of "out and proud" links pride to self-disclosure, so that coming out and pride become nearly synonymous. Critics of this "out and proud" mandate argue that it inappropriately privileges sexual identities above all others, including race, class, or gender identities, and that, in contrast to the deconstructive agenda of queer theorists and activists, it reifies sexual distinctions into essential markers of self.[73]

Queer scholars drawing on affect theory, which explores the connection between unconscious feeling and conscious action, argue that feelings of pride and shame have shaped the collective identity of gays and lesbians. The construct of gay pride mandates the rejection of negative emotions like grief, loneliness, and shame in connection to LGBT identity. Heather Love contends that this suppression of negative affect is dangerous, as it separates us from the realities of a queer past that might be instructive and, indeed, productive for moving a queer politics forward.[74] Paying greater theoretical attention to the moments of shame and humiliation that coincide with the emergence of a homosexual identity makes more space for an internal critique of LGBT politics and identities than the doggedly defensive concept of gay pride does. Shame, as a theoretical and political foundation, might "provide a basis for collective identity [that spans] differences in age, race, class, gender, ability, and sexual practice" and moves away from simplistic pride politics.[75]

Despite the troubling limitations of the gay pride mantra, it continues to have considerable social influence. In many circumstances, anyone who does not comply with the imperative to come out risks being marked as a traitor to his or her sexual community. This directive—be out and proud or else—helps fuels the dilemma faced by gay and lesbian teachers. External and internal pressures to be out and proud in the classroom collide with the countervailing pressure to be professional, which, in the teaching context, usually discourages the disclosure of sexual identity.

STUDYING GAY AND LESBIAN TEACHERS

To find out how gay and lesbian teachers make sense of their experiences both as teachers and as gays and lesbians, I needed to capture the complex, messy, and even contradictory realities of those experiences. I approached this goal in two ways. First, I conducted in-depth interviews with teachers, which allowed me to access their own understandings. Interview methods are ideally suited for examinations of social context and meaning making.[76] In in-depth, interpretive interviews, "two individuals come together to try to create meaning about a particular topic."[77] The interpretive method of interviewing encourages the researcher to solicit and analyze stories, metaphors, contradictions, and what Arlie Hochschild calls "magnified moments" of epiphany or heightened emotion.[78] The interviews were semistructured, which means that although I followed a rough outline of questions, interviews were conversational in tone and structure. In the interviews, I asked participants to talk about their decisions to become teachers, their experiences as teachers, and their survival strategies as legally and socially vulnerable workers.

In addition to these in-depth interviews, I also was a participant observer in the workplaces and social spaces of some of the teachers.[79] Participant observation is a highly useful complement to interviews. Robert Zussman argues that the best qualitative sociology considers "people in places"—research participants in their own social contexts—because "places are typically the manifestations, or, perhaps more precisely, the instantiations of institutions and policies."[80] Such manifestations, and the discursive battles that create them, are critical for understanding the dilemma of pride and professionalism confronted by gay and lesbian teachers. For this reason, a closer look at teachers in their actual work and social environments was necessary to this project.

The "people in places" approach helped me to recreate teachers' experiences in more concrete detail. It also allowed me to witness what the research participants described, giving me further insight into their work worlds. Their physical workspaces were an important source of information. The ecology of the classroom is a fascinating site of study, especially given the heightened surveillance in schools today. Teachers are caught in a complex web of constraint, formed by school administrations, educational policies, parents, students, and communities. How they navigated this web on a day-to-day basis was a crucial piece of this research.

In the end, I conducted in-depth interviews with forty-five gay, lesbian, and bisexual-identified teachers and administrators (twenty-four in California and twenty-one in Texas) between June and December 2008.[81] In addition, I interviewed six straight allies, including GSA chairs and educational advocates, to compare their perspectives. I sought to include participants of a variety of race, class, gender, and age positions and was successful to varying degrees. I was not as successful at recruiting teachers of color as I would have liked, perhaps because their intersecting marginalities as both gay or lesbian and people of color made them less visible as potential research participants and less willing to assume the possible risks of being interviewed by a stranger. The sample did not include bisexual- or transgender-identified participants.[82] While their perspectives are important, their experiences are probably in some respects analytically distinct from those of gay and lesbian teachers. Transgender and bisexual teachers open up additional challenges to the binaries of sexual and gender identity, making their experiences even more fraught.[83] While I initially attempted to recruit them for the study, I ultimately decided to limit my analysis here to gay and lesbian teachers.

I chose California and Texas as research sites because of their similar demographics and different legal and political circumstances. At the time of my research, California and Texas were both majority-white states with larger-than-average Latino and African American populations.[84] They were home to two of the

TABLE I

TABLE I
Demographic Characteristics of the Sample

	CA Sample	TX Sample
Age		
40 or under	11	12
Over 40	15	13
Race/Ethnicity		
White	17	19
Latino/a	6	3
Black	0	3
Asian	2	0
Biracial (Black and white)	1	0
Gender		
Man	14	11
Woman	12	14
Sexual Identity		
Gay	14	11
Lesbian	9	10
Straight	2	4
Bisexual	1	0
Teaching Level		
Elementary school	4	8
Middle school	3	7
High school	13	5
Administration	6	1
Not a teacher	0	4

ten largest US school districts, Los Angeles Unified and Houston Independent, both of which had been pioneers in school policy. Despite these similarities, the two states differed significantly with respect to policy and practice.

California had statewide statutes and local ordinances that protect gay and lesbian teachers from discrimination and harassment. These laws prohibited employment discrimination and harassment on the basis of sexual identity and/or gender expression. In addition, the 2000 California Student Safety and Violence Prevention Act, AB 537, amended the California Education Code to add protection on the basis of "actual or perceived sexual orientation and gender identity" to existing school non-discrimination policies.[85] In the Los Angeles Unified School District, districtwide programs such as Project 10, an educational support services program for LGBT youth, and the Gay and Lesbian Administrators Alliance Administrators (GALAA) supported LGBT students and teachers. Local and nationally affiliated teachers unions, such as the American Federation of Teachers (AFT), the National Education Association (NEA), and United Teachers Los Angeles (UTLA), had been vocal in their support of LGBT teachers and LGBT rights in schools.[86]

In contrast, Texas had some city or countywide but no statewide protections against antigay discrimination and harassment at work and in schools. A few local school districts did have district-specific protections and policies against discrimination. The Dallas Independent School District, for instance, had a nondiscrimination employment policy that explicitly forbade sexuality-based discrimination and harassment, but most districts did not. The Texas school system further differed from California's in that it was an independent district model (as opposed to California's unified districts), so districts were exempt from municipal regulation and had more autonomy in school policy making. Another difference was that Texas was a right-to-work state, so teachers unions had very little political power. Unlike in California, unions could not represent teachers in labor disputes, including disputes about sexual harassment and discrimination on the basis of sexual identity. Overall, gay and lesbian teachers in Texas occupied a more vulnerable legal position than their peers in California.

While these different political contexts offer the opportunity to make a meaningful comparison, I do not mean to overstate the differences between them. My data suggest that, by and large, gay and lesbian teachers feel more comfortable and secure coming out in California than Texas, particularly when it comes to students. However, they also show that the culture of the schools themselves, as well as individual experiences and embodiments, are often more meaningful factors in their experiences.

Stereotyping California as a liberal "safety zone" and Texas as a conservative "danger zone" is overly reductionist. For example, in 2008, California voters passed Proposition 8, which invalidated same-sex marriages in the state, suggesting that it might not be as politically progressive and gay-friendly a state as it is often characterized. Cultural stereotypes and legal histories do not always reflect the on-the-ground realities. Consequently, this book will unpack differences *and* similarities between the two contexts, showing how the sociopolitical contexts of schools affect individual experience, while also revealing the contours of the general experience of gay and lesbian teaching in the United States. Both strands of this analysis help us understand the relationships between sexuality, schools, and work. Organizing the book by theme rather than region enabled me to consider similarities and differences in context.

ORGANIZATION OF THE BOOK

In the following chapters, I consider the various factors that shaped the experiences of the teachers I interviewed. In chapter 2, I review in greater detail the history of gays and lesbians in the teaching profession. Teachers are expected to model moral behavior for their students, which has led to strict surveillance of their personal lives, including their sex lives. This chapter considers how this unique professional history affects gay and lesbian teachers today. I also outline the legal history of the rights of LGBT teachers, who have long been subject to discrimination and harassment on the basis of sexual identity and/ or gender nonconformity. In the ongoing battle over gay rights, antigay activists have frequently scapegoated LGBT teachers to rally support for their cause, rhetorically constructing gay rights as antithetical to child welfare. I discuss the consequences of this discursive battle in the day-to-day lives of gay and lesbian teachers.

Chapter 3 reveals that gay and lesbian teachers make sense of themselves and their classroom experiences in the context of both their professional expectations and contemporary sexual identity politics. As noted above, the prevailing politics of gay pride calls for being out and proud at all times, leaving gay and lesbian teachers understandably conflicted. They respond to this conflict in three ways—by *splitting* their sexual and professional identities, *knitting* them together, or *quitting* classroom instruction altogether. This chapter explains each of these strategies and argues that the underlying tension between gay pride and teaching professionalism limits the possibilities for challenging heteronormativity and homophobia in schools.

Regardless of the strategy they ultimately choose, all gay and lesbian teachers face initial decisions about coming out on the job, including whether, how, when, and to what extent. Chapter 4 discusses the various ways teachers negotiate this process. Despite some sociological research that suggests the closet is decreasing in power as a metaphor for the LGBT experience, it continues to be a relevant symbol for gay and lesbian teachers making sense of their lives.[87] Teachers make decisions about coming out in the context of interrelated but analytically distinct factors: the legal and political climate of their school, district, and state; the social/microcultural context of their workplace; and their own gendered and raced presentations of self. Teachers must consider how their gender performances affect their intentions to disclose or withhold information about their sexual identities. Teachers of color must negotiate their in-school identities from a location of multiple marginalities, making decisions about coming out and presentation of self with conscious consideration of how race mediates the process.

In chapter 5, I discuss in greater detail how the performance of gender and sexuality on the job affects a teacher's ability to avoid antigay working conditions. The teaching context rewards certain performances of gender and sexuality and stigmatizes others, thereby implicating the embodied performance of gay and lesbian identities in the structuring of inequality regimes.[88] Gender normativity often acts as a buffer against harassment and discrimination for out teachers, while the pressures on visibly gay and lesbian teachers to appear just like their straight counterparts results in the continued marginalization of "deviant" sexualities. This pressure comes not only from the dictates of teaching professionalism but also from the mainstream gay rights movement, which emphasizes normality, productivity, and assimilation as the pathway to equality. This constrained version of gay and lesbian visibility perpetuates what Lisa Duggan calls *homonormativity,* a mode of LGBT identity that does not challenge but rather is wholly compatible with the raced, classed, and gendered inequalities of neoliberalism and thus limits the challenge to gendered and sexualized inequalities that visibility hopes to achieve.[89] This "virtually normal" model of LGBT identity comes up frequently when gay and lesbian teachers discuss visibility in the classroom.[90]

While I discuss the intersections of race and sexual identity throughout the book, chapter 6 focuses sustained attention on the ways teachers use race both to anticipate and to discredit homophobia. Teacher narratives often included racialized explanations of potential homophobia, including the expectation that Black and Latino coworkers, parents, and students were more likely to be homophobic. By taking an intersectional approach to understanding these deployments of race, this chapter shows how racism and homophobia are mutually sustained through racialized discourses of homophobia. By perpetuating the linking of gayness and whiteness, this process not only further alienates gay and lesbian teachers of color but also limits the possibilities for coalitional politics that might challenge both racism and homophobia in schools. In addition, many research participants used racial discrimination as a comparative rhetorical strategy to make sense of the discrimination they experienced as gays and lesbians. While this strategy is often useful for combating discrimination, it is also problematic. First, it assumes a false dichotomy between race and sexual identity that further erases the experience of teachers of color, who must contend with both kinds of discrimination. Second, it posits a false equivalence, when in fact the unique histories and operations of each kind of marginality resist such simplistic comparisons.

Finally, chapter 7 discusses the implications of my findings for sociological theory, pedagogical practice, and the political advancement of sexual justice. The findings of this book suggest that sexuality inequality will not be remedied simply through expansion of "gay-friendly" policies and practices, which leave homonormativity and racist exclusion more or less intact and are therefore limited in their reach. I suggest that the bigger and more important challenge is to reach for the possibility of a truly *"queer*-friendly school." I conclude by explaining how queer-friendly schools differ from gay-friendly schools and offering some suggestions for their realization in the US public school system.

CHAPTER TWO

"Like a Fox Guarding the Henhouse"

The History of LGBTs in the Teaching Profession

When Virginia Uribe began teaching high school in Los Angeles in the late 1950s, she could not have imagined how the teaching profession—and her life—would transform over the course of her career.[1] Virginia was married to a man when she began teaching, but within a few years she had divorced her husband, fallen in love with a woman, and begun to identify as a lesbian. She soon came out to close family members and friends, but it would be another two decades before she began to come out at work. She explained, "I just thought being in the closet was just part of what you were supposed to be if you were lesbian—you were just in the closet, and that was just it."

Things changed radically for Virginia in 1984, when an openly gay student dropped out of her school after repeated harassment by students and staff. Discussing the harassment with a coworker, Virginia realized she had had enough of the silence around homophobia in schools. During an interview in her sunny Los Angeles home one summer afternoon, Virginia explained, "We began to talk, we began to just, discuss this whole issue. And [my coworker] said, 'That's just what happens to gay kids.' I wanted something to change where that wasn't the case." Virginia and her colleague brought the idea of a gay and lesbian student support group to their principal, who gave them permission to start it. They called the group Project 10, a reference to Kinsey's estimate of the percentage of homosexuals in the US population. Project 10 has since grown into a districtwide program that serves as a model for similar efforts nationwide.

While Virginia was successful in institutionalizing support for LGBT students, she eventually found herself ensnared in the emerging culture war over the impact of gay rights on children. After several years of operating quietly under the radar, Project 10 came under fire from the Religious Right in 1988, targeted as a danger to children by groups like the Traditional Values Coalition, the Moral Majority, and Focus on the Family. Virginia was bewildered by the virulence of these attacks: "I kept saying to myself, my God, you're trying to start a program to keep kids from killing themselves, you know, trying to do something good, and they are saying I'm like a pedophile, like a fox guarding the henhouse." These organizations demanded that the state of California deny funding to the school district until Project 10 was disbanded. Fortunately, the board of education refused to withdraw their support, and Project 10 prevailed.

Still, the experience sensitized Virginia to the war brewing over gay rights, a conflict that rests in part on the idea that the advancement of gay rights and the protection of child welfare are at odds. For Virginia, this was baffling; to her, not only were the two compatible, they were the same fight. Project 10 was intended to protect child welfare by advancing gay rights and protections in schools. Nonetheless, advocates on both sides assumed that gay rights and child welfare were separate—and often conflicting—interests. This chapter explores the history of the teaching profession in the United States and, more specifically, the history of LGBTs in the profession to show how this discourse of incompatibility between gay rights and child welfare developed. Understanding these historical forces is the first step to understanding the pride/professionalism problematic faced by today's gay and lesbian teachers.

THE POLITICS OF PROFESSIONALIZATION

Teaching has long held an uncertain occupational status. "Special but shadowed," it is at once considered uniquely virtuous and denigrated.[2] Initially a job of last resort for upwardly mobile men, teaching evolved into a "women's profession" in the United States during the late nineteenth century, a transformation that emphasized the moral and maternal aspects of teaching, deflated wages, and by the 1960s, relegated teaching to semiprofessional status.[3]

While this gender shift reinforced the relationship between teaching and morality, the connection between the two has existed in the United States since the colonial era. When formal schooling was first established in the colonies, ministers often did double duty as schoolteachers.[4] Over time, colonies passed laws that prohibited ministers from teaching, but many remained involved in schools in supervisory capacities. One of their priorities was to monitor teachers for sinfulness in their public and private lives. While homosexual identity did not yet exist, homosexual behavior was considered a grievous sin against God and classified as a crime punishable by death.[5] Any teacher engaged in or even suspected of committing homosexual sex acts would have been severely punished.

The common-law tradition of in loco parentis gave teachers both the permission and the responsibility to strictly regulate student morality; along with this responsibility came close scrutiny of their own morality. Concurrently, the emerging doctrine of childhood innocence portrayed children as "innocent, vulnerable, and in need of protection from adult sexual knowledge and practice."[6] As a consequence of these conjoined ideologies, teachers were closely scrutinized during the hiring process, made to sign morality contracts, and supervised throughout their tenure by community members who watched carefully for any lapses in moral behavior.

Although women had been moving into the teaching ranks in the United States since the mid- to late eighteenth century, the feminization of teaching began in earnest around the time of the Civil War.[7] By the late nineteenth century, the transformation of teaching into a "woman's job" was complete. This transformation accompanied a transformation in teaching itself, as Progressive Era education reforms led to the application of rational and scientific techniques to teaching, which in turn increasingly formalized the teaching process. The emerging expectation that teachers needed specific skills they could acquire only through standardized training helped to support the push to accord teaching legitimate professional status. Occupations with professional status tend to have a monopoly over a body of knowledge and provide an expertise that can be accessed only through formal training; this had never before been true of teaching, at least at the primary and secondary levels.[8]

In a strategic bid to increase the status of teaching and improve its standing as a legitimate profession, teacher training programs and schools began recruiting and promoting men, white men in particular, in the late twentieth century.[9] Today,

teaching professionalism maintains much of its feminized character—teachers should be nurturing, caring, altruistic—but
increasingly, professionalizing bodies and teaching training
programs emphasize stereotypically masculine skills, including
authority, discipline, and technical rationality.[10] As a result,
white (and presumed straight) men experience a "glass escalator" effect of being propelled up the ranks into higher-paying
positions of authority in teaching administration.[11]

Teaching professionalism is not only gendered but also raced.
Black men and women were all but excluded from teaching at
the turn of the century and were later relegated to all-Black
schools and ignored as viable professionals.[12] After *Brown v. Board
of Education* prohibited educational segregation, Black teachers
from now-closed all-Black schools were forced to undergo educational retraining, under the assumption that their professional
skills were not up to par for teaching white students.[13] As a result
of this history of professional exclusion, Black teachers continue
to be treated as professional Others.[14] These politics of professionalization established unequal access to power and authority
for teachers of color, and the legacy of these politics continues to
have bearing on the experiences of gay and lesbian teachers of
color.

MCCARTHYISM AND THE PURGING OF GAY AND
LESBIAN TEACHERS

Alongside the racialized and gendered preferences noted above,
heterosexual teachers have been preferred throughout the history of education.[15] While earlier teaching policies did not allow
women teachers to marry, since the mid-1950s marriage has been
seen as a career benefit because it guarantees an upstanding

heterosexual image.[16] The 1950s also saw mounting Cold War fears of communist infiltration, as the newly formed House Un-American Activities Committee and others attempted to root out communists and their sympathizers in government, the movie industry, and more. Gays and lesbians were particularly targeted as potential sympathizers or spies because of their supposed deviance from traditional American values.

Karen Graves explores how this "lavender scare" affected gay and lesbian teachers of the era.[17] She focuses on a widespread purge of gay and lesbian teachers in Florida, at a time when, according to fellow historian Jeff Woods, "Segregation and anti-Communism acted as mutually reinforcing components of an extreme southern nationalism."[18] In Florida, one manifestation of these ideologies was the Johns Commission, which was ostensibly intended to root out individuals and organizations that disrupted the "orderly pursuits" of businesses and citizens but was widely acknowledged as an effort to attack the NAACP and other Black Power organizations that were pushing for school desegregation. When the NAACP successfully blocked its attacks, the commission turned its attention to another group that threatened the southern status quo, initiating a statewide investigation and purge of gay and lesbian schoolteachers, who were considered a powerful threat to American values.

The Johns Commission operated with impunity, ending the careers of many gay and lesbian teachers, until 1962, when the Florida Supreme Court ruled that the commission and the board of education had overstepped their bounds.[19] While the decision terminated the commission, the board of education continued the purge on the basis of standardized criteria and protocols, as demanded in the court decision. Florida's circumstances were particularly dramatic, but similar purges were going on across the country: in a nationwide review of teacher dismissals in the 1950s and 1960s, John Davis found that "immorality," a charge that often included suspicions of homosexual behavior, was the most common cause of dismissal.[20] These dismissals were often based on the morality clauses teachers were forced to sign, which commonly forbade homosexual behavior or association.

The Cold War ushered in formalized systems of social control that kept teachers in the closet for decades to come. It also brought the "problem" of gay and lesbian teachers to public attention, foreshadowing subsequent waves of moral panic over gays and lesbians in education. At the same time, McCarthyism's atmosphere of fear and intimidation helped inspire the beginnings of a formal gay rights movement. Though their ability to defend gay and lesbian teachers was limited, emerging homophile organizations like Mattachine, Daughters of Bilitis, and *One* magazine began to agitate for changes in the social status of gays and lesbians.[21] These opposing social forces—Red Scare–inspired homophobia and homophile resistance to discrimination and harassment—set up the bitter discursive dispute between gay rights and child welfare that continues to dominate the conversation about gay and lesbian teachers.

OUT OF THE CLOSET AND INTO THE CLASSROOM

By the late 1960s, gays and lesbians were reaching a breaking point. Police harassment, street violence, and social stigma were commonplace, but what had once been accepted as an inevitable risk of living a "homosexual lifestyle" was growing unbearable for many. The homophile movement had created community; more importantly, it had introduced the promise of a life of dignity, respect, and acceptance. Revolution was already in the air, as the

US civil rights and women's movements challenged the mistreatment of women and people of color, protests against the Vietnam War and American imperialism grew ever louder, and student activism on college campuses nationwide threatened to dismantle business as usual. In 1969, the police raided the Stonewall Inn, following common practice against public gathering places for gay, lesbian, bisexual, and transsexual people.[22] What was not so common this time was that the patrons fought back, inciting a riot. Together with a few similar incidents, this riot jumpstarted the burgeoning gay liberation movement. The following year, a march held to commemorate the riot was the first of what ultimately became today's Gay Pride celebrations, held across the country and abroad in the month of June.

Gay liberationists of the time rejected the predominant political model of homophile organizations, favoring more radical goals and in-your-face tactics. The group Gay Liberation Front (GLF), formed in the aftermath of Stonewall, envisioned the universal dismantling of sexual distinctions and roles and advocated for sexual liberation for all. This more radical grand vision was hampered by internal skirmishes over GLF's affiliation with the Black Panthers and other militant antiracist and antiwar groups; the subsequent splinter group Gay Activists Alliance (GAA) focused more narrowly on securing human rights and social acceptance for LGBTs.[23] Although GAA's model would ultimately win out over the GLF's more expansive vision, in that moment the scope of gay liberation was yet to be determined.

Morrison v. State Board of Education

Before gay liberation, states and local school boards had the last word in defining "acceptable" teacher behavior, which meant that targeted gay and lesbian teachers had little legal recourse for challenging terminations. Earlier victories like the Florida court decision that stemmed the gay and lesbian teacher purge asked that school boards develop a fair protocol for firing suspected homosexuals but did not speak to what fair criteria might be. In 1969, the California Supreme Court decision in *Morrison v. State Board of Education* answered the question of criteria and in the process redefined the legal terrain by limiting school board powers in the termination of gay and lesbian teachers.

In the *Morrison* case, a teacher's board certification had been revoked after administrators discovered a short-lived affair with another teacher of the same sex. While prior case law supported the school's prerogative to fire a teacher on the basis of immoral conduct or moral turpitude, the *Morrison* decision limited such terminations to circumstances involving a significant danger of harm to students, school employers, or others who might be affected by his or her actions as a teacher.[24] While *Morrison* did not prohibit morality terminations outright, it did significantly curtail schools' abilities to fire gay and lesbian teachers. Shortly thereafter, the National Education Association (NEA) and the American Federation of Teachers (AFT) publicly announced their support for gay and lesbian members and their employment rights.[25]

Morrison had a huge impact: it initiated the legal right to a private life for gay and lesbian teachers, so long as that life did not interfere with their public duties, and it set in motion a new legal and social framework for contesting gay and lesbian teacher dismissals. Sexual behaviors had to cause direct danger or harm to students to warrant termination. *Morrison* followed the emerging legal doctrine of individual rights to privacy in the absence of a compelling and contravening public interest. Unfortunately, the vague definition of "harm" left some room for the continued termination of gay and lesbian teachers. The notion that children need to be protected from sexual "deviants" had picked up steam since homosexual behavior had crystallized into the existence of homosexual persons. This notion, along with lingering Cold War fears and emerging anxiety over the successes of gay liberation, coalesced in a moral panic over gay and lesbian teachers among some constituencies. As long as exposure to gay and lesbian people could be conceived of as harmful to children, *Morrison* could not fully prevent school boards from coming up with termination rationales.

In appealing to the right to privacy, *Morrison* and similar decisions began to frame homosexuality, in both law and the cultural imagination, as a fundamentally private concern, rather than a public issue of social justice. *Morrison*'s redefinition of employment termination criteria implicitly encouraged gay and lesbian teachers to distinguish between their public lives as teachers and their private lives as gay and lesbian citizens.[26] At the same time, new antidiscrimination legislation was beginning to constitute gay and lesbians as members of a protected minority class.[27] The *Morrison* decision became part of an emerging legal tradition that addressed gay and lesbian employment interests in terms of individual minority rights.

Although this framework successfully shored up employment rights and job security for gay and lesbian teachers, it came at a cost. By implicitly encouraging gay and lesbian teachers to keep their sexual identities to themselves, *Morrison* established an educational policy akin to the military's "Don't Ask, Don't Tell."[28] The shift to minoritizing politics represented by *Morrison* further solidified sexual politics into two fixed and mutually opposed camps, heterosexuality and homosexuality. This binary construction of sexual identity severely limited the kinds of claims teachers could make and forced sexuality into the purview of law.[29] So long as the state had the power to define acceptable sexual identities, the terms of the debate remained frozen as private rights versus public injury.

*Anita Bryant, Save Our Children, and
the Briggs Amendment*

The gay liberation movement significantly advanced legal protections for gay and lesbian citizens, mostly in the form of ordinances against discrimination and harassment. Unfortunately, a backlash movement came directly on its heels. The nascent organized antigay movement made its debut in Dade County, Florida, under the leadership of television personality Anita Bryant. In 1977, Bryant started the Save Our Children campaign to repeal a local gay rights ordinance barring housing and employment discrimination against gays and lesbians. Bryant took the stance that gay rights ordinances would harm children, saying "As a mother, I must protect my children from their evil influence.... They want to recruit your children and teach them the virtues of being a homosexual."[30] She argued that the ordinance would allow gay male teachers to "wear dresses to work and flaunt their homosexuality in front of [her] children."[31] After months of campaigning, the ordinance was repealed by a landslide referendum vote, striking a serious blow to the momentum of gay rights initiatives.

Buoyed by their success, Anita Bryant and Save Our Children helped pass similar repeals in Minnesota, Kansas, and Oregon.[32] Just as in Dade County, antigay activists raised the specter of the sexually abusive and morally corrupting gay teacher, even as city officials tried to explain that the ordinances did not even cover public school teachers. Using psychological "experts," distorted data, and horror stories to support their claims, these campaigns successfully mobilized child welfare concerns to repeal gay rights ordinances. With each antigay victory, gay and lesbian teachers became increasingly vulnerable scapegoats for Far Right political action, and in 1977, they became an explicit target.

In June of that year, California state senator John Briggs introduced a statewide ballot initiative that sanctioned the firing of any public school employee found guilty of engaging in "public homosexual activity" (openly revealing homosexual identity or behaviors) or "public homosexual conduct" (advocating or supporting gay rights in any public manner). Proposition 6, also called the Briggs Initiative, would have expanded the post-*Morrison* termination criteria of "harm" to include the mere acknowledgment of the existence of gay and lesbian teachers.

Until this point, gay activists had largely ignored Bryant's claims about homosexual recruitment and sexual abuse, focusing instead on making their political claims within a human rights framework.[33] In the Briggs fight, though, Bryant's position became impossible to ignore, since interactions between children and gay and lesbian adults were the very subject of the battle. Instead of brushing them off, gay activists began to directly respond to Bryant's claims: when Harvey Milk, the first openly gay politician to be elected to public office, debated John Briggs over Prop 6 in a series of "town hall meetings," he rebutted Briggs's assertion that gays and lesbians were more likely to abuse children by quoting law enforcement statistics showing that most pedophiles were heterosexual. He also used jokes to discredit Briggs's concerns about a gay "recruitment agenda," saying, "If it were true that children mimicked their teachers, you'd sure have a helluva lot more nuns running around."[34]

Despite the best efforts of Milk and other gay advocates, the measure was initially projected to pass. Then, in a surprising turn of events, Governor Ronald Reagan publicly opposed it,[35] and it failed to muster enough Election Day support. Still, the Briggs Initiative was a warning to gay and lesbian teachers who were considering coming out. Gay rights might have been changing the climate of other workplaces, but schools remained dangerous places for openly gay and lesbian employees.

Both the Save Our Children campaign and the Briggs Initiative discursively established harm to child welfare at the level of *exposure* to gays and lesbians, which in turn defined the very existence of gays and lesbians in schools as a threat to children. Antigay activists worked to incite fears that gay rights would lead to the abuse and indoctrination of children by gay and lesbian educators and child care workers. In response, gay rights advocates attempted to debunk the myths underlying such claims and to assert the respectability and moral worth of gay and lesbian teachers. Their use of crime statistics and expert authorities struck a blow at the Christian Right's pedophilia charges. This strategy was eminently reasonable, but it also represented a missed opportunity to expand the meaning of child welfare to *include* gay rights. That is, activists could have supplemented their defensive response with proactive support for gay rights as child welfare and focused on the ways that gay rights protections could benefit children and make schools safer environments. Because the movement did not capitalize on this opportunity to expand child welfare claims, instead dismissing concerns about child welfare as irrational, gay rights discourse emerged as contrary to, or at best entirely separate from, concerns about child welfare. In the decades to come, this lost opportunity would come to haunt the push for employment nondiscrimination protections.

The AIDS Crisis and Reagan-Era Retrenchment

The backlash to gay liberation picked up new steam in the 1980s, as conservative political leadership, the growing strength of the Christian Right, and the AIDS crisis made the United States feel like a hostile and dangerous place for LGBTs. Shortly after the fanfare—and failure—of the Briggs Initiative, Oklahoma quietly passed the nearly identical Helm's Bill. Even before it became law, Oklahoma administrators began firing suspected gay and lesbian teachers; the bill only empowered them further. The public outcry was surprisingly minimal. In the conservative political climate of Oklahoma, gay activists were more wary of speaking out than they had been in California, where openly gay San Francisco county supervisor Harvey Milk had led the charge. It took several years for a small contingent of critics to find litigants and begin the process of legally challenging the bill.[36]

Six years after it passed, legal advocates for gay rights succeeded in overturning Helm's Bill. A US Court of Appeals decision deemed the bill unconstitutional on the basis that using "public homosexual conduct" as a termination criterion violated First Amendment rights. However, the court affirmed that the state had a responsibility to "not [allow] public homosexuals or public advocacy of homosexuality to influence school children."[37] Although the decision was appealed, a split decision among the US Supreme Court upheld it by default. The bill's defeat was a victory for gay and lesbian teachers, but that victory was bitter-

sweet; the wording of the decision ultimately did little to affirm
their rights to employment. Shortly after, the US Supreme Court
upheld the constitutionality of sodomy laws in *Bowers v. Hardwick,*
striking another blow to the advance of gay rights.

Meanwhile, fear and dread replaced the sexual exuberance of
the 1970s, as a "gay cancer" later identified as AIDS ravaged the
community. Health care, treatment, and medical research
became the main priorities of gay rights activists. Ronald Reagan, now president, remained silent on this emerging public
health crisis until the very end of his second term; by then, more
than thirty-five thousand Americans had been diagnosed.[38]
Presidential adviser and Christian Right leader Pat Buchanan
declared that AIDS was nature's "awful retribution" against
homosexuals, who had themselves "declared war upon nature"
first.[39] The Center for Disease Control and the National Institute of Health routinely denied funding for AIDS research, and
the administration's policy of nonresponse severely hindered
efforts to fund research, treatment, and care. Gay activists
formed their own networks and organizations to care for AIDS
sufferers and became increasingly confrontational and angry in
their political tactics. Eventually, the government responded to
the crisis, but too much damage had already been done. In addition to provoking a hostile political context for gays and lesbians, AIDS contributed significantly to public stigma around
homosexuality, and advances in gay rights initiatives were
severely stunted as a result.[40]

In such an environment, gay and lesbian teachers were understandably circumspect. The AIDS panic further intensified the
already tense debate over children's exposure to gays and lesbians. However, some brave gay and lesbian educational advocates
fought back. In 1984, Virginia Uribe began and successfully

defended Project 10 in LA. Gay and lesbian students began forming their own student associations and taking same-sex dates to school functions such as proms; when denied access, they successfully petitioned the courts to uphold their rights.[41] The National Education Association (NEA) bolstered its support of LGBT members, speaking out against proposals for mandatory AIDS testing of teachers.[42] These acts of rebellion against homophobic backlash were small but significant milestones on the road to more significant employment protections for gay and lesbian educators.

THE CONSOLIDATION OF LGBT EMPLOYMENT RIGHTS

In the mid-1990s, the Employment Nondiscrimination Act (ENDA), which would have settled the question of the legality of sexual identity discrimination once and for all, was introduced in the Senate. Once again, teachers became scapegoats. Antigay activists evoked a recent scandal involving a schoolteacher who had performed in gay porn to dissuade senators from supporting ENDA. In an attempt to distance themselves from the scandal, ENDA advocates amended the bill's language so that it wouldn't prevent employers from terminating employees on the basis of "nonprivate sexual contact." Relying yet again on the language of privacy, the 1996 incarnation of ENDA was severely limited in its power to protect workers. ENDA supporters also agreed to leave transgender workers out of the bill's protections, for fear they would hinder its success. Had it passed, ENDA might have provided additional protection for some teachers, but it would have left others vulnerable to continued harassment and discrimination. In the end, though, the bill was defeated.[43]

After decades of legal limbo, a series of high-profile court cases in the late 1990s finally upheld the rights of gay, lesbian, bisexual, and, at last, transgender teachers to equal protection from employment discrimination, strengthening the legality of coming out on campus. Although US teachers still lack federal protections, these cases established a strong case law against firing teachers on the basis of sexual identity or gender expression.

First, in *Glover v. Williamsburg Local School District* (1998), the court overturned the termination of an openly gay school-teacher in Ohio. Glover, a white middle school teacher, was the target of a rumor claiming he had held hands with his partner at a school dance (a claim Glover said was false). After the rumor surfaced, he experienced an increasingly hostile and discriminatory work environment. Despite glowing teaching evaluations, his teaching contract was not renewed at the end of the academic year, a decision he challenged in court. Glover argued that he was being discriminated against on the basis of sexual orientation, gender, and race, in violation of the Equal Protection Clause of the Fourteenth Amendment. He contended that the fact that his partner was African American helped fuel the rumor and its fallout. Ultimately, the court agreed with Glover that his termination did indeed violate the Fourteenth Amendment, even though the amendment does not explicitly mention sexuality. This was a historic legal moment for gay and lesbian teachers; unlike the tepidly worded *Morrison* and earlier court decisions, this decision overturned the termination not on the basis of a right to privacy but on the basis of a right to protection from discrimination and harassment.[44] In other words, it established a right to be *publicly* lesbian, gay, or bisexual in the educational context.

In a similar decision in 1998, a Utah court upheld a lesbian teacher's right to honestly answer student questions about her sexual identity. Wendy Weaver had been removed from her position as a high school volleyball coach after a student asked if she was gay and she answered affirmatively. As a condition of her continued employment as a teacher, she was prohibited from discussing her "homosexual orientation or lifestyle" with parents, students, or staff. In *Weaver v. Nebo School District*, the district accused Weaver of "encouraging or supporting criminal behavior ... sexual abuse ... [and] child abuse" by disclosing her sexual identity to a student.[45] For once, the trope of child endangerment was not enough to suppress the right to be openly gay, lesbian, or bisexual. The court found that the school district's actions violated Weaver's constitutional rights under the First and Fourteenth Amendments. With this decision, the Utah court established a firmer criteria of harm than *Morrison* had: simply answering questions about one's sexual identity was not a potential harm to students.

Transgender teachers were finally acknowledged and affirmed in a 1999 court case. When Dana Rivers, a California public school teacher, came out as transgender to colleagues, she was suspended and then fired. Rivers challenged this decision, again on the basis of First and Fourteenth Amendment rights, and the school board capitulated and awarded her a settlement.[46] She later went back to teaching in a different school district and was still teaching in the California public school system as of 2014.

These cases represented significant advances in the fight against the use of morality clauses and harm criteria to fire LGBT teachers. They established a teacher's right to protection from discrimination and harassment on the basis of sexual orientation and gender expression. In the absence of a federal

LGBT nondiscrimination policy, many school districts began adding sexuality and gender identity protections to their own employment policies. It began to seem as if the question of LGBT employment rights in schools was all but decided.

Then, in 2002, *Schroeder v. Hamilton School District* cast these rights into question yet again. Wisconsin teacher Tommy Schroeder faced repeated antigay harassment from students, staff, and parents, even after transferring to a new school. At his new placement in an elementary school, parents distributed a memo questioning his fitness as a role model for young children. Rumors that he was a pedophile began to circulate in the community. Administrators did little to protect Schroeder, and his principal allegedly told him that he might be barred from being alone with boy students on the basis of these rumors, despite the lack of supporting evidence.[47] When Schroeder sued, a panel of judges concluded that the school administration had not violated the equal protection principle by leaving Schroeder open to harassment. One judge's concurring statement argued that LGBTs were not deserving of the same equal protections under the law as other groups such as women and people of color. This was a blow to the emerging case law that interpreted the Fourteenth Amendment to include sexuality. The court argued that since the language of the amendment did not specify sexual identity or gender expression as a basis for protected status, equal protection did not apply. The school administration's minimal intervention on Schroeder's behalf was thus deemed adequate.

The *Schroeder* ruling demonstrates that the right to be out in schools is yet to be firmly established. It also illustrates the need for federally mandated employment protections, as teachers remain dependent on a generous interpretation of the Equal Protection Clause for legal recourse against discrimination and harassment. Whether they are legally protected from discrimination depends on the state, county, or school district where they work. Where protections do exist, the legal precedents largely frame these protections in terms of the balance between the individual's right to privacy and the public well-being of children. As a result, the very laws intended to protect gay and lesbian teachers from discrimination contribute to the continued exclusion of gay and lesbian identities from schools.

THE LEGACY FOR CONTEMPORARY GAY AND LESBIAN TEACHERS

This brief legal and political history illustrates how the emergence of the gay rights movement has been met with varying levels of resistance, from the overt hostility of the Save Our Children campaign and the Briggs Initiative to the inconsistent application of equal protection for gay and lesbian teachers in the 2000s. The belief that gay rights are a threat to child welfare continues to have traction in other arenas, including contemporary debates over nondiscrimination protections, marriage equality, and military policy. In these battles, LGBT teachers have again been scapegoated by antigay activists who continue to argue that gay rights are dangerous to children.

In his dissenting opinion in *Lawrence v. Texas*, the US Supreme Court decision that struck down sodomy laws, Justice Scalia asserted that "many Americans do not want persons who openly engage in homosexual conduct as partners in their business, as scoutmasters for their children, as teachers in their schools."[48] Commercials and flyers used in the 2008 campaign to invalidate California same-sex marriages played on fears that marriage equality would lead to the "overt indoctrination of children" into the gay agenda.[49] In a 2011 editorial, Bryan Fischer of the conservative American Family Association argued that the repeal of Don't Ask, Don't Tell would lead to LGBT teachers and "pro-gay indoctrination" in military classrooms.[50] In 2013, in Supreme Court hearings on the constitutionality of Proposition 8, Justice Scalia invoked roundly discredited antigay research to counter marriage equality arguments, inaccurately claiming that "there's considerable disagreement among sociologists as to what the consequences of raising a child in a single-sex family, whether it is harmful to the child or not."[51] The idea that gay rights run counter to child welfare continues to circulate, often in powerful ways, contributing to the continued vulnerability of LGBTs in education.

One difference, however, is that since the mid-2000s some activists have begun to merge child welfare into gay rights advocacy. This was particularly true in the "No on Prop 8" campaign, which drew heavily on images and testimonies of happy, healthy children with gay and lesbian parents. Campaigners argued that supporting marriage equality is, in effect, supporting children, in that marriage provides more stability and benefits to their families. Similarly, proponents of LGBT adoption have argued that such adoptions are better for children's welfare than the overcrowded, underfunded, often damaging realities of foster care and group homes. While this has been another useful strategy, and the lives of these children certainly should be taken into account in determining sexuality-related policies like marriage and adoption, this rhetorical turn has its own limitations as a gay rights strategy. Comparing the 1977 Dade County gay rights ordinance repeal and the marriage equality battles, Patrick McCreery argues that the way gay rights advocates have adopted the rhetoric of child protectionism (formerly the purview of antigay activists) does a disservice to both LGBTs and children. By deploying the "symbolic child," the gay rights movement forecloses "opportunities to change the social, legal, and ethical conceptualizations of family in the United States."[52] Additionally, it contributes to the rhetorical exploitation of children, rather than empowering them as agents who can speak on their own behalf. I would add that this strategy evades the opportunity to transform not only families and adult-child relationships but teacher-student interactions as well. While these considerations of children's welfare are a good first step, they don't go far enough toward dismantling the presumed antagonism between gay rights and children's rights.

Even in the face of these new efforts to change the terms of the debate, child welfare remains largely in the domain of the antigay movement. The resulting definition of gay rights as opposed to child welfare is potentially damaging for everyone, and it certainly leaves gay and lesbian teachers in a vulnerable position vis-à-vis their work with children. The social construction of childhood as sacrosanct in Western culture means that in a discursive battle between gay rights and child welfare, child welfare will almost always inevitably win. The ironclad child welfare strategy of antigay activists continues to legitimize job discrimination against LGBT people and solidify heterosexual privilege. Further, as long as gay rights discourse continues to rely primarily on rights to privacy, the debate remains one of private rights (of LGBTs) versus public injury (of children and morality). Defining gay rights apart from the best interests of the public severely limits the scope and success of LGBT activism. Finally, this strategy precludes children from the constituency of gay rights activism, leaving LGBT and gender-nonconforming children more vulnerable to external and internal forces of homophobia.

Ultimately, these discursive tensions ask gay and lesbian teachers to either enact sexual invisibility to protect child welfare or enact visibility in the name of promoting gay rights. A number of professional categories share this pressure, but it is especially pronounced for teachers because of their proximity to children and assumed responsibility for their moral education. The gay and lesbian teachers I spoke with in the course of my research repeatedly referenced this tension between invisibility and visibility, professionalism and pride. In subsequent chapters, I examine how teachers interpreted and enacted this forced choice in their performances of gay and lesbian identity in the classroom.

CHAPTER THREE

Splitters, Knitters, and Quitters

Pathways to Identity Making

In his twenty-two years as a teacher and an administrator in California public schools, Mark's feelings about how to negotiate his
sexual identity in schools ranged from wanting absolute separation
to wanting complete integration. In the early days of his career,
Mark did not yet identify as gay: "I started teaching when I was
twenty-three, and I didn't start that whole process [of becoming
gay] until I was about twenty-seven or twenty-eight. So I was not
only closeted for those first four years, I wasn't even identifying."
Once he did actively identify as gay, Mark was careful to keep his
personal and professional lives separate: "It was very exhausting to
do things like switch pronouns at school. Like, I'm really talking
about a guy that I think is good-looking I saw last night, or my date
last night, and I'm switching pronouns for teachers that wanted to
know more about me. And I think that's the thing, too—that's a
very typical thing when you get to know other adults on campus,
naturally they want to know more about you."

At this stage of his career, Mark was what I would categorize
as a splitter—he took pains to maintain a strict split between his

life as a gay man and his life as a teacher. He was especially vigilant about this split as it pertained to his students, because he worried, "If they knew that I was gay, how would they look at me? And as a coach, would they be comfortable with me? Because I had to go through the locker room to do supervision. And then as a teacher, are they going to be making comments to me? Are they going to be talking about me?" After several years of successfully splitting these two domains of his life, a chance encounter disrupted the neat division:

> I remember my last year of teaching, one of my students, who was eighteen at the time, saw me at Gay Pride. I'm there with five hundred thousand people and I feel this tap on my shoulder! And he says, "I knew it!" That's what he said. And so for about three months, the kids knew because he went back and told.... It made me feel a little uncomfortable for the first week, because a couple female students came up to me in the first week and said, "We know something about you and can we ask you?" And I said no! I was really evasive about it.

After those three months, Mark transitioned into administration, where the increased distance from his students led him to relax the split between his sexual and professional identities. Still, he says, "I think it wasn't until I started working with [LGBT educational initiatives], really, I think, that really brought me out of the closet. Because you cannot do this work without some level of integrity and honesty with people." At this point in his life, Mark's perspective shifted to favor a more integrated approach to thinking about sexuality in professional context—he became what I would call a knitter, someone who attempts to knit together the seemingly disparate identities of gay/lesbian and teacher (or in this case, administrator).

Mark's experience illustrates the various paths to identity making that gay and lesbian teachers can take—they can split their sexual identities, knit them together, or quit classroom instruction in order to evade the difficulties of the first two. For Mark, splitting gave way to quitting, which later enabled him to embrace knitting as the ideal strategy. In this chapter, I explore each of these pathways and their implications in greater detail. Mark's story also shows how the tension between pride and professionalism shapes the pathways available for teachers. As described in the previous chapter, gay and lesbian teachers have been scapegoated by antigay activists since the first gay rights struggles in the United States. In this chapter, I offer a sociological explanation for the persistence of this scapegoating, arguing that gay and lesbian teachers are in the crosshairs of two simultaneous sex panics, one about children's sexuality, the other about queer sexuality. Mark's fears about being found out as gay, given his role as a locker room supervisor, exemplify the kinds of dangers gay and lesbian teachers face because of the historical connection between homosexuality and immorality, most starkly demonstrated in the specter of the gay pedophile.

However, at the same time that gay and lesbian teachers are a prime focus for these ongoing sex panics, they are also venerated in progay circles as frontline role models for LGBT and questioning students. Mark's characterization of coming out as matter of integrity and honesty echoes the language of role modeling that underpins contemporary notions of gay pride. This role-modeling imperative, which I will critically examine, can weigh as heavily on gay and lesbian teachers as scapegoating.

As a result, depending on context, a gay or lesbian teacher can feel like a villain or a hero, an enemy or a savior, sometimes even both in the same moment. It should hardly be surprising, then, that these teachers are conflicted about merging their sexual and professional identities. In this chapter, after outlining the historical and social forces that set up their dilemma, I look at how teachers respond to these pressures and find three distinct responses, each of which comes with its own set of limitations. I examine each of these responses and explain how they demonstrate an underlying tension between the professional expectations of teachers and the dictates of gay pride, a tension that, until it is resolved, will limit the possibility of challenges to heteronormativity and homophobia in schools.

GAY AND LESBIAN TEACHERS AND THE SEXUAL POLITICS OF CHILDHOOD

The prevailing belief that children are sexual innocents is a relatively modern construct in Western history, yet today this belief is so firmly ingrained in our understandings of childhood that it's hard to believe there was a time when children were routinely exposed to sexual knowledge and behavior.[1] Prior to the late nineteenth century, children were often treated as "little adults" and were hardly shielded from knowledge of sexuality.[2] James Kincaid argues that the social construction of the innocent child in the late Victorian era was not about discovering developmental difference but about projecting fears, needs, and anxieties about sexuality onto the fantasy of childhood.[3]

Even the seemingly self-evident concept of child sexual abuse did not regularly circulate until the 1970s, when feminists fought to bring attention to the sexual abuse of women and girls.[4] The Catholic Church's very public abuse scandals and media coverage of women teachers having sex with boy students brought concerns about boys into the conversation.[5] This shift has had a significant impact on parenting practices. Parents now routinely warn their children—daughters and sons—about sexual abuse from an early age.[6]

This concern about cross-generational sex has raised public consciousness about sexual trauma and the power dynamics of sex in helpful ways. However, some argue that it has also foreclosed the possibility of recognizing childhood sexuality as valid and real. Steven Angelides contends that the fever pitch of contemporary pedophilia fears disempowers children as much as it protects them.[7] The legitimation of the concept of child sexual abuse, he writes, was made possible only through "rigorous efforts to conceal, repress, or ignore the realities of child sexuality."[8] Paradoxically, this move has left children in some ways more vulnerable by abrogating any sense of sexual agency they were once afforded. As a result, it is nearly impossible to grant children authority over their own sexual selves, or even to introduce them formally to the concept of a sexual self. Under the Clinton and Bush administrations of the late 1990s and early 2000s, sex education in the United States took a sharp turn toward the "abstinence-only" model, which emphasizes sexual abstinence as the best and safest choice.[9] While states and school districts vary in their approaches to sex education, research suggests that few US public schools offer truly comprehensive sex education.[10]

The level of cultural anxiety over children and sex amounts to what scholars of sexuality call a sex panic.[11] This is a form of *moral panic*, which emerges when an event or group threatens social order.[12] *Sex panics* occur when disruptions of the established norms of appropriate sexual behavior threaten to transform the hegemonic order. Because the norm of childhood sexual innocence is so rigidly enforced in the United States, children are at the heart of a number of related sex panics. However, as Roger Lancaster argues, sex panics are "less about the protection of children than about the preservation of adult fantasies of childhood as a time of sexual innocence."[13] Alarm over teenage pregnancy and rates of sexually transmitted infections, media sexualization of children, and changing norms of teenage sexual behavior all constitute sex panics, which often entail false or exaggerated claims about the phenomenon at hand that are then used to justify more stringent punitive and surveillance practices.[14]

In the 2000s, for instance, media reports of so-called "rainbow parties," during which adolescents participated in group sexual behavior, helped solidify abstinence-only policies in schools, even though there was no actual evidence for the existence of such parties.[15] Sheila Cavanaugh documented the explosion of media attention since the 1990s devoted to school sex scandals involving women teachers having sex with their students and the way this attention has led to increased surveillance and stricter codes of behavior for teachers.[16] In Cavanaugh's analysis, this sex panic, which is ostensibly about protecting child welfare, is actually about the regulation of gender, sexuality, and race. Similarly, Angelides argues that the construction of childhood innocence is fundamentally about preserving hierarchies of power.[17] Further, Judith Levine argues that these "sexual politics of fear" do more harm than good to children, who come to associate sex with fear and danger in the absence of a more sex-positive model for understanding their own sexual experiences and identities.[18]

Sex panics over homosexuality are myriad and ongoing, as the previous chapter demonstrated. The pursuit of the so-called lavender menace of the McCarthy era, public responses to the AIDS crisis, and antigay initiatives to quell gay rights ordinances and marriage equality are just some of the most prominent examples in the twentieth and twenty-first centuries. Much like the alarm over children's sexuality, these panics serve as outlets for channeling anxieties about social change. In fact, as queer activist/scholar Amber Hollibaugh has argued, homophobia is a "convenient cloak" for dealing with bigger "forbidden erotic themes" on a societal level.[19] Arlene Stein, who studied an Oregon ballot measure to deny civil rights protections to gay and lesbian citizens, uncovered the curious fact that many of the towns where residents were fighting passionately to deny "special rights" to gays and lesbians had little visible gay and lesbian community presence.[20] Stein's observations and interviews with the ballot's supporters revealed that their fight was largely symbolic. The ballot measure was a way for them to take a stand against perceived attacks to their morality and material well-being. Stein shows how contemporary sex panics over homosexuality are as much a protest against changes wrought by globalization, the evolution of the family, and the increased power of civil rights discourse as they are a challenge to LGBT people and communities.

Gay and lesbian teachers are at the locus of these two incredibly powerful triggers of sex panic: children and homosexuality. In addition, schools as socializing institutions are committed to both liberal and communitarian philosophies, which emphasize sameness over difference and the protection of "community values."[21] As a result, schools work to contain sexual expression that veers from the normative. Not surprisingly, then, gay and lesbian teachers have to be incredibly cautious about their public presence. Indeed, queer sexuality has come to be defined as inherently unprofessional in the teaching context. In other words, these sex panics have shaped the norms of professional behavior in the classroom to exclude any visible trace of homosexuality. Instead, the archetype of the ideal teacher is determined by heteronormativity: he or she should act, dress, speak, and self-present according to normative gender and sexual expectations. Although some teachers try to redefine professionalism to be more inclusive, almost every teacher I interviewed referenced the heteronormative teacher archetype, even if they didn't refer to it as such. Many of them internalized this ideal and came to see overt displays of homosexuality as inherently unprofessional. Teachers, they said, should present themselves as asexual in the classroom, an expectation that, on the surface, applies to all teachers, gay or straight. However, in reality, the teaching context implicitly legitimizes some expressions of sexuality and not others, a distinction that privileges heterosexuality and further marginalizes gay and lesbian teachers.[22]

I arranged to meet Hugh at an LGBT-affirming church in Houston that had offered up space for conducting my interviews in the area. Hugh walked in, trim and impeccably dressed, and greeted me with a wide smile that immediately set me at ease. Hugh was a Latino high school teacher in his midthirties who had been teaching for a little over a decade. After some small talk, we turned to his experiences as a gay teacher. When I asked if his students knew he was gay, he shook his head no, explaining, "I don't approach that with my kids. I don't bring up anything personal with my kids, just because ... children are impressionable and I don't want to have to explain myself to a child. So I never come out to my students. I just don't think it's appropriate to bring up." Hugh defined his sexuality as "personal" and therefore beyond the bounds of appropriate classroom discussion. While "personal" is ostensibly a neutral descriptor that might apply to hetero- or homosexuality, Hugh's comment about not wanting "to explain myself" is telling. A heterosexual teacher would presumably be able to "come out" about his girlfriend, fiancée, or wife without explanation, yet for Hugh, who had been with his partner for even longer than he had been a teacher, that kind of disclosure felt inappropriate. Further, in referring to children as "impressionable," Hugh seemed to implicitly reference the common belief that children must be protected from (homo)sexuality for fear of disrupting the so-called natural development of a healthy sexual identity.

This type of response was common among teachers in both states, who defined their sexuality as "personal" and thus irrelevant to their teaching responsibilities. Cheryl was a thirty-seven-year-old Latina lesbian who had been teaching in the Los Angeles area for a couple of years. She was especially adamant about distinguishing between her personal life as a lesbian and her professional life as a special education teacher. She explained, "No, [I'm not out at school] because I think, first and foremost, I see myself as a teacher. I don't mix my sexual orientation with my career. You know, it's my career first. I've never even thought about it." Cheryl's statement implies that sexual identity and career are mutually exclusive—and mutually opposed—components of identity and self. The fact that she had "never even thought about" revealing herself to be a lesbian at work suggests that her idea of teaching professionalism entirely precluded such a consideration.

Some teachers felt that being visibly gay or lesbian was especially unprofessional with younger children. Phillip, a thirty-four-year-old white gay elementary school teacher in Texas, explained, "I just don't think it's appropriate for them to know about me at seven or eight years old." Perhaps drawing on the same rationale of impressionability that Hugh used, Phillip defined his sexual-

ity as inappropriately premature knowledge for elementary
schoolers. Barbara, a forty-four-year-old white lesbian middle
school teacher in Texas, concurred: "The older kids, like high
school, maybe.... I know there's a lot of teachers who are out to
kids, and that seems okay. But middle school? Not so much. I
would have loved to have been out to the kids, but that's just ...
[in middle school?] Yeah, right!" Like Cheryl, Barbara found the
idea of coming out to middle schoolers almost unfathomable.

Ironically, just as elementary and middle school teachers
cited their students' young ages in defining homosexuality as
unprofessional, high school teachers cited adolescence as a similarly prohibitive factor. If their students' sexual innocence pre-
vented elementary school teachers from coming out, the sexual
awareness attributed to high school students provided a rationale
for their teachers to remain closeted. In particular, some gay
men worried about vindictive students targeting them with
allegations of sexual abuse and directly referenced the controlling stereotype of pedophilia successfully deployed against gay
teachers by antigay activists in prior decades.

I visited Larry's condominium in a tony Los Angeles neighborhood early one morning shortly after the close of his academic year. The living room windows provided a sweeping view
of LA, which I admired as we settled in for the interview, Larry's small dog curled happily at our feet. Larry was a forty-two-
year-old white gay man who had been teaching high school in
the area for several years. In discussing his presentation of self
in the classroom, he referenced a specific stereotype that puts
gay men in a vulnerable position in high schools: "[The stereotype is that] you're there to recruit, if you are a gay man, you
like teenage boys." In an interview over lunch in downtown Los
Angeles, Mike, a forty-seven-year-old white administrator,

explained how advances from students, even if carefully handled, can be devastating to gay men's careers:

> You know, especially as a male teacher, you never want to be a target. And I had to be careful. Like, for one example, one of the kids that was in my group—he approached me and tried to, I don't know, he was kind of hitting on me. And I wasn't sure what to do. And he wasn't real stable, anyway, and I thought, "All it would take would be for him to say 'He touched me' and I'm done." So you feel really vulnerable. In that situation, I went immediately to my administration and let them know, you know, what's transpired, here it is in writing, here's what I did. And any further correspondence or contact with this kid, I'll make sure someone is there. And so I think that's one of the fears, if a student gets pissed off, if he fails your class, he'll say, "I'm just going to make an allegation."

Gay teachers like Larry and Mike worried about sexual advances and sexual harassment accusations from older students, who they believed had a more advanced understanding of sexuality than elementary students. Thus even as age consistently served teachers as a rationale for not disclosing, it did not do so unilaterally. Rather, teachers of younger and older students had distinct concerns about how the age of their students might jeopardize them if they were out.

Gay and lesbian teachers used words like *personal, unprofessional,* and *inappropriate* to argue that their sexuality had no place in the classroom context. They didn't always tie this argument to homosexuality; some contended that the demand for a sexually neutral ideal teaching performance applied to all teachers, gay or straight. But when pressed about displays of (hetero)sexuality, they readily identified the ways straight colleagues referenced their sexual identities in daily interactions at work. Rufus, a white gay middle school teacher in California, was thirty-one and only a few years out of his teacher training program when we met up in a Silver Lake coffee shop. When talking about his straight colleagues, he eloquently captured the invisible privileges granted straight teachers: "[Heterosexuality] is a range of experience, a way of being. [Straight teachers] talk about their husbands, wives, their straight lives in way that has an impact on their students and their ideas." Rufus recognized that, unlike homosexuality, which continues to be shaped by expectations of how to be gay, heterosexuality is allowed to be unique to each person, as straight people are granted a "range of being" often denied to LGBTs.[23] He also saw how little things, such as talking about one's partner or life outside of work, can have a significant effect on students, who are learning how to be by example. Rufus called out the seemingly casual ability to reference partners and personal lives for what it is: a heterosexual privilege that passes unquestioned through the supposed sexually neutral standards of teaching professionalism.

Mary, a sixty-year-old white lesbian in California, had, by the time we met, retired from her position as a health teacher to run a nonprofit for LGBT youth. Not surprisingly, she was a strong advocate for breaking down the heteronormative ideal of teaching professionalism. She justified her position by referencing the ways straight teachers make their sexualities known at school: "The assumption is that you are heterosexual until proven otherwise. For the most part, people assume heterosexuality. And so that's why teachers who are heterosexual don't feel the need to 'come out'; it's just assumed. [Heterosexual teachers] talk about their husbands and wives and their children and have photos of their families in the classroom. I think, likewise, we need to participate in that in the same way." As Mary pointed out, the same family displays that married straight teachers engage in are considered unprofessional if performed by gay and lesbian teachers. How do we make sense of this? Sociologists of gender and work have shown how the ideal worker norms of various workplaces depend on gendered expectations that ultimately disadvantage women.[24] Similarly, Rufus and Mary pointed out the subtle but unmistakably heterosexual character of the ideal teacher norm. This is certainly not unique to teaching; Nick Rumens and Deborah Kerfoot's analysis of gay men in the corporate world found similar incompatibilities between homosexuality and professionalism.[25] Yet there is something distinct—and, I would argue, more stubborn—about the heteronormativity of teaching professionalism, given its relationship to moral panic over children and homosexuality. As a result, gay and lesbian teachers must find a way around the heteronormative ideal teacher norm, either by trying to fit into it or by redefining it on their own terms.

GAY PRIDE AND THE ETHICS OF ROLE MODELING

The ideal teacher norm is not the only challenge gay and lesbian teachers must grapple with as they make decisions about their behavior at work. They are also deeply affected by the imperative to act as "role models" for their LGBT and questioning students. Today the language of role modeling is so ubiquitous that it has taken on the quality of a commonsense notion, but it actually originated in sociological theory. Robert Merton first coined the term in his 1957 study of medical students, arguing that medical schools were not just repositories of medical and scientific knowledge but social institutions that teach students how to accurately perform the role of doctor.[26] Likewise, primary and secondary schools are socializing institutions where students learn various role performances, including how to be LGBT.[27]

Role modeling is integral to the rhetoric of gay pride. Coming out of the closet, the quintessential act of gay pride, is predicated on the importance of role modeling. LGBTs, especially those in high-profile positions, are expected to come out as a matter of civic responsibility. Gay pride advocates argue that by coming out they become role models for other LGBTs, who feel encouraged and empowered by the visibility of their successful and happy peers in all walks of life. Such rhetoric often envisions LGBT and questioning youth as the recipients of this role modeling. For example, when NBA player Jason Collins came out in April of 2013, out athlete Martina Navratilova declared in response, "One of the last bastions of homophobia [men's basketball] has been challenged. How many LGBT kids, once closeted, are now more likely to pursue a team sport and won't be scared away by a straight culture?"[28]

The importance of role-modeling LGBT identities for students was not lost on gay and lesbian teachers, even those who vehemently opposed coming out as an unprofessional act. For example, Hugh, who said that talking about his partner or otherwise coming out to students was too personal, spoke about the importance of role modeling:

CC: *What other things could be done to make [the school] climate more hospitable for [LGBT] teachers and kids?*
HUGH: Um … [long pause]. You know, I'm kind of a hypocrite, because—teachers coming out. Teachers coming out to their students.

CC: *How do you think that would make a difference?*
HUGH: It would definitely give them a positive role model. Me? I don't want to come out to my students. But if more people were doing it, maybe I'd be more comfortable doing it.

Despite his own reservations, Hugh invoked the rationale of role modeling, noting that having gay and lesbian teachers as positive role models might empower not only his students but also himself.

The terms *role model* and *role modeling* came up frequently in interviews. In fact, they were mentioned in thirty-two of my fifty-one interviews. In twenty of those interviews, respondents brought up the terms, without my prompting, to explain why the visibility of gay and lesbian teachers is important in schools.[29] Mark, forty-five, identified as gay and Latino, and his work in the central administrative office for the LA Unified School District reflected his commitment to advocating for LGBT students and students of color. Reflecting on the importance of having gay and lesbian teachers in the classroom, he moved beyond role modeling for LGBT students: "We want gay youth, LGBT youth, to have role models on campus, but most importantly, we want the straight students to see positive role modeling of LGBT persons on their campus, because it demystifies— you know what a gay person is. They are no longer this stranger; it's their administrator, it's their teacher, it's their teacher's aide." Mark's comments illustrate the far reach of the role-modeling work expected of gay and lesbian teachers, who are responsible to LGBT and straight youth alike.

What are the role-modeling implications of *not* asserting oneself in the classroom as an out and proud educator? Amy, a forty-eight-year-old white bisexual California high school teacher, laid out the consequences: "I think it's up to the individual teacher, but I think the more that we're visible, the better it will be for everybody. And I think that, you know, we help our students, too, by being visible. Because, you know, if they don't see adults feeling comfortable with their own sexuality, what's it saying to them? How does it affect them? If you're coy about it or secretive or whatever." Amy implicitly references the discourse of gay pride, which holds that being "coy" or "secretive" about one's sexual identity is counterproductive with regard to the wider mission of LGBT acceptance. Although she acknowledges the varying contexts that make visibility more or less possible, the role-modeling discourse leaves little room for nuance. Ultimately, she frames visibility as an individual choice, and also as the *right* choice, which by and large ignores the institutional and professional constraints teachers face.

Héctor was one of the teachers I interviewed who belonged to an advocacy group for gay and lesbian teachers and administrators. He was a thirty-five-year-old Latino gay man who worked in central administration for a large California school district. When we spoke, Héctor stressed the importance of gay visibility not just for teachers but also for administrators. He suggested that administrative gay visibility promotes a culture of safety in schools: "[My colleagues and I] always felt that if there were out administrators, out principals, out assistant principals, superintendents, directors that were out, then teachers would then feel safe to come out and then those teachers that are out can serve as direct role models for their students, as well as the school site administrators. So that was our plan, our strategy to make the students feel safe in the school, to make a safer environment." Héctor underscored the role-modeling argument and added another rationale for visibility: the creation of a safe school environment, beginning with the visibility of high-profile figures in the district. This "trickle-down" argument was fairly common across my interviews, echoing the arguments of mainstream LGBT politics, which often demand that public figures such as politicians, artists, and actors come out, on the basis that their visibility fosters a safer climate for other LGBT people.

The kinds of arguments these teachers presented demonstrate the influence gay pride discourses have on how gay and lesbian teachers think about their professional responsibilities. Yet at the same time these divergent norms of teaching professionalism contradict each other, creating countervailing pressures for these teachers. This ambivalence—good teaching *requires* coming out, good teaching *prohibits* coming out—lies at the heart of teachers' decisions about how to present their identities in school.

PATHWAYS TO IDENTITY MAKING

As the previous discussions of professionalism and role modeling reveal, gay and lesbian teachers are subject to the demands of two competing identities: LGBT and teaching professional. However, they respond to this unique pressure in different ways that can be categorized into three pathways, which I call *splitting, knitting,* and *quitting.* Each of these pathways addresses the identity dilemma in its own way, providing teachers with a measure of relief, but none of them fully resolve the underlying tensions, nor do they truly challenge homophobia and heteronormativity in schools.

The Splitters

Mauricio, a forty-year-old Latino gay teacher, worked in a county in central Texas that, unlike much of the state, did have a nondiscrimination policy for LGBT employees. Mauricio invited me to meet him in his middle school science classroom, which was large and colorful. Student art and letters from past classes hung on the walls alongside posters of the periodic table and charts of climate change. Mauricio had been teaching for fifteen years, and his face still lit up whenever he talked about the job. He seemed to love being in the classroom and was very invested in his identity as a teacher.

Mauricio was what I categorize as a splitter, which means that he drew a very strict line between his identity as a teacher and his identity as a gay man. Splitters believe that sexuality can be checked at the school gates; when they come to work, they leave their sexual selves behind and replace them with asexual teaching selves that abide by the tenets of teaching professionalism. In practice, however, splitting is not always as simple as this metaphor suggests. Mauricio was in a complicated position: despite his interest in keeping his sexuality out of the classroom, he was, as he put it, "gay-acting," which caused his students to gossip. Still, no matter what they surmised, he was adamant about not coming out to them. He felt that discussion of his sexual identity in the classroom was dangerous and inappropriate, and he worried about parental reactions. He also feared that other teachers who knew he was gay would out him to students, but he continued to insist that his sexual identity had nothing to do with his schoolhouse self.

Mauricio's experience was a clear example of bifurcating identities, a common phenomenon noted in research on gay and lesbian teachers.[30] Mauricio ardently defended this splitting strategy as not only necessary but the only appropriate way to be a gay teacher. Yet when asked about how schools could be improved with respect to LGBT issues, his answer revealed an undercurrent of conflict in his position:

> This is going to say a lot about me, but I wish there were more openly gay men and lesbians in the field. I'm not one of them, obviously, not to my current students, anyway. Because we have to be

role models. We definitely have to be role models. I don't remember a single teacher growing up that I even *suspected* of being gay or lesbian. I met my first, my first, openly gay person—who is my cousin—in college. And it was like, whoa, *that's* what it is! I get it now! Again, I'm not going to run out and out myself because I still believe my job here should be to be your science teacher, not your gay science teacher. But, no, that's important though. Wow, listen to myself.

Mauricio's statement showed the power of the contradictory identity demands placed on gay and lesbian teachers. At the same time that he tried to perform the ideal teacher archetype, he felt the tug of gay pride's role-modeling discourse. As he tried to avoid being characterized as the "gay science teacher" by limiting the personal information he shared with students, he recognized that his mannerisms and way of speaking already probably identified him as gay. He occupied a glass closet,[31] in which he tried—and failed—to keep his sexuality out of the classroom in the name of professionalism.

The suppressed tensions in Mauricio's performance surfaced when we talked about ways to improve schools for LGBTs. As he talked, he became increasingly uncomfortable with the dissonance between his suggestions and his practice. He began by saying, "This is going to say a lot about me," and ended with "Wow, listen to myself," seemingly recognizing the tension he had just articulated. At the end of our interview, he revealed his uneasiness with the contradictions he had unearthed, asking me, "I'm not the only one who doesn't come out, am I? There have to be others like me, right?"

Peter and I met in his office on a California college campus, where he taught preservice teachers. Before becoming a professor, he had taught in secondary schools for twenty years. Peter, a sixty-year-old Asian gay man, stressed that being out was not something he felt was important or relevant to his own teaching process, in his current college instruction or his former secondary school classroom: "I guess, for me, that's not a cross I choose to bear. I mean, most heterosexuals, they don't bring that out, they don't self-identify to their students. So I mean, I don't see why [gay and lesbian teachers] would [identify themselves]." Instead, he said, he focused on the significance of race and ethnicity for himself and his students:

> If you don't know who you are, then how are you going to deal with people, [with] students who come from a different cultural background? [I also focus on] awareness of what is portrayed in the curriculum and how that impacts how they feel about themselves and their identity. Knowing how that had a big impact on me, I think it's really important for people to be aware of who they are, and of how awareness can either help or hurt what they do. But if you don't know who you are, for whatever reason, because it's not pleasant to deal with or whatever, how are you going to deal with people who might also be wrestling with their sense of identity?

Peter found the experience of moving from Hawaii, where he grew up, to the mainland United States profoundly unsettling. "Coming here," he said, "I think I kind of lost sense of who I was, because more of the people I ran around with [in college] were white." This experience sensitized him to the importance of thinking about race and racial privilege in the teaching context. He explained, "If you're going to work in areas where the people don't resemble you at all—culturally, ethnically, even socioeconomically . . . and if your experiences don't mirror [your students'], then you need to be cognizant of that." For Peter, racial/ethnic identities were more salient to the classroom than sexual identity, which was "not a cross [he] chose to bear" on top of his diligent efforts to draw attention to racial privilege and oppression.

Peter experienced teaching as a master identity that largely precluded not only other identities, including his sexual identity, but also other interests and parts of himself. In discussing why he had chosen not to come out on the job, he explained, "I feel like I've devoted so much of my life to my profession, and to getting here, in many cases, I feel like I don't know who else I am because my identity is so tied to being a teacher for so many years." At the beginning of the interview, Peter was adamant about separating his sexual and professional identities, even a bit angry to be asked about a possible relationship between the two. Over the course of our conversation, though, he warmed up to the topic. Once he did open up, he expressed an uncertainty similar to Mauricio's:

> I don't know if [this is] a sad testimony on my part, but I feel like there are other parts of me that I would like to explore, that I have not made time for or I have chosen not to explore. I don't know. Getting back to this whole thing about—because I'm now thinking about the role models thing—maybe it would have [been better if I'd been out]. But I think in the era I grew up in, that was very difficult for people to do, so I don't know. It just wasn't, it just seems like whatever was out there was totally unacceptable to the way you thought about yourself, you didn't see yourself that way. And maybe that's your point—you know? That if you only see the stereotypes of what society perceives, then you are horrified ... "Am I like that?" So maybe in answer to your question, it would [have helped to have role models]! It would have, you know? If it were people that you could identify with and saw that, oh yeah, they're just like me! You know? ... So I think yeah, in answer to your question, it would have helped. You wouldn't feel so badly growing up [with] a range of ways you could see and you could identify with. I think it would be much easier to cope. That there are good people in the community,

that contribute to the wealth of the community and so forth. But I think because of the generation I grew up in, that was very difficult to find. And maybe that's why my own attitudes are reflective of the generation I grew up in, you know what I mean?

In thinking through the implications of splitting, Peter considered the negative consequences of his decisions, recalling his own lack of role models as a young gay man growing up in the 1960s. Ultimately he framed his commitment to splitting generationally. His experiences of racial marginalization had been formative for his pedagogical approach and teacher identity, while his experiences of sexual marginalization had not. For Peter, splitting was an inevitable choice, but that didn't mean he had no regrets about the limitations of his path.

Similarly, Charles, a white gay retired high school teacher in his seventies, described his experience teaching in California public schools as influenced by the era:

CHARLES: Well, until the last of the 1980s, [coming out] was a very indiscreet thing to do. Now, up until the '70s, they could fire you for that reason. In the 1970s, they couldn't fire you, for those reasons, but they could find other reasons for firing you, and they did in instances that I knew of.

CC: *So there were some practical reasons for not coming out.*
CHARLES: And also, social. Social relationships with other people. Now, the teachers there, most of them obviously realized I was gay, but it was still a situation of—it's better not talked about. And that was clear to me. Now there were people who find that emotionally difficult, but I never did.

CC: *Were you friends with other teachers?*
CHARLES: Yes. Several.

CC: *And were you out to those teachers?*

CHARLES: No. No, because as I say, they certainly did know, but they expected me to be by myself when we went to a play or a show. And when they invited me to dinner or lunch or whatever, they expected me to be by myself.

For Charles and others, splitting did not feel like a choice; rather, it felt like a necessity driven by the internalized and external homophobia of a particular era or context. In contrast, thirty-seven-year-old Latina lesbian teacher Cheryl was deliberate and resolved in her splitting strategy. Cheryl insisted on not "mix[ing] [her] sexual orientation with her career," a position she contrasted with that of a "very flamboyant" colleague who was "very public about [his sexual identity]." She explained that her coworker often talked about his sexual identity, "even at board meetings and stuff, which I felt very uncomfortable with. He was like, setting the tone, setting the stereotype for what people thought about gays and lesbians. He was setting it, he was our example. And it was pretty bad." Cheryl considered this kind of public identity making to be unprofessional and inappropriate, and she believed that out gay and lesbian teachers were too uncensored about their sexuality.

While Cheryl did not believe her sexuality was relevant to her career, forty-four-year-old Barbara, a white lesbian, worried more about appropriate pedagogy. Barbara had only recently taken her current position at a Texas junior high school, having moved from another part of the state. She worried about the appropriateness of talking about sexual identity in the classroom, saying, "I don't think it's my place as an educator in a classroom to be educating them on those things. Whether or not I agree with what they teach them, it's not my choice. These children are their parents' children, and their parents have the right to teach them what they want." In Barbara's case, splitting was an outcome of her philosophy of teaching, which considered gay and lesbian identities to be outside the bounds of what should be taught in schools.

It's worth noting that gay and lesbian teachers' narratives of splitting sound strikingly similar to the ways women who work in male-dominated environments talk about their professional and gender identities. Gender sociologists argue that women who make it in these kinds of jobs are reluctant to think about how their status as women affects their experiences.[32] Successful professional women often have struggled for professional legitimacy, as their job performances are read through a gendered lens that disadvantages them in comparison to their male colleagues.[33] Women lawyers are punished for trying to be "Rambo litigators," while men lawyers are praised, yet if women act too much "like a woman," they are dismissed as ineffective.[34] Women who make it in such treacherous terrain manage to strike a tenuously effective compromise between professionalism and femininity, and they are often loath to disrupt this delicate balance. Women also face a motherhood wage penalty, which encourages some in male-dominated workplaces to avoid visible reminders of their parental status (such as family pictures) in the same way some gay and lesbian teachers feel pressure to hide evidence of their family.[35] Thinking about gay and lesbian splitters in this light, the reluctance to even consider how sexuality affects professional identity makes considerable sense. Gay and lesbian teachers are the subject of keen scrutiny and suspicion, perhaps even more so than women in male-dominated professions in the twenty-first century. Keeping their sexuality out of the workplace is a wholly reasonable survival strategy.

As these examples demonstrate, there was no one route to splitting; rather, splitters had a variety of motivations and feelings about their decisions to separate their sexual identities from their classrooms. They were united, though, by a general sense that the dictates of teaching professionalism required them to exclude their sexual selves from their teaching. Some teachers engaged willingly in this process; others were less comfortable but did not feel as if they had other options. Regardless of how they came to the process or how they felt about it, splitters were bound by a belief that sexual identities—and LGBT identities in particular—were incompatible with the teaching context. The splitting pathway thus suggests that the historically tenuous position of gay and lesbian teachers maintains real purchase in the experiences of contemporary teachers.

The Knitters

Despite their historical vulnerability in the classroom, some gay and lesbian teachers employed a strategy I call knitting, which wove together their sexual and professional identities. These teachers were intent on bringing their sexuality into the teaching context, feeling strongly that doing so was their responsibility as gay and lesbian role models. At a minimum, knitting could mean coming out to colleagues to ease some of the awkward tensions that splitters identified. At the other end of the spectrum, it could entail the full incorporation of sexual identity into a teacher's pedagogical mission and teaching strategies. It is important to note that, much like splitters, knitters often felt ambivalent about their pathway: that is, knitting also did not entirely resolve the fundamental tensions of being a gay or lesbian teacher. What distinguished knitters from splitters, however, was their core commitment to bringing the two identities together, regardless of the penalties or drawbacks.

Rufus took his first teaching position with the intention of being an out LGBT advocate at all times, despite his fears that being out to students would be difficult. When I asked why he felt it was important to be out, he said, "Just from my own personal experience, I think that it has really benefited my teaching by being out. And I see and hear from my students, just them knowing that it makes them more comfortable with gay people." Rufus connected his gay role modeling to his success as a teacher, unlike splitters, who saw visibility as a potential threat to their authority and teaching. Rufus's first experiences were not easy. Students yelled pejorative gay epithets into his classroom as they walked by and used homophobic language to challenge his classroom authority. He came into school one morning during his first year and found "Mr. [Brown] is gay" spray painted on his classroom door. Despite—or perhaps because of—this kind of harassment, Rufus decided to come out to students earlier, eventually including his sexuality in an introduction exercise at the beginning of every year. Knitting may have created a sense of authenticity and pride for Rufus, but it also subjected him to consistent harassment; as a result, he felt he had to be especially vigilant about maintaining classroom discipline at all times, which he admitted felt burdensome.

Like Rufus and others, Karen, a thirty-four-year-old white lesbian teacher, framed her commitment to knitting in terms of role modeling. Karen worked in a large high school in West Los Angeles, where she chaired the school's GSA. While she ultimately believed in the knitting strategy, she struggled with how to put it into practice without overemphasizing her sexual identity at the expense of other salient identities:

I haven't explicitly said, "I'm a lesbian," but I do say, "my partner," and they know I'm the head of GSA. But I struggle with those issues sometimes because does that mean I'm like, am I still closeted? What does that mean? But if I were married to a man, would I say [that I was married]? Straight teachers do! They always say "my husband and I," "my husband and I," "my husband and I." But also, I don't—I don't agree with mixing—even if, I think, if I were dating a man, I don't think I'd be like, "My husband, my boyfriend!" because it's not about me, it's about them. And also, no students ever ask me, because if they're curious, they go to [GSA]. So some of my students, I've talked explicitly to them because they are in club meetings and it's about LGBT stuff, but otherwise, I'm trying—I don't know. Trying to be a role model and not have that be my sole identity, just have that be another part of me.

Karen's hesitation—not wanting to be closeted, but also not wanting to have her sexual identity become her "sole identity"—demonstrated a common struggle for knitters. As they try to knit together their sexual and professional identities in a way that feels authentic and empowering, knitters must constantly negotiate "how much" sexual identity is enough. Karen did not want to foreground her sexual identity over other components of her classroom self, nor did she want to make herself the focus over her students. The careful calibration of being open without oversharing sometimes left her unsatisfied. In our interview, she wondered whether this pathway might sometimes leave her in the closet. Her worries about her own internalized homophobia were likely fueled by the demands of gay pride, which "require[s] an unfailing repetition of a 'homo self' at every possible iteration."[36]

Chelsea, a twenty-eight-year-old white lesbian teacher in California, emphasized authenticity and wholeness as primary motivators for choosing knitting:

For me, to not be open would be just defeating the purpose of going to work. So I, on the first day of school—I think in the first and second year I actually said, "And I'm a lesbian," in my introduction, you know? And they were like, wow. They were excited by that, like, "Oh my God," because they'd never had a teacher say that.... I'm not embarrassed of myself, I'm not embarrassed of who I am. I can talk about it anytime to anyone because it's not something I'm hiding, it's just part of who I am.... I just think that's really, really important, that teachers need to be out and open in order to support their kids, and right now it's really hard for them to do that.

Chelsea cited the same sense of pedagogical effectiveness Rufus emphasized, saying, "I think the purpose of being a teacher is to connect with other human beings and guide them. And you can't do that without being an honest person. And you're not being honest if you're not being yourself." For Chelsea, part of "being yourself" was sharing your sexual identity, and not "being yourself" was a hindrance to one's ability as a teacher.

For knitters like Chelsea and Rufus, splitting would defeat the purpose of being a teacher or would at least severely limit their abilities to teach. In this way, knitters saw their sexual identities as a fundamental part of their teaching selves, rather than something that got in the way of their teaching. This way of understanding their careers resonated with notions about authenticity and openness that undergird gay pride discourse. It is important, however, to note that fifteen of the nineteen teachers in my sample whom I consider to be "knitters" were white, which undoubtedly aided their ability to choose knitting—and its attendant risks—over other strategies. Rufus, Karen, and Chelsea were able to trade on their racial privilege to mitigate some of the hazards of being out in the classroom. While they did not talk explicitly about how their white privilege informed

their decisions, it no doubt made it easier to choose the vulnerability of being out as gay or lesbian.

The Quitters

In addition to splitting and knitting, a third alternative for gay
and lesbian teachers attempting to reconcile their sexual and
professional identities was quitting. If teachers could not find a
way to split or knit that felt comfortable for them, they sometimes quit education or moved into administration in search of
more supportive working conditions.[37]

John, a twenty-four-year-old Asian gay middle school teacher
in California, was referred to me by his straight coworker Joan,
who told me in hushed tones during her first-period English
class that John had been having a tough time since starting at
their high school. A few days later, I met John in his empty science laboratory classroom at the end of the school day. When I
told him that Joan had mentioned he'd had a hard year, he concurred. John had begun his career as a splitter but after a year of
teaching decided to knit. He explained:

> I didn't want to come out, to label myself as a gay teacher. My first
> year, I was definitely in the closet. I was *so* in! … But after a while, I
> just so tired of lying to them and lying to myself…. In college I was
> completely out. And you know, I felt very comfortable. I felt like I
> didn't have to hide anything. But when I started teaching, it was
> kind of like, I had to go back to the closet. Like, almost eight hours
> a day, I had to hide who I was. And I'm a very happy-go-lucky per-
> son, but to facilitate a class of students who aren't listening to you,
> and who don't know you, I had to turn into this person who was
> very militant, and, you know, militantly *not* homosexual. And it
> was really hard. I'd come home and I'd be like, you know, "What am
> I doing?" At the beginning of this year, though, I really wanted to

change my outlook, change my approach with the students. So this year, I'm much less militant, I'm still strict, but I'm less militant. And I wanted to just be honest with them, you know, this is who I am. And I'm still your teacher, I'm still the same person, and you know, accept me or not accept me.

John found that trying to keep his sexual identity separate from work to avoid the label of "the gay teacher" was hampering his "true" self, a comfortably out gay man. Bringing his sexuality into the classroom more actively by mentioning his partner, he discovered that he "can build so much more rapport with the students, because they see that I can trust them with my personal life." As a result, he said, his teaching was "much more effective."

John's explanation fit well with the preferred gay pride narrative: in coming out, the individual eschews shame, lives a more "authentic" life, and is subsequently happier. John's experience differed from that narrative, however, in that coming out had also had a negative impact on his job satisfaction. Since coming out, John had been bullied by some students and was engaged in ongoing power struggles with administration that he linked to coming out. In large part because of these experiences, he was planning to leave teaching at the end of the school year and go to medical school. For John, neither splitting nor knitting resolved the dilemma of being "the gay teacher." As a splitter, he felt fraudulent and stifled; as a knitter, he felt targeted and harassed. Ultimately, he found that being gay and being a teacher were irreconcilable, and he chose another career path that would not be so fraught.

When Kenny, a twenty-four-year-old Black gay teacher, invited me into his apartment in Houston, he was in a convivial mood. He made us some tea, showed me around the apartment,

and asked me about my research. His mood became more sub-
dued when we settled in to talk about his teaching experiences.
As it turned out, Kenny was having a difficult time figuring out
whether to split or knit. Though he lived in a district that had a
sexual identity nondiscrimination policy, he was wary of the
repercussions of coming out not only to students but also to staff
members. Like several other teachers, he also worried about
being pigeonholed as the gay teacher. He explained, "I [am] not
trying to make [my sexuality] a focal point of who I am—I [don't]
want people to think that Kenny equals gay or gay equals Kenny."

Nonetheless, Kenny felt conflicted about keeping this part of
himself a secret in school. In particular, he was good friends
with a fellow teacher but was afraid to come out to her, which
bothered him a lot. Of teachers who do come out, he said:

> I'm very much in support of teachers who are comfortable enough
> to do that. I only wish I could be.... You serve as a role model and
> you break the stereotypes for gays and straights alike. Just being
> able to be true to yourself is a very important value to demonstrate
> to kids. Maybe not so much at the high school level, where their
> values are already kind of ingrained. But where they are in that
> stage of development where they could really learn some things
> and internalize them—like you said, at the age I teach, prepubes-
> cent, to know that our kids are probably having the same questions
> I had as a high schooler, probably in sixth grade. Lord knows prob-
> ably a lot of kids have those ideas and are struggling with them at a
> young age. So I only wish I could be that role model and maybe in
> another learning environment, another school, I could be. Which
> makes me almost embarrassed that I haven't done that.

When I asked him what would have to be different for him to
feel more comfortable, he admitted that he wasn't sure anything
could make a difference. He explained, "The policy that my district has, that was very encouraging for that brief moment [when

I started the job] and I never really took advantage of it, but it was very comforting to know I have that to fall back on if something happens. That the district supports me as a gay individual. And it's almost like, if I can't come out in a school like that, where could I come out in?" This dilemma had spurred him to think about other career options; when we concluded our interview, he mentioned he wasn't sure he would continue teaching after the school year ended.

Several years later, I ran into Kenny and discovered that he had decided to continue teaching and had been at that same Houston area middle school for five years. Since our interview, he had reconsidered his initial splitting strategy and was now trying to knit his identities together more publicly. "I always think back to that interview and how what I said then is so different than how I feel now," he said, demonstrating that even the most adamantly held position that emerges in an interview can represent a moment in time rather than a lifelong belief. It is important to bear in mind the fluidity between strategies that John's and Kenny's experiences demonstrate.

When I met James, a twenty-three-year-old Black gay teacher in Texas, he had already decided to leave teaching. Like Kenny, James had struggled over deciding whether to split or knit. In his first year, students taunted him about his presumed homosexuality and called him homophobic slurs during conflicts, but the students in his second year of teaching, he said, "also [seemed to know] I was gay, but they liked me more because of it and they wanted to know more." With both groups, though, James maintained a "don't ask, don't tell" policy, refusing to confirm his students' assumptions about his sexuality, whether their intent was positive or negative. When I asked him why, he explained: "I feel like [explicitly coming out] would have done more harm than help. I realize that it's an opportunity to influence, to be the first out gay person some of them know. But I'm just more concerned about teaching, about getting through the lessons.... I just think it would be harder to do both at the same time."

Like splitters, James felt that being out would be a distraction, but at the same time he wanted to be a role model to his LGBT and questioning students. Of one such student he said, "I can really relate ... to this kid in particular, he's like, really out, kind of effeminate. He's isolated, and all of his friends are girls, which I can really relate to." James wished he had been more open so students like this one wouldn't feel as isolated, but he was wary about changing his strategy. In other words, James could be called a reluctant splitter who then became a quitter—the discomfort of splitting led to his decision to leave teaching after two years. He decided to pursue a career in law, where he hoped to work in education and LGBT advocacy. He explained, "I never want to forget what I've learned here, and I'd like to be an advocate."

Sometimes quitting meant not leaving education entirely but moving up the ranks into administration, where there were fewer potential conflicts. Mike, a forty-seven-year-old white gay administrator, had a rocky experience as a relatively early knitter teaching in Los Angeles in the 1980s. Mike was involved with his school's Project 10 chapter and ended up "out by association." He explained, "When I got involved in the organization, you know, the kids talk!" Eventually, he began experiencing conflicts with administration: "[I had] administrators that were particularly homophobic and made it known. One that was extremely hostile towards me and I couldn't figure out why until I spoke to one of my colleagues, and she was like, 'Oh, by the way ...' You know, I couldn't figure it out. So that's why I took a lower profile. But you know, it was different times. In hindsight, and as I've matured, I think maybe I would have done it differently. But you know, the times were also a little bit different." When an opportunity to move into administration arose, Mike jumped at the chance:

> Some of the administrators approached me and said, "By the way, we think you should consider getting an administrative credential." And I was like, "Well, why, why would I bother doing that?" But then I started to enjoy working with people.... I do well building relationships and communicating, so it was just kind of a natural path at that time. And it provided for other opportunities. It's more lucrative, but that's not really why I did it. You can impact kids on a different level. You know, the classroom's wonderful, but there's something about impacting policy at a larger level that is satisfying.

Mike did not decide to move into an administrative role solely because of his struggles under a homophobic administrator, but those struggles did influence the move: "It was just easier, you know, not having to bother anymore with all that." When I asked if he was out now, he answered, "Oh yeah! I have a picture of my partner at my desk, and actually a lot of the people in [my department] are out." Mike's story shows how moving out of the classroom, into positions that require less contact with students and are therefore less fraught with anxiety, can take some of the pressure off gay and lesbian teachers who are struggling with the decision to knit or to split.

The experiences of John, Kenny, James, and Mike reveal just how irreconcilable gay and lesbian teachers' interests can feel. For these gay men, neither splitting nor knitting provided a satisfying resolution to the problem of being a gay teacher. Instead, they ultimately chose to leave teaching or at least direct classroom instruction, in large part because of this irreconcilability. Christine Williams theorizes that gay men working in education are often propelled from classroom instruction into administration by a "glass escalator" because of homophobic discomfort with their working with young children.[38] In our interview, Mike spoke of feeling vulnerable and wary of possible accusations of pedophilia by virtue of being a gay man in the classroom (as described earlier in this chapter). Mike's experience suggests that the glass escalator effect may also be part of the quitters' experience; in fact, all of the respondents I classify as quitters were men who had moved either up the ranks or out, often into more prestigious and higher-paying careers.

The splitters, knitters, and quitters I interviewed all wanted to see LGBT role models and curriculum in schools. Almost none were opposed to the idea of visibility, regardless of whether they personally wanted to be visible. They knew that the historical suppression of gay and lesbian voices in the educational context, detailed in the previous chapter, was wrong, yet they still faced its legacy in their own no-win situations, where they could either take on the stress and loneliness of the classroom closet or risk job discrimination and harassment for a highly constrained version of visibility.

This chapter has documented the three pathways by which teachers tried to resolve the fundamental identity tension between teaching and homosexuality. Some gay and lesbian teachers engaged in a splitting strategy, in which they attempted to check their sexuality at the school gates. While splitting allowed them to cultivate a professional demeanor that was more or less untainted by the stigma of queerness, it came with a psychological burden that added another layer of stress to their jobs and could generate uneasiness and even shame about their perceived failings vis-à-vis the expectations of gay pride.[39]

Other teachers attempted to knit their sexual and professional identities together into a cohesive schoolhouse self. These teachers often positioned themselves as "positive role models" for LGBT and questioning youth, as well as for straight students, who might otherwise characterize LGBTs according to negative stereotypes. This integrating strategy psychologically liberated teachers from the "classroom closet,"[40] but it had its own costs. Individual teachers engaged in knitting worried that their sexual identities would become a distraction for their students. More broadly speaking, it is important to note that not all teachers have access to this strategy. As the following chapter will show in more detail, limited legal protections, hostile work environments, economic vulnerability, and raced and gendered marginalization mean that only a relatively privileged subgroup of teachers can risk it.

Finally, those who could not find a satisfying location between splitting and knitting chose quitting. For some teachers, the relief of quitting and the satisfaction found in another job resolved much of the discomfort engendered by splitting and knitting. However, quitting is not viable for teachers who do not have the resources to leave a steady income and subsidize a career change. Furthermore, opting out is not a viable strategy for creating systematic change in schools.

This chapter has described the various pathways gay and lesbian teachers took in reconciling their professional and sexual identities, with a focus on how internalized beliefs about teaching professionalism and sexual identity influenced their strategies. The next chapter broadens the scope to consider how the *context* of teachers' working experiences further shapes their decisions about integrating their sexual and teaching selves.

CHAPTER FOUR

Dangerous Disclosures

The Legal, Cultural, and Embodied
Considerations of Coming Out

In the winter of 2008, I interviewed Barbara in her seventh-grade Texas classroom, after her last class of the day. I sat across from her at her desk, which was piled high with homework and reports, as well as pictures of her dog and drawings from past students. Barbara had been teaching for four years, but she had just transferred to her current school at the beginning of the semester. Her demeanor was brisk but pleasant, with an air of efficiency she attributed to her busy schedule, which included classroom instruction along with frequent classroom observations and teacher meetings on behalf of a caseload of special education students.

When I asked Barbara if she was out as a lesbian at work, she shared an experience from a previous job at a private school. The director of her school was hostile to gay and lesbian employees; as she described it, at the time she left the school "he'd already gotten rid of a bunch of people on campus that were openly gay." Barbara wasn't open about her sexual identity, nor, she believed, was she "visibly gay." One afternoon, the director made sexual advances toward her and wouldn't accept her refusals. Finally, she felt forced to tell him, "Listen, I'm very flattered, but I'm gay." The next day, Barbara said, the director trumped up charges of unprofessional conduct against her and she was fired.

Understandably, Barbara was extremely wary in her subsequent school placements. By the time she got to her current school, she had, as she put it, "learned her lesson." In the first few weeks, she "didn't know what the climate was … [she] hadn't gotten a taste for the environment yet." As a result, she kept personal details to a minimum and evaded questions about her sexuality and relationship status. Once she became comfortable with a small group of liberal-minded young teachers, Barbara came out to them at an off-campus social gathering.

About half an hour into our interview, another teacher opened the classroom door and popped in to ask Barbara a question about a student. At the sound of the door, Barbara straightened up into a rigid posture and stopped speaking in midsentence. After she saw who it was, her shoulders relaxed, and she laughed. She said to the teacher, who was one of the young teachers she had mentioned, "Oh my God, here I am talking about being a lesbian on campus and you walk in! But you're okay. Thank God it was you."

Although Barbara lived in a Texas county that protected LGBT employees from workplace discrimination, she was still reticent about disclosing her sexual identity in school. Her previous experiences suggested to her that legal protections were meaningless, since discriminatory and sexually harassing employers could evade the law using roundabout methods of dismissal. She was afraid to be out or to discuss LGBT issues, except with a select group of close-knit colleagues. She also worried that her students' parents would find out about her sexuality and "accuse [her] of changing the course of their child's development."

Barbara's story raises important questions about the experiences of gay and lesbian teachers, namely: How is the tension between pride and professionalism mediated by policy protections and the on-the-ground reality of teachers' classroom lives? And how does this relationship shape whether one becomes a splitter, like Barbara, or a knitter, or a quitter? In this chapter, I argue that teachers make decisions about coming out on the basis of the complex relationships between policy protections, school culture, and individual gendered and raced embodiment. This chapter demonstrates how the clash between pride and professionalism is not simply ideological but is also affected by the political and embodied realities of teachers' lives. Before delving further into these interrelationships, however, we must critically examine the meaning and importance of "coming out" as a personal and political act.

THE MEANINGS OF COMING OUT

What does it really mean to "come out" as gay or lesbian? According to George Chauncey, the term first emerged in the 1920s to refer to one's debut into underground gay societies in cities like New York, much as debutante balls introduced young women to a social circle of similarly raced and classed peers.[1] In both cases, coming out signaled initiation into a new sexual culture: the twilight world of homosexuality or the rituals of heterosexual courtship and marriage. The myth of isolation, as Chauncey calls it, holds that there was virtually no public gay culture until gay liberation demanded one, but in fact, he argues, gay culture was thriving in places like New York City, as demonstrated by "coming out balls" held in public spaces like nightclubs. The closet was an invention of the 1940s and '50s, when awareness—and fear—of homosexuality became more widespread. "Coming out" did not even reference a "closet" until the 1970s.

Today, the metaphor of coming out of the closet is so familiar that other groups have adapted it to name their own identity disclosures: people now routinely talk about coming out as Christian, kinky, an alcoholic, and so forth, to the point it could be argued that the metaphor is so overextended as to have lost its original meaning. Steven Seidman suggests that coming out of the closet has lost relevance as a metaphor even for the experiences of gay, lesbian, and bisexual people.[2] If the closet implies a lifelong pattern of concealment from close relatives and friends, significant social isolation, and abiding feelings of shame and fear, he argues that it is no longer a prevailing feature of gay, lesbian, and bisexual lives in the contemporary United States. Nonetheless, many of the people Seidman interviewed still used the language of coming out to explain their experiences, though they described not a lifelong effort to disguise their homosexuality but rather episodic patterns of concealment to avoid socially uncomfortable or risky situations. The metaphor of the closet implies that disclosure of one's sexual identity is a straightforward and singular experience: you open the door, step out of the closet, and are revealed. But for most people in the United States today, coming out is a continual, context-specific practice rather than a stable, linear process.[3]

Along with its dubious accuracy in capturing the contemporary experience of sexual identity disclosure, some critique coming out of the closet as a political strategy. Seidman argues that the individual strategy of gay, lesbian, and bisexual visibility is a flawed solution to the institutionalized problems of heterosexism and homophobia. Further, the near-ubiquitous imperative to come out negates the intersecting identities and life circumstances, including raced, classed, and gendered hierarchies, that may make coming out more difficult.[4] The material possibility of violence, harassment, and loss of financial and familial resources can weigh heavily on those who are not able to leverage race, class, and/or gender privileges. Finally, the language of the closet problematically relies on a binaristic and static conceptualization of identity. The movement from in the closet to out of the closet suggests an essentialized sexual identity: people are always already gay or lesbian, and once they realize it they must step out of the closet into their "true" and essential identities.[5] As a metaphor, then, the closet upholds flawed and essentialist identity politics.

Despite these limitations, the metaphor of the closet and the sociopolitical meaning of coming out held significant explanatory power for my research participants. Without prompting, teachers repeatedly drew on the language of coming out to explain their experiences and decision-making processes. It was thus important that I engage with the term and its conceptual framework in this book. Bearing in mind that the coming out metaphor is both limited and powerful, I define it as the partial, ongoing, and dynamic process of staking a public claim to an LGBT identity, and I recognize that the contemporary emphasis on coming out lacks contextual considerations. Coming out is synonymous here with disclosure, the process of purposefully signaling one's gay or lesbian identity to coworkers, administrators, and students. Coming out is thus distinct from being inadvertently read as gay or lesbian by virtue of one's gender performance because disclosure requires intent.

That is not to say that disclosure and gender performance are mutually exclusive processes. As I will discuss in greater detail later in the chapter, a nonconforming gender performance can encourage some teachers to disclose. These teachers chose to step out of the "glass closet" because they felt that they were inevitably "read" as gay or lesbian and there was thus no point in continuing to hide their identity. Stanley, a thirty-seven-year-old white gay man, was a substitute teacher in Southern California; as a result of his position, he met new groups of students fairly regularly. His approach was to come out to students often and early. He explained, "It's easier to get it out. You know, I can't hide. I am too effeminate. I don't hide my sexuality very well. So it's better to just deal with it out front and have it out in the open and not have people snickering and laughing and causing who knows what kind of problem." For Stanley, hiding his sexuality was not a possibility, so he tried to get ahead of the gossip and speculation by disclosing it outright.

In contrast, teachers who do not appear to be gay or lesbian have more freedom to disclose at will. For Ruben, a sixty-year-old Latino teacher at a California alternative school, "being gay is a constant process of outing oneself." Muscular and gruff-spoken, Ruben did not fit many people's stereotypes of gay men. As such, he had more control over his disclosure process than Stanley did. When he came out to coworkers at his current school, he said that one teacher remarked, "I never would have thought you were gay. You're very masculine!" as if the two were mutually exclusive. As Stanley and Ruben's experiences demonstrate, disclosure was distinct from gender performance, but gender performance often influenced disclosure.

COMING OUT ON CAMPUS

All teachers, regardless of sexual identity, engage in an ongoing negotiation of self-disclosure with their students, who are inevitably curious about the personal lives of their teachers. In the last few decades, the influence of critical pedagogy has empowered teachers to draw on personal history to engage students and make their teaching material relevant.[6] Developed in the early 1970s, critical pedagogy seeks to empower students to understand and challenge inequality. It interrogates traditional hierarchies of authority in the classroom, particularly the imbalance of power between teacher and student.[7] A critical pedagogical approach also brings autobiography into the classroom as a way of helping students understand their own privilege and oppression. The influence of critical pedagogy in teacher training programs has relaxed some of the formerly strict boundaries between teacher and student as well as "personal" and "professional." Still, teachers have to balance the value of self-disclosure against the danger of revealing something that could bring them under fire from parents and administrators. As a result, even the most ardent devotees of critical pedagogy must learn to temper the amount of intimacy they foster with students.

For gay and lesbian teachers, the practice of critical pedagogy is even more fraught. Coming out is a powerful biographical tool that can be used to teach students about heterosexism and homophobia.[8] But at the same time that it has the potential to break down walls between teachers and students, it can also build new ones. In his reflections on teaching as a gay man, Jonathan Silin argues that "by making teaching a 'very personal experience,' we give up being like our students or even being liked by them in order to foster authentic dialogue with them."[9] Disclosure may foster engagement for some students, but it is likely to alienate others. In addition, the restricted modes of disclosure available to most teachers make room for only a tightly regulated, sanitized, and normalized depiction of homosexuality.[10] Some argue that although coming out's pedagogical goal is to destabilize heterosexuality, it may inadvertently reinforce it by presenting homosexuality as a fixed, stable entity, thereby upholding the homo/hetero binary.[11]

Education scholar Mary Lou Rasmussen argues that debates over coming out in the classroom oversimplify teachers' moral, political, and pedagogical considerations.[12] As well, they leave little room for exploring how a teacher's race, class, and age are significant filters for interpreting their coming out and its pedagogical value. While the coming out discourse is limited, a deeper examination of how coming out operates in the educational context is a worthwhile endeavor. In understanding how teachers make decisions about disclosing their sexual identities and lives, we can also understand how institutional contexts produce visible gay and lesbian selves, which in turn produce discourses of gay and lesbian subjectivity. Gay and lesbian teachers negotiate the process of disclosing their sexual identities largely on the basis of three interrelated and interacting factors: the policy environment, the microculture of their schools, and their own gendered and raced embodiment.

Policy Environment

As described in detail in chapter 2, employment nondiscrimination policies currently protect only a portion of LGBT workers in the United States, and these protections are unevenly distributed and defined more or less narrowly depending on location. Some policies include only sexual identity and not gender identity and expression, thereby leaving transgender and genderqueer workers vulnerable. In some places, only public employees are protected, so private employees must rely on employer nondiscrimination policy if available. Without a clear and inclusive federal policy, individual LGBT employees are often left in confusing and legally ambiguous positions with respect to their employment rights.

The existence of nondiscrimination policy also does not eliminate the ongoing bias, exclusion, and marginalization experienced by LGBT workers.[13] The critical race critique of racial nondiscrimination law is instructive in this regard. For example, Alan Freeman argues that nondiscrimination and hate crime law and policy sustain a "perpetrator perspective" on racism by relying on the notions of discrete "perpetrators" and "victims" of racism.[14] Consequently, such laws and policies *individualize* racism rather than showing how it is in fact an *institutionalized* phenomenon. Gender and sexuality nondiscrimination laws suffer similar limitations. In addition, nondiscrimination policy's inability to accommodate intersectional claims to discrimination—for example, the raced and gendered harassment of Black women—further hinders its effectiveness.[15]

Queer critics of the Employment Nondiscrimination Act (ENDA) and other LGBT nondiscrimination efforts point out that such efforts truly protect neither the sexual rights of workers nor the right to freedom of gender expression.[16] Rather, they protect a very limited class of LGBT workers who conform to the standards of homonormativity. Of the 1996 version of ENDA, key supporter Senator Edward Kennedy explained, "Like other civil rights laws, the Employment Nondiscrimination Act does not protect bizarre behavior.... School systems can discipline teachers who appear in pornographic movies or other kinds of activities, but they must discipline both homosexuals and heterosexuals similarly."[17] My research showed how this narrow conceptualization of sexuality discrimination limits ENDA's effectiveness in protecting LGBT workers.

When I interviewed Kyle, a forty-seven-year-old white straight organizer for the teachers' union in Austin, Texas, he mentioned a recent controversy over the termination of a lesbian art teacher. Austin High School teacher Tamara Hoover was fired by the Travis School Independent School District when partially nude photographs, taken by her partner and posted to her partner's professional photography website, came to light.[18] Because the district argued that Tamara had violated "standards of professional conduct," the county's nondiscrimination legislation did not apply, although, as Kyle explains, the termination appeared to be related to the fact that the photos highlighted her same-sex relationship:

> [Tamara's] case was all kinds of—you know. She wasn't *really* being fired because of her sexual orientation. She was being fired because photographs had been posted on that website, Flickr. But it was all balled up, because the photographer was her partner, and you know, some of them were sexually explicit, although I don't remember them being—the school district told us that we never saw the "real" pictures because the most graphic stuff got pulled down. But I don't think that it was like … I think she was depicted either alone or with a man, but it all got balled up. Again, it's like, teaching while human. You know? It's like, you're not allowed; once your sexuality is revealed to students, then all of the sudden, it's like, you've crossed this line. It's very bizarre, it really is. Working with kids, it's just, the standards are different.

Because Tamara's sexual identity was tangled up with participation in a public display of sexuality, nondiscrimination protections were powerless against the strict codes of "professional conduct" that regulate teachers' extracurricular expressions of sexuality.

James, one of the quitters described in the previous chapter, told a story that further revealed the limitations of existing nondiscrimination policies:

cc: *Do you know if your school has a nondiscrimination policy?*

JAMES: I don't know. I don't think I would be fired, though, for being gay. So that's not the reason I'm not out, it's more just comfortable. Although, now that you mention it, last year, there was this incident in Houston where Fox News did an exposé called "Teachers Gone Wild." They went on Facebook and searched "teachers" and "Houston" and then got all these crazy pictures of teachers, you know, doing the normal twenties thing, drinking, partying and stuff. And one of the pictures was of a teacher who was gay, and the picture was from Pride and he was holding a dildo. Just like, you know, being silly at Pride and whatever. And it was on the news and everyone was all outraged. And his school—they didn't fire him, but they asked him not to teach for the rest of the year and they paid him anyway.

While James wasn't worried that he would be fired for coming out, he realized that the dangers of being a gay teacher go beyond questions of intentional disclosure. Attending Gay Pride events, posing for pictures with a sex toy, and leaving the evidence in a semipublic forum like Facebook can lead to suspension or nonrenewal of your teaching contract, regardless of whether you disclose your sexual identity at work. As with the Tamara Hoover case, nondiscrimination policy did not protect this teacher's right to pose for sexually charged pictures on his own time. James's example demonstrates a very literal clash between pride—attending a Gay Pride event and posing for pictures—and professionalism that even extensive policy protections cannot mediate.

Despite the obvious limitations of current policy, previous research suggests that policy does benefit some gay, lesbian, and bisexual workers. Studies show that gay and lesbian employees

who work in companies with LGB or LGBT-inclusive nondiscrimination policies are less stressed and display lower levels of
internalized homophobia than workers without such policies.[19]
Where protections do exist, gay and lesbian employees are more
likely to come out at work, which is significant, as research
shows a negative relationship between being in the closet and
job satisfaction.[20] Statewide policies appear to be especially
important to perceptions of gay-friendliness, ability to be out at
work, and internalized homophobia.[21] However, these benefits
do not appear to apply equally to workplaces involving children.
In 1986, Beth Schneider found that employees who worked with
children, such as teachers, were especially reluctant to be out on
the job;[22] this appears to still be the case, even in states with a
nondiscrimination policy.[23]

While this research provides important context for understanding gay and lesbian teachers, it offers only a partial account.
These studies rely on survey data, which provide a broad, but
not necessarily deep, picture of the LGBT employee experience. While they demonstrate that, for many, policy does have a
relationship to employee health, happiness and job satisfaction,
they don't offer much information about how and when policy
matters. In the case of teachers, how does policy interact with
school cultures, teachers' unions, and neighborhoods? How do
teachers find out about policy protections? When does policy
trump a homophobic work environment? My research allowed
me to explore these questions.

I was especially interested in whether the disparate policy
environments of California and Texas played a role in how
teachers made decisions about disclosure. California's gay-
friendly policy context included nondiscrimination policies at
the state, local, and district levels. The California Student

Safety and Violence Protection Act of 2000, AB537, added a provision to the existing nondiscrimination educational code stating that "all students and staff in public education facilities have the same right to a safe learning environment, regardless of their sexual orientation or gender identity."[24] The California Teachers Association (CTA), the largest affiliate of the National Education Association (NEA), had an LGBT caucus and protected its members from unlawful discrimination on the basis of sexual or gender identity. California's slightly more conservative American Federation of Teachers (AFT) affiliate also had an LGBT caucus and a nondiscrimination position, so union support was a given, regardless of which union a teacher belonged to. The LA Unified School District's Educational Equity Compliance Office had a specialist on sexuality-related harassment and discrimination of students and employees. California had one of the, if not *the*, strongest policy environments for the protection of gay and lesbian teachers.

Rufus chose to teach in California because of its extensive nondiscrimination protections. When asked about the challenges he faced as an out gay man working in a middle school, he said: "Yeah, I heard a lot of put-downs from students, and just like, really rude things. And I immediately was like, 'This is against the law.' That's one of the reasons I choose to live here and not in [my home state of] Wisconsin. I don't know if Wisconsin has something like AB 537 or other progressive laws like California does, but that was a conscious choice." The protections in California public schools influenced not only Rufus's decision to teach in the state but also his choice to come out to students. After threats and classroom vandalism by students who inferred Rufus's sexual identity on the basis of his mannerisms and mentions of his partner, Rufus decided to take a proactive approach to coming out. In addition to disclosing his sexual identity to students, he began educating them about LGBT policy protections and helping them understand that harassment would not be tolerated by the school and district administration. He explained, "I'm trying to teach fairness and respect and equality in my classroom, and, thankfully, I have the law on my side, and I tell my students. So I let them know that's against the law. And I didn't know I had to be so forward when I first started. And now I spend my first week—weeks!—of every school year, and in a fun way, we look at the law." By incorporating policy directly into his curriculum, Rufus demonstrates the protective power of nondiscrimination policy for some gay and lesbian teachers.

By contrast, the lack of protections in Texas was a deterrent for some teachers there. Unlike California, Texas had no statewide protections for LGBT employees, and teachers were perhaps more vulnerable than most. Some parts of the state (Austin, Dallas, Houston, and Fort Worth) had nondiscrimination protections for all employees at the time of my research, but most of the state was not covered by such statutes. Teachers' unions also had far less power in Texas. As Kyle explained to me:

> The fundamental difference in the legal structure in terms of teacher unions [in California and Texas] is this. California has enabling legislation that has created a system for collective bargaining. And it's mandatory; school districts have to collectively bargain with their teachers, and teachers' unions have negotiated for agency fee. Which means even if you don't join the union, you still pay the dues. So basically, when you go to work as a teacher in the California public school system, you're going to pay union dues. In Texas, it's the polar opposite. Collective bargaining is illegal. We're one of only two or three states that say out and out, it's against the law to do this. You are not allowed to do this. You could elect the best school board on the planet, and they could say, "But we want to, you know, recognize the rights of

our teachers." Can't do it. Against the law. So what we have done in Austin and several other urban areas is we've gotten the school board to adopt consultation policies, which kind of allow you to walk right up to the line without stepping over it. So our union, since 1999, has been elected three times, by all the teachers in the school district and all the support employees, to be the consultation agent, similar to the collective bargaining agent in California, the principal difference being we don't negotiate a contract. We negotiate with the administration around single-shot issues, and then, as the budget comes up, we present a budget package and try to get things in the budget. But at the end of the day, we either get in an agreement with the administration or we don't, and then we have an impasse agreement that lets us go to the school board. But we are much, much weaker, because of the laws, than they are in California. And because teachers can choose to join the union or not join the union or quit the union whenever they get mad or frustrated with us or the administration—it makes it very, very difficult to build an organization and exercise collective strength.

Although Education Austin, the Austin union affiliate, was supportive of gay and lesbian teachers, it could not demand nondiscrimination protections in employment contracts or offer much legal aid for teachers who alleged sexual identity discrimination. Overall, in contrast to California, Texas had one of the weaker policy contexts for supporting gay and lesbian teachers.

Melissa's experience as a forty-four-year-old white lesbian teacher in a small Texas town exemplified how vulnerable teachers without legal protections can feel, especially in a hostile work environment. Before she even started her first job, she was warned not to come out to anyone on campus:

> I couldn't be out at that school. My sister was a principal's secretary there. And my sister told me [that] the year before—well, she was like, "Melissa, you can't come out here." She goes, "It's not safe for you to come out here," and I said, "Well, why?" I didn't really know. And she says [that] the year before I came, there was a

volleyball coach, a female volleyball coach, that got pregnant out of wedlock and they fired her. Because all the parents were ganging up on her, coming to school board meetings, and you know, they didn't want her there. She wasn't a good role model for the students because she got pregnant and she wasn't married. And they didn't just come out and say that's why they fired her, but my sister was like, "I know that's why they fired her. I'm the principal's secretary." So they found reasons to get rid of her. And she said, "You know, if you come out, they'll do the same thing to you."

From this story, Melissa learned that evidence of nonmarital, nonheterosexual sexuality, which fell outside the bounds deemed appropriate by the community, was a career killer. This was driven home in her next job, where, she explained, "there was a teacher who was fired in this district when I first started and the newspaper said, 'homosexual teacher' and assumed that [all gay people] are pedophiles." In such a context, without any legal recourse against discrimination, she was vigilant about hiding her sexual identity and her relationship with another woman, although it caused her pain and stress.

These examples show how policy can empower or deter teachers in their decisions about coming out to administrators, coworkers, and students. However, the relationship between law and disclosure was complicated by the fact that a significant number of teachers, in both California and Texas, had incomplete or inaccurate knowledge of their legal rights as gay and lesbian school employees. Some California teachers did not know about the educational code barring antigay discrimination. Mark, the California administrator in charge of educating teachers about AB537, recounted the following story about a training session, which he said was typical of many such sessions: "I just did this training two days ago, and I said to them that these laws apply to employees and students, and I started the presentation. And at the end, this lesbian teacher raised her hand and I went, 'Yes?' and she said, she looked at everyone and she goes, 'So. I'm a lesbian teacher. Can I come out to my kids?' And I said, 'Absolutely, you are in a protected class!' And she looked at everybody and she said, 'Starting tomorrow I am coming out to my students.' And I thought, wow."

Given the extent of nondiscrimination protections for California teachers, I assumed that the teachers I interviewed would know they existed. Mark, who was my first interviewee, quickly disabused me of that assumption. Of the sixteen gay and lesbian teachers employed in California at the time of data collection, thirteen knew they were protected by nondiscrimination legislation at either the local or the state level, but three did not. The teacher at Mark's session, who he said was not unusual, suggests my sample may have been more informed than the norm. Indeed, one morning I sat in on one of Mark's sessions and a similar incident occurred. While it is difficult to generalize with such a small and nonrepresentative sample, it seems that even though California's nondiscrimination laws are well publicized, some teachers are still not aware of them.

California teachers also had varying levels of knowledge and enthusiasm about their union's ability to protect them from discrimination and harassment. Ruben, for example, was aware of his union's progay stance but also frustrated that more gay and lesbian teachers weren't taking advantage of union power to demand improvement:

CC: *What do you think UTLA's position is on protecting gay teachers? Are there any policies to protect gay teachers?*
RUBEN: Well, [United Teachers Los Angeles] is a very progressive union, first, let me start off by saying that. Now, UTLA was one of

the first unions to have domestic benefits. UTLA has been extremely progressive in that way. But one of the things that has to happen—there's actually a gay group called the Gay and Lesbian Issues Committee, GALIC. But what happens is, like every other group that's trying to create equality, gays must organize themselves. They have to come out and rally.

Others, like Alfred, a twenty-seven-year-old Latino gay teacher, were not as well versed in their union's LGBT position. When I asked Alfred, who was in the same union as Ruben, to describe what rights he had as a union member, he answered: "We have elections that come up about increasing benefits, fighting for a raise, vote yes or no, should we combine the secretary and treasurer position, just simple elections like that." He had not heard about GALIC or other LGBT-specific protections, although he did know that, generally speaking, the union would represent him in a conflict with administration.

In Texas, only eight of eighteen currently employed gay and lesbian teachers knew whether they benefitted from local or state nondiscrimination policy. Ten did not know, although some correctly guessed that they did not have any protections. Most interestingly, a surprising number of teachers in the places that *did* have local protections—Austin, Dallas, Houston, and Forth Worth, at the time—did not know about these policies. For example, when I asked Barbara, who lived in one of these cities, if she was aware of her district's or county's policies on nondiscrimination, she said, "No, I haven't got a clue. I haven't got a clue. I have no idea whether or not I could be fired outright by the school district for being gay." She was not alone in her lack of awareness: six of the ten teachers who did not know about regional nondiscrimination policies were actually protected at the city, county, and/or district level. It seems possible that the absence of more visible state-level policies affected their awareness of their overall legal status as gay and lesbian employees.

Barbara was the only Texas teacher to mention belonging to a union, though the group she paid dues to was actually a teachers' association, not a union. Teachers' associations provide liability insurance to teachers but do not negotiate (or in the case of Texas, consult) with school districts as unions do. Barbara did think of this membership as a potentially protective factor, but only in a worst-case scenario:

> They tell you if you are a [special education] teacher, the potential for litigation is so much higher because we have to restrain kids and we also deal with emotional disturbed kids who might turn around and say anything they want. And that's another reason—because if the kids found out I was gay, they could so go home and say, she's gay and she touched me here. Because I work with [emotionally disturbed] kids and they do that. So that's maybe part of it, too, but yeah, the legality of working with kids in [special education], so it's highly recommended we have some kind of representation through the unions.

While membership in the association helped Barbara feel protected against false accusations, it did not help her feel as if she had the choice to disclose her sexuality at work more broadly than the few close friends she had told.

Even teachers who worked in gay-friendly legal contexts and knew their rights could be wary of disclosing their sexual identity at school. Suspecting dissonance between policy and practice, they worried that they would still have to contend with quiet bias. Elizabeth, a soft-spoken thirty-year-old white lesbian, taught in the Dallas School District. Although she said her school offered nondiscrimination protections on the basis of sexual identity, she wasn't out to any of her colleagues and was nervous about the possibility of being outed. She explained: "Even in the hiring paperwork that I signed, it says they don't discriminate on the basis of sexual orientation. But it's just one of those things that—just because it says it, doesn't mean they wouldn't find other reasons, you know? So I still watch it."

For teachers like Elizabeth, the existence of a policy wasn't sufficient protection. Hugh, who defined his sexual identity as fundamentally personal and inappropriate for classroom discussion, agreed that even though his district had a nondiscrimination policy, "it could be overturned … or [they could] look the other way. I think principals wouldn't support you, the administration wouldn't support you." Ironically, teachers in less legally supportive regions sometimes had the opposite perspective. Debbie, a fifty-three-year-old white lesbian elementary school teacher in a medium-sized town an hour outside Dallas, did not benefit from any local, state, or district LGBT ordinances. However, her long and esteemed tenure in the school gave her the confidence to subtly come out to staff members. She commented, "I feel like I'm pretty well respected. I guess I just hit some point in my career, and I guess it was when I started being older than most of the people I was working with…. It's not like I go around telling everyone my personal life, but I'm still not afraid to put the rainbow sticker on the back of my car, for example." It seems clear that, in both states, relative knowledge of the legal context was a contributing, but by no means deciding, factor in teachers' decision making.

These examples suggest that nondiscrimination policy empowers some teachers to feel protected from harassment and discrimination at work. However, the fact that some teachers in the sample did not know whether these policies existed is troubling. If teachers don't know their own policy contexts, they can't make informed decisions about coming out on campus. This research suggests a need for greater policy education for teachers, and, by extension, for LGBT employees in general.

School Microcultures

As I began traveling through California and later through Texas to conduct interviews and observations, I was immediately struck by the incredible diversity of school contexts. Especially in urban areas, like Los Angeles or Houston, school conditions, student demographics, and politics could vary dramatically, even within a couple of miles. These variations made it difficult to characterize the school climate in a particular state, region, or even district. As Ruben put it, "LA Unified is extremely progressive, but there's a big difference between having a resolution that says that everyone is going to be treated equally and translating it down to the school site." It became apparent in my interviews and observations that school context shaped how teachers made their self-disclosure decisions much more than regional context. I use the term *school microcultures* to refer to the school-specific practices that influence disclosure decisions. These include staff and student interactions, administrative support for LGBT issues, and the presence or absence of other openly gay and lesbian staff members.

Alfred worked in an elementary school in Pico Union, an economically depressed neighborhood in downtown LA. He spoke at length about the gay-friendliness of the school environment. During one school visit, he introduced me to the front office staff, explaining that he was being shadowed as part of a "study of gay teachers." He also pointed out an announcement about the district's Gay Pride Month posted outside the principal's door. In the library, he chatted with the librarian about the Los Angeles Pride March, which had taken place the day before, while his students read nearby. As kids and staff streamed by us during the final bell of the day, he snagged another teacher by the arm, told him about the study, and encouraged him to participate. Alfred's school microculture was so formally and informally supportive that he and his coworkers could speak openly and casually about LGBT issues. In such an environment, the day-to-day tensions between pride and professionalism were minimal.

In contrast, Elizabeth, who worried about being fired from her Texas school, felt that, regardless of its policy protections, the school had a microculture of homophobia and heteronormativity. When asked why she led students and staff to believe she was married to a man rather than a woman, she said interactions with fellow teachers made her most wary of coming out. She described an instance of heterosexism from an orientation session at the beginning of the school year:

> Ms. [West], who is the other special ed teacher, goes, "Well, isn't that how it's supposed to work? Girls are supposed to like guys and guys are supposed to like girls." And coming from the special ed teacher of all things, you think she'd be more sensitive like that. I was just a little put off by it.... I'm fairly confident that most of my teaching staff is very conservative, so I only share very little.... Part of [the reason I didn't come out was because] the week prior to school, I was kind of testing the waters, listening to other teachers, and especially that comment Ms. [West] made let me know it wouldn't be okay.

Elizabeth felt that Ms. West's comment was representative of the climate of her new school, where heteronormativity was not just tacitly accepted but openly endorsed by school staff. In addition, she said, "My kids will make comments in conversations among themselves about 'gay' and how that's gross." In this climate, she lived in fear of being exposed as a lesbian; even though she and her partner lived in another town, she was afraid of being seen by parents, students, and staff, or somehow being outed. For teachers like Elizabeth, the coming out mandate associated with pride discourse came into direct conflict with the norms of professionalism endorsed by the school environment.

While Alfred's and Elizabeth's schools had different geographical contexts (California versus Texas, urban versus suburban), such microcultural divides did not occur solely along state and regional lines. John, the twenty-four-year-old Asian gay high school teacher who was about to quit teaching, taught in the LA Unified School District at a school not far from Alfred's that was markedly less gay-friendly. John encountered regular and explicit homophobia and harassment from students and staff. When asked about specific incidents of harassment, John recounted:

> [The harassment] started with a male African American student, he got mad one day. He was writing, passing notes in class, and I took the note and threw it in the trash. And he stood up and he said that [I was a fag]. I kicked him out and asked for a suspension. And then another incident happened, a kid doodling on the table ... something graphic about me "sucking dick." ... I've noticed some students are less comfortable, you know, with me being who I am. Like, certain things I would do, they would kind of give me a face.

Such incidents, both before and after he came out, played a significant role in John's decision to leave teaching and pursue a career in medicine.

These experiences make it clear that the microcultural practices of schools affect how gay and lesbian teachers negotiate sexuality in their own classrooms. Sometimes, the school micro-culture seamlessly matches the legal context, and the two work together to reinforce an atmosphere in which teachers like Alfred feel more comfortable referencing their sexuality. But for Elizabeth, a conservative and heteronormative microculture trumped any legal protections her school offered. Teachers like John, who decided to come out in antigay microcultures, often relied on legal protections as a protective shield against homo-phobic work environments. But even that shield was not enough to make John feel comfortable staying in the teaching profession. Each of these experiences illustrates the complex interrelationship between legal and microcultural context.

Gendered and Raced Embodiment

While policy and environment might seem like obvious factors in the process of coming out in the classroom, my research uncovered another factor: teachers' own gendered and raced embodiments. The experience of coming out is not just an institutional experience but an embodied one; how coworkers and students interpret a teacher's gender and race mediates decision making about disclosure.

A teacher's ability to manipulate gendered identity cues affects his or her decision-making process around coming out. Whether teachers could successfully perform a normative gender identity had significant bearing on how and when they disclosed their sexual identity. The term *gender expression* refers to the ways in which people perform masculinity and femininity in their daily interactions. Gender expression is being added to nondiscrimination policy more frequently, to cover discrimination and harassment on the basis of non-normative gender presentation and transgender status. The significance of this addition is twofold; first, it symbolizes a growing political awareness that transgender and genderqueer employees need employment protections too—today, perhaps more so than gender-normative gay, lesbian, and bisexual employees, whose rights and identities are increasingly normalized. It also symbolizes a shift from seeing sexual identity as the motivating force for violence and harassment against LGBTs to thinking about how such behaviors can also be responses to gender non-normativity.

Concurrently, gender and sexuality scholarship has moved from documenting the existence and histories of LGBT people to interrogating the relationship between gender performativity and sexual identities and practices.[25] In this literature, *gender expression* is sometimes used interchangeably with *gender performativity* to refer to the "stylized acts" we engage in to perform gender for ourselves and others.[26] Gender expression or performativity is an important component of one's *habitus*, the durable ways of standing, speaking, walking, and general deportment that are sedimented in childhood.[27] These dispositions are part of the embodied self, not behaviors that are displayed in particular situations. Such embodied mannerisms are imprinted not just on the body but *in* the body. Some gender expressions (often unwittingly) signify homosexuality through gender-atypical gestures, hair and clothing styles, speech patterns, and so forth. In the classroom, such embodied distinctions can lead students to "read" teachers as gay or lesbian. These interpretations can be another factor in teachers' decisions about whether to come out.

Mauricio referred to himself as "gay-acting," which conflicted with his desire to withhold his gay identity from his students. He said:

MAURICIO: Do they know [that I'm gay]? Current students, I think about 80 to 90 percent suspect and the other 10 percent don't care.

CC: *Why do you think they suspect?*
MAURICIO: I hear what they talk about, they talk about me. It's almost like, well, Mr. [Lopez], he's gay, well, so what.

Mauricio's students were likely (and correctly) deducing his gay identity by reading his gender expression cues. In *How to Be Gay*, David Halperin argues that the distinct history and culture of homosexuality produces certain camp-influenced mannerisms, aesthetics, ways of speaking, and tastes in many gay men.[28] This gay "sensibility" is as much a part of gay community as political or sexual practices. Mauricio in many ways exemplified the stylized performance Halperin references. The pitch and variability of his voice along with his use of what linguists call the California Vowel Shift (popularly recognizable in "Valley Girl" speak) marked Mauricio's speech as gay.[29] His teaching style was very physically expressive: to emphasize a point, he would hold his hands to either side of his face and wriggle his fingers for emphasis. When he was exasperated with a student, he would roll his eyes exaggeratedly and sometimes tilt his head to the side, mouth open and eyebrows raised, until the student answered him or stopped talking with friends. During our interview, he sat with his legs crossed, arms straight, and wrists crossed at the knee. Overall, his voice, mannerisms, hand gestures, and body language were consistent with a gender performance that is often read as gay when seen in men.

Phillip, the elementary school teacher who, like Mauricio, was an adamant splitter, also acknowledged that students speculated on his sexuality. The fluid, elegant way he carried himself, coupled with how he spoke, had the hallmarks of the gay aesthetic. He recounted, "One day, there were two boys passing a note back and forth to each other. I got a hold of it and it was about me. It said, 'Do you think Mr. [Bloom] is gay?' and the other boy, he wrote, 'Well, yeah.'" When I asked if he was surprised, he replied:

> No, not particularly. I mean, fifth graders, they're about ten or eleven years old, they have enough clues from the world, and TV, and the Internet. By the time you are in fifth grade, you kind of know what gay is, and you kind of know what it looks like, what it sounds like. I think it was something in my voice, the way I talk, that led them to this conclusion.... That's part of why I won't teach anything probably above third grade. That quickly clued me in to an age that I don't need to be around because I felt that would always be an issue. And I thought the best way to sidestep that is to be teaching kids a little younger than that. Before puberty, before hormones, before ... they just get to an age where they know about these things.

Phillip was upset that the older students had interpreted his embodied dispositions as gay because it "invites trouble I don't need, trouble they don't need, their parents don't need." He also felt it was inappropriate and irrelevant, saying, "It's not, it just doesn't seem pertinent to what I'm trying to do. I'm just trying to teach them to read and add and subtract a little bit."

Stanley, the California substitute teacher, faced a similar dilemma but had decided to solve it by outing himself early and often. In one classroom, "this kid who sat right in the front of the class, said 'Mr. [Miles], when you do this'—and he made a swishy hand motion, because I tend to gesticulate when I talk— he said, 'When you do this, you look like a fag.'" Another time, he came into the classroom to see "Mr. [Miles] is fat and gay" scrawled across the chalkboard. While Mauricio tried to maintain the open secret of his sexuality in the face of his gender performance, Stanley resigned himself to coming out (regardless of his own preference) because, in his own words, "I can't hide. I am too effeminate."

Some teachers transformed what Stanley saw as an inevitable impediment into an important teachable moment about accepting difference. They saw what felt like their natural and comfortable gender expression as an important political opportunity. Taylor, a thirty-year-old white lesbian health teacher in California, wore men's clothing and kept her hair very closely cropped. Because she did not remove facial hair, she had a light beard on her chin and cheeks. Her small stature meant that she was sometimes mistaken for an adolescent boy student. Taylor considered her atypical gender expression an opportunity to critique conventional notions of "appropriate" gender displays, and she used it as a way to come out to her students. In particular, her facial hair often prompted this discussion. She explained

> I [bring LGBT issues into the classroom when I] come out—I mean, it's kind of hard not to. I always say on the very first day to my students, "I know that I don't look like most female teachers that you've had, but I choose to look this way because it makes me feel more comfortable in who I am. If you ever have questions, feel free to ask—I'm totally open to that. And if you ever want to talk after school, or in class, if you have questions, let me know." So sometimes kids will say, "Do you like guys or girls?" and I'll be like, "I'm a lesbian, I like girls, I have a partner," and so on. And some of them ask, "Well, why do you have a beard?" or "How did that happen?" and I explain.... I had a beard when I went through puberty, and I plucked it for a long time and shaved it, went through electrolysis, everything that a "good girl" does. You know, I tried to fit in. And then I came out as lesbian, and I realized ... maybe I would like to grow it out, and I did and I felt comfortable with myself. I

frame it as a self-esteem thing, because I teach about self-esteem. So I tell them that I really liked the way I looked, I feel a lot more comfortable in who I am and that's really important. And that I think it's really important for them to feel comfortable with their body, the way they look.

Taylor's use of her gender performance to come out was further enabled by supportive policy and school microculture. She was able to practice what Janna Jackson calls the "enactment of queer pedagogy," or queering the classroom space and pedagogical practice by bringing sexual identity and experience into the teaching process.[30]

Conversely, some teachers who believed they didn't present as gay felt less pressure to comment on their sexual identity in the classroom. I met with Ian, a sixty-one-year-old white gay man, in the sitting room of his ranch-style Texas home. Ian's voice had a deep, rumbling gravitas and authority that reflected his three decades of teaching. Only recently retired, Ian had taught from the early years of gay liberation until 2006, and he was able to speak to teaching in Texas across various eras of gay history. Even in the 2000s, Ian felt he needed to stay in the closet to exert authority at work, but at the time he began teaching in 1974 he believed it was an absolute necessity. He explained that, unlike other coworkers, he was able to remain closeted at school because of his normative gender expression. Of his fears of being outed, he said: "It didn't really matter with students, because most of the time I pulled off seeming straight to them without too much of a problem. I mean, I'm not too effeminate. To be effeminate would be just a disaster. You would never get hired. It's just . . . the kiss of death."

Christi, a thirty-year-old white lesbian, had been teaching in the same Texas town as Ian since the early 2000s, but she was much less worried about keeping her job and was out to coworkers and administrators, though not students. Where Ian called on his normative masculinity to secure and maintain his job, Christi described using her normative femininity as a buffer against homophobia and a way to control when and how she came out. She explained, "I think if I were butch, it would be very difficult. You have to work twice as hard. I know we had a very, very, very butch woman who taught in the position across from me for the first three years.... But I don't think ... that would be a battle. I don't think I could do that." Unlike her coworker, Christi believed she could leverage her conventional gender presentation not only to control disclosure but also to make herself less threatening and more approachable to students. She was considering coming out to her students in the next year, believing they would be more open to accepting her as a feminine-presenting lesbian than they would have been to her butch coworker, had she been explicitly out.

Some teachers spoke of consciously trying to correct their non-normative gender habitus and body postures. Kenny, who was not out, reflected on his classroom disposition:

cc: *Do you think that your sexual identity impacts your teaching in any way?*
KENNY: I don't think so. Maybe in ... the only ways I've noticed, well, how I stand? I don't know if you are talking on that level, but how I talk to my kids. Sometimes I may do something effeminate and the kids laugh at it and are like, that's cute and whatever....

cc: *It's interesting you mention gestures—are there things you do that students read as gay?*
KENNY: On occasion. But it's almost like I'm aware of it, and—what's a good example—and these are all so stereotypical, but like, gay male behaviors, like put my hands on my hips or something like that.

And I don't do it very often, like no one is like, Mr. [Johnson] is gay—well, maybe they are, but I haven't heard anything....

CC: *In terms of those gestures, is it like, you're doing them unconsciously and then you stop yourself, or you do them on purpose?*

KENNY: Both. Definitely both. There are times that I've done it and I realize they like it and they giggle, but there's definitely times, you know, and I'm talking about something as miniscule as—I'll be like, posted up on the wall, leaning against it, and I'll take myself out of body for a second and I'll think, "If I were looking at myself right now ...," or I see someone walking down the hall and I think, "I wonder what that looks like to them as they walk by."

Kenny's description of himself demonstrated a self-conscious engagement with gender expression that exemplifies the fraught relationship between choice and embodiment. He noticed his own moments of gender non-normativity and asked himself how his students or fellow teachers might interpret them. By "taking [himself] out of [his] body for a second," Kenny recognized that he unwittingly demonstrated a gay self-presentation. Sometimes he tried to correct these signs, but at other times he played them up for comedic effect. Overall, though, he attempted to manipulate his gender expression to prevent questions about his sexuality.

The men in the sample talked about being read as gay much more often than the women did. This makes sense, given that men are held to a stricter standard of gendered behavior in which any failure of hegemonic masculinity leaves them open to suspicion and derision.[31] Héctor, the gay Latino former classroom teacher turned administrator, observed, "I don't think lesbians are singled out as much as gay men are. Women are kind of ignored, and that goes for both gay and straight women. In that sense, I think it's easier for lesbian teachers, because it's not as recognized as gay men." Men also spoke of "acting gay" while women referred to "looking like a lesbian." This distinction between "acting" and "looking" may reflect the active/passive dichotomy that constructs our language of gender, in which men act and women are acted upon.[32] Regardless of these gendered distinctions, it is clear that gender expression shapes whether, how, when, and why gay and lesbian teachers disclose their sexual identity to students and staff.

Race also has a profound effect on the process of disclosure. Previous research on LGBT people of color strongly suggests that the intersecting inequalities of racial and sexual marginality make their experiences distinct from those of white LGBTs, whose voices otherwise predominate in the literature on sexual identity.[33] This research demonstrates the importance of including the specific experiences of people of color when theorizing about sexual identity. To fully understand how context shapes the coming out experiences of gay and lesbian teachers, it is essential to consider whether and how racial marginality shapes disclosure decision making.

Sometimes race is implicated in the reading of gender performance. Racialized expectations of masculinity affected how and when gay men of color came out. John explained, "The first year, it was like, okay, I'm Asian American, so they might perceive me as gay." During his first year of teaching, John wanted to keep his sexual identity out of the classroom, but feminized stereotypes of Asian men made him worry that his students might already presume he was gay.[34] This complicated his decision-making process in a way that white gay teachers did not have to contend with. James, a twenty-three-year-old Black gay teacher, was cognizant of how his gay sensibilities were read in the context of his Blackness by his mostly Black and Latino students. When James was preparing to begin his first job, he thought about race and gender:

JAMES: I knew the community I was coming into, I was going to act differently than the other Black men these kids have in their lives.

CC: *How so?*
JAMES: Well, like, I wear tight clothing, not many of the men in their community dress like me. And I guess some of my mannerisms.

James was conscious that his gender performance would be interpreted through the lens of race and that expectations of Black masculinity would be part of his classroom life. For both John and James, the intersection of race and gender performance informed their self-presentation and their decisions about coming out.

At forty-three, José had earned his master's and doctorate in education. He began his career as a classroom teacher but left for about a decade to pursue his EdD and teach in an education master's program. By the time we met, José had returned to teaching at the primary level, though he continued to teach part time in the master's program. This dual perspective gave him valuable insight into the experience of being a gay teacher of color. José had lived in Mexico until he was ten, when his family moved to the United States. In the transition, he went from a successful student to a struggling one, mostly because of the language barrier in his US classroom (the school he attended did not have a bilingual education program). As an adult, he was motivated by this experience to become a teacher and work with non-English speakers. In addition to his passion for bilingual education, José was interested in incorporating antiracist and antihomophobic lessons into both the teacher training program and the elementary school. Perched on the tiny chairs in his elementary school classroom, we thumbed through the children's book *The Sissy Duckling* by Harvey Fierstein, which his first-grade class had read that year. The book is about a boy duck who is ostracized for having feminine interests but is celebrated in the end when he saves his injured father using his nurturing skills. José was excited about the opportunity to teach his young students about difference and begin to deconstruct homophobic notions about what boys and girls should do. True to his other passion, he continued to work with non-English-speaking students, despite the fact that California had been dismantling bilingual education in public schools since 1998.

In the master's program, which was heavily invested in critical pedagogy, his students of color were complaining about the undue burden of educating their fellow students about race and racism. He explained: "[Professors say] 'Let's talk about oppression, let's talk about, say, racial inequality, that a lot of sensitive issues do come up,' and I think it does bring up a lot of discomfort with students [of color] in the program.... That students say, 'Well, all of a sudden, I become the token person [of color] and all of the other students see me that way.'" Such students often told him, "I refuse to talk in Such-and-Such's class anymore, because everyone, when we're talking about X issue, everyone looks at me, as if I were the representative for the group." The experiences of José's students suggest that gay and lesbian teachers of color have already experienced racial Othering by the time they enter the classroom and that even well-meaning professors and fellow students can participate in this process while ostensibly trying to challenge racism. Indeed, previous research has identified the injuries this kind of tokenizing engenders.[35] Such experiences may deter gay and lesbian teachers of color from coming out and potentially being subjected to further tokenizing.

As for his own experiences with elementary school students, José said, "I can't separate my personal background from my professional, because I can't separate being Latino and having been raised in a Latino family from how I teach in a Latino community." His strategies for dealing with questions of sexuality in a predominantly Latino school and community were very much influenced by his own experiences growing up gay and Latino. He explained, "Part of me is bringing my internalized homophobia [in] because I think I know how oppressive the Latino community can be, and [I have to ask myself,] am I willing to tackle that, to take that on?" José acknowledged that his own experiences of oppression in a Latino family and community shaped how he, in turn, dealt with questions of coming out to his students.

David, a forty-three-year-old Latino gay Texas teacher, also made sense of his decision to stay in the closet at school in the context of his own family experience, which he extrapolated to be representative of "Hispanic culture":

DAVID: So ideally it would be great if I could share that part of my life with [my students], but I don't think I'll live to see that.

CC: *Because of . . . ?*

DAVID: Parents, society's attitudes. The reason I say that is because of Hispanic culture, I know the culture pretty well, and it's basically just very unacceptable. They are more into the male machismo thing and mom's in the kitchen, barefoot and pregnant and making tortillas and that's it, that's the way life is. You know? That's kind of how my family was.

Like José, David was reluctant to come out to students because his own experience suggested to him that his students' parents, who were also largely Latino, would be intolerant of his sexuality. I discuss this phenomenon of predicting homophobia on the basis of race and ethnicity in greater detail in chapter 6, but it is important to acknowledge here that it is part of the disclosure decision-making process for some teachers of color. The intersectional considerations of gender and race reveal the complex considerations that gay and lesbian teachers must undertake alongside their negotiations of the structural and microcultural factors discussed above.

What my interview respondents call "coming out" is in fact an always partial, ongoing negotiation of disclosure that is contingent on a variety of contextual factors. For gay and lesbian teachers, coming out at work involves decisions about both staff *and* students; both kinds of disclosure come with their own dilemmas. Coming out to coworkers can help teachers feel comfort and camaraderie among their peers, but it can also open them up to discrimination, harassment, and stereotyping. Coming out to students can be a powerful teachable moment, exposing straight and LGBT students alike to positive role models. Yet this coming out also has the highest stakes, because of the immediate risk of harassment, as well as adult concerns about exposing children to homosexualities and attendant fears of polluting or corrupting their development. The issue of coming out in schools is steeped in the tensions between pride and professionalism at the heart of this book—the rhetoric of gay pride demands coming out, while the expectations of teaching professionalism stifle it. The specific constellation of local conditions that teachers experience on the ground are implicated in this larger discursive struggle.

My analysis of the coming out considerations of gay and lesbian teachers reveals the ways in which workplaces—in this case, schools—can shape sexual identity disclosure. For these teachers, negotiating a public self as both a teacher and a gay or lesbian person involved navigating a series of legal, cultural, and embodied considerations. Three context-specific factors interacted to shape their decision-making process: legal protections or vulnerabilities, the culture of school environments, and their gendered and raced embodiments.

This finding contributes to previous organizational research that has shown how occupations and organizations are structured in a manner that perpetuates gender inequality.[36] By considering how sexuality-related inequalities are also sustained through occupational factors, this chapter extends our understanding of the relationship between organizations, individuals, and the maintenance of inequality regimes.[37] Far from being sexually neutral, workplaces shape sexual expression in meaningful ways. The sociological aspects of coming out at work should be examined within other jobs to further outline the operation of heterosexuality privilege across occupational contexts.

Coming out is more than a political or a psychological process; it is also a social phenomenon that is shaped by structural, cultural, and embodied context. Social institutions contribute to the production of sexualities, and workplaces legitimize and stigmatize expressions of sexuality in a manner that reproduces gender and sexuality inequality. Still, the experience of being a gay or lesbian teacher is about more than just decision making about coming out; it is also about the everyday performance of sexuality, as the next chapter will show.

CHAPTER FIVE

"A Bizarre or Flamboyant Character"

Homonormativity in the Classroom

In the summer of 2008, I attended a meeting of the Gay and Lesbian Allied Administrators (GALAA) in a nondescript office park in downtown Los Angeles, not far from the LA Unified School District central administration office. Since 2006, when it began as a support group for gay and lesbian administrators, GALAA has broadened its scope to include all educational professionals in the distinct, including teachers and school staff. Although I followed the directions to the meeting given me by one of the group's coordinators, when I walked into the conference room, I hesitated, unsure if I was in the right place. At the front of the room stood a podium draped in heavy velvet brocade embroidered with the words "Jesus Christ is our Lord and Savior," as if to create a makeshift pulpit. Otherwise, the room looked like a typical conference room with a long table in the middle, inoffensive seascapes on the walls, and carpet and chairs in muted shades of beige and green. I was the first to arrive, which added to my confusion about the location, but within a few minutes, I was joined by one of the coordinators, who assured me that this was not, in fact, a surprise religious service.

The podium and brocade caught the attention of others as they entered the room, causing many double takes similar to my own. As we waited for everyone to trickle in, someone joked that we should leave a note to make sure the religious group knew they were sharing their meeting space with "a bunch of gay teachers." Someone else gestured to the embroidery and asked, "Is this our new motto?" Everyone laughed. Amid the jokes and small talk, two teachers introduced themselves to me and we began to talk about their experiences. June had been teaching special education at South Central High for five years. Stanley had taught English at Eastside High for two years before he was moved into substitute teaching after a classroom confrontation with students. Stanley raised the issue of coming out to students and asked how others dealt with whether and how to come out. June replied that she initially hadn't wanted to raise the issue of her sexuality in the classroom, but eventually, she said, "I did it for the kids. When I see what they go through, I had to come out." After about fifteen minutes of chatting, the coordinator called the meeting to order. A total of ten members were present, including a mix of teachers, principals and vice-principals, and central district administrators.

I introduced myself to the group and spoke about my research, asking people who were interested in participating to get in touch after the meeting. My brief presentation spawned an impromptu discussion about what it was like to be gay or lesbian in the classroom. Mark, the central administrator who had formerly been in the closet in the classroom, posed the question, "Why won't teachers come out?" June responded that coming out brings a new dimension into teachers' relationships with students, where they suddenly become "the gay teacher." "What used to be seen as strengths," she explained, "are suddenly interpreted as 'dyke-ness.'" She complained that students are distracted by this new information and that they focus on asking personal (and invasive) questions about her sexuality, rather than on their work. June said she faced an additional dilemma because she worked in a co-teaching classroom: she worried that her co-teachers might resist working with a "gay teacher." Her comments reminded me that, for gay and lesbian teachers, the battle for legitimacy and acceptance continues long after the initial decisions about coming out outlined in the previous chapter.

When the conversation turned to teachers' confusion over how to handle gay issues in the classroom, Mark shared a concern that frequently comes up in the professional development trainings he runs at schools across the district to inform teachers about the laws and policies that protect LGBT staff and students. He explained that "people get uncomfortable [with LGBT teachers] because they think you are going to start talking about sex" with students. When he said that he tried to dispel this hypersexualization of LGBT teachers in his professional development sessions, and started to describe his efforts, Stanley interrupted him. "But at the same time," he exclaimed, "we *need* people who *are* going to be talking about sex!" Stanley was frustrated that kids, and in particular LGBT kids, do not get adequate sexuality education because teachers are afraid of addressing the issue of queer sexuality. With this sudden turn in the conversation, the group began to ponder a critical dilemma: How do you present LGBT sexuality in schools without either hypersanitizing or hypersexualizing?

While the previous chapter explored how schools shape the coming out process, this chapter focuses not on disclosure but on the everyday performance of gay and lesbian identity in the classroom. Although, as the last chapter demonstrated, the performance of gender and sexuality is an important aspect of disclosure, its significance is not limited to decisions about coming out. As with coming out, the tensions between gay pride and teaching professionalism shape the ways teachers talk about gay and lesbian visibility, both their own and others'. However, these discourses shape visibility differently than they affect coming out. In coming out, the two are pitted against each other: the ethos of gay pride demands it, while the expectations of teaching professionalism discourage it, especially to children. But when it comes to how gay and lesbian teachers should behave in the classroom, the two curiously coalesce, reinforcing rather than fighting each other, but in ways that ultimately discourage the project of transforming the gender and sexual politics of schools and workplaces.

By now, it should come as no surprise that schools inhibit gay and lesbian teachers' expressions of their sexual selves. As previously discussed, the professional norms of teaching call for strict adherence to a presentation of self in the classroom that is supposedly "neutral" but in reality is deeply imbued with heterosexual and gender normative expectations. These norms disadvantage gay and lesbian teachers, who must either try to conform or risk failure, which can entail discrimination and harassment. What may be more surprising, though, is that the mainstream gay rights movement also works to constrain the ways teachers present themselves in the classroom. As marriage and family have come to dominate the political agenda of the movement, gays and lesbians are increasingly expected to look and act the same as their straight counterparts and even to have the same desires. This "white picket fence" vision of equality, dubbed the new homonormativity by Lisa Duggan, has all but replaced the radical critiques of monogamy and procreation that flourished during gay liberation.[1] Rather than distance itself from the neo-liberal values of consumption, individualism, and privatization, the movement has embraced them, as demonstrated, among other things, by the extensive corporate sponsorship of Pride celebrations and the pursuit of marriage equality to the near exclusion of other political projects.

Critics of this shift argue that the political emphasis on marriage equality, military service, and procreation reflects an over-investment in the concerns of those who can—and want to—afford the privileges of normativity.[2] This investment trades complicity with the racist, classist, and sexist status quo to secure gains for those willing and able to participate in it. The result is a steep hierarchy of worthiness within LGBT communities, with those privileged by race, class, and gender at the top. Gender normativity, or the performance of being a "very straight gay," has become increasingly important in this context.[3] Trans people, bisexuals, genderqueers, queers of color, queer sex workers, and others have become eyesores on the whitewashed, upper-middle-class aesthetic of homonormativity.[4] This hierarchy puts pressure on all LGBT individuals to mimic the new norm, lest they be accused of hindering the progress of the gay rights movement.

The single-oppression model of LGBT organizing encourages homonormativity by assuming that shared sexual behavior creates a shared experience of oppression. As Cathy Cohen argues in her classic article "Punks, Bulldaggers, and Welfare Queens," queer politics should be about "one's relation to power, not some homogenized identity."[5] In the past few decades of LGBT organizing, the political turn toward the state as a vehicle for social change has further embedded the politics of homosexuality in homonormativity.[6] This will to institutionality, as Roderick Ferguson terms it, disciplines queerness through the proliferation of legal and political apparatuses that govern who counts as a legitimate sexual subject.[7] The rhetoric of gay pride facilitates this process by demanding that LGBTs eschew feelings of shame, self-loathing, and despair as relics of the repressed "before," unnecessary in today's liberated "after." To feel proud of being LGBT today requires ignoring those who aren't thriving under the new regime. This dissonance, which Kevin Murphy calls the melancholy of homonormativity, is the dark underbelly of the spectacle of gay pride.[8]

Accordingly, gay and lesbian teachers in schools must negotiate not only the performative demands set out by antigay forces but also those of the gay rights movement. In determining their everyday performance of sexuality, the teachers in my study had to make decisions about their visibility as gays and lesbians in the classroom in the context of strict expectations about what that visibility should look like. In interviews, they made it clear that the dividing line between acceptable and unacceptable presentations of a gay or lesbian self hinged largely on conventional presentations of appearance and behavior, which were in turn interpreted through a racial lens. White teachers contrasted their performances of gay identity with the imagined performance of queers of color, whom they portrayed as gender nonnormative—and less evolved. Teachers of color, in turn, had to juggle both racist and homonormative expectations when making sense of their own classroom selves. The appearance of "virtual normality" downplayed the sexual aspects of gay and lesbian identity,[9] which was what Mark attempted to do in his professional development trainings. In these complexities, we see how expectations of homonormativity emerge from both anti- and progay discourses.

Teachers not only felt accountable to these normalizing expectations on campus but also were frustrated by their constraints. Stanley's comments in the GALAA meeting demonstrated this frustration. His specific concern was that removing sexual content from LGBT school discussions denied students the possibility of adequate sexuality education. I argue that, along with its pedagogical limitations, this emphasis on normality limits the visibility permitted in schools to a very specific—and finite—set of classroom performances and practices.

In this chapter, I consider two interrelated questions that gay and lesbian teachers must answer in the process of constructing a classroom presence. First, how did homonormativity shape their understandings of gay and lesbian identity? And second, how did these understandings operate in the day-to-day lives of visibly gay and lesbian teachers? I find that, theoretically and practically, there are acceptable and unacceptable ways of being a gay or lesbian teacher. The acceptable gay or lesbian teacher, an occupationally specific version of what Steven Seidman would call the "normal gay," is married or partnered, monogamous, productive, and gender normative;[10] he or she has the same interests and tastes as heterosexual teachers. The unacceptable gay or lesbian teacher is politically radical, sexually promiscuous, and gender ambiguous—and in so being endangers gay rights for everyone else. This binary tightly controls the kinds of gay and lesbian representations that are allowed to emerge in the school context and affects pedagogical opportunities around LGBT issues. These limited classroom identities ultimately support the systems of privilege that many hoped gay and lesbian visibility would challenge.

ACCEPTABLE—AND UNACCEPTABLE—GAY OR LESBIAN TEACHERS

Mary, a sixty-year-old white lesbian retired teacher, was instrumental in bringing many LGBT initiatives to the LA Unified School District. I met with her and her partner, another retired teacher, in their split-level cottage in the Hollywood Hills. After showing me photos of their early teaching days and giving me a tour of the house, they each sat down with me in the living room for interviews. As someone who had spent such a long time working on LGBT issues in schools, Mary had clear ideas about the potential obstacles to full inclusion. Part of what needed to happen, she argued, was that gay and lesbian teachers had to "put a face on ourselves that we are normal and productive citizens like everyone else. So people can begin to know that we exist, and who we are and that we're teachers and neighbors and family members, aunts and uncles, and you know, whatever career we're in." This emphasis on "normal and productive" resonates with the discourse of homonormativity: look, act, and work like everyone else in order to secure rights. In attempting to distance herself and her peers from the limiting stereotypes they encounter, Mary reinforced a gay and lesbian code of conduct that narrowly dictates how teachers should present themselves.

Charles, also retired, reiterated Mary's position, saying, "The thing is that we need to keep working, to get people to see that we are regular people." Likewise, David, the Latino gay teacher who pointed to the influence of machismo culture on his decision to deemphasize his sexuality at school, spoke of the relationship between the growing visibility of gay and lesbian teachers and the projection of an image of normality:

CC: *What do you think we could do to improve the way schools are organized or the culture around schools to make it a more gay-friendly climate?*

DAVID: I think really what we need, and this is hard to say because I think it would jeopardize a lot of people, is we need more media coverage. And positive coverage. Because a lot of time, the public, all they see, and there's nothing wrong with this, but all they see is our friends out there marching in Gay Pride and they've got a wedding dress on and a beard, and it's like, they need to know that we're people, too. And we're fighting for the same goals they are, educating our children and making our lives better. A lot of times I think when straight people look at us, they look at us as deviants. And that bothers me, because I feel, I personally feel that I would have more in common with a straight man that likes to do the things that I do than with a gay man that likes to do the complete opposite.

David hesitated when describing the image he felt gays and lesbians should project, because he realized how it could jeopardize more marginalized LGBT people. Although his frustration at feeling limited by stereotypes about gay and straight men was valid, in discouraging attention to those who would wear a wedding dress with a beard—in fact, in defining *personhood* in opposition to such gendered displays—David ultimately rejected in-your-face political advocacy and gender non-normativity as possible routes to achieving progress. In arguing that LGBTs should avoid behavior that could label them as deviants and instead package their media representation to emphasize conventional dress and behavior, he articulated an agenda very much in line with the ideal of homonormativity.

David and other teachers understandably struggled with the constraining power of stereotyping. David himself was, in part, reacting to the stereotypes of gays and lesbians as gender transgressors, which, as someone who did not fit the stereotype, he found limiting and frustrating. Teachers referenced these stereotypes frequently when they talked about their experiences. Elizabeth, the thirty-year-old white lesbian teacher from Texas, lamented, "One of the biggest things is public perception about what being gay is. Because those stereotypes ... you have those even with high schoolers and those carry on into your adult life.... For instance, every lesbian has short hair or a mullet and plays softball, things like that." Ideally, representations of gays and lesbians would include a wide range of being, embracing a spectrum of normative and non-normative images. The problem, though, with the position David articulated is that it depicts gender non-normative LGBTs as complicit in their own stereotyping and therefore damaging to the gay rights agenda. The person with a beard in a wedding dress becomes a distracting spectacle, rather than a person who has his own legitimate needs that also fall under the umbrella of gay rights.

June articulated a vision of progress that demonstrates the pervasiveness of homonormativity. When asked what kind of future she would like to see with respect to LGBT rights, she explained:

> I think that as children are growing that they need to see gays in every walk of life, doing all of the things that they aspire to do and that they understand that, again, just as we don't look at heterosexual people and say, "There's a heterosexual police officer," we don't look at gay people like that. The word becomes a secondary aspect. In talking to one of the teachers who was like, "I don't see what the big deal is about gay marriage," I said that to me, what gay marriage represents is that for every parent and every child, for every parent who thinks that their child is gay and for every child who figures out or realizes that they are gay—that the only thing that that will change in that parental book of their child's life will be the figures

on the top of the wedding cake. And that's the only thing that will change. And then there will be the prom and there will be the heartache. There will be everything else. And then the ultimate goal is there won't need to be a GSA, there won't need to be gay pride. There won't be need to be those things.

June's vision of ultimate victory would be the complete assimilation of LGBTs into the monogamous, heterosexualized institutions of prom and marriage. The only thing different for gays and lesbians would be the figures on top of their wedding cakes, a far cry from the more radical visions of dismantling the institutions of marriage and family posed by the gay and lesbian liberationists of the 1960s and '70s.

The troubling aspect of this emphasis on normality was the corresponding disdain for those who did not toe the line. When I asked what advice he would offer newly minted gay and lesbian teachers, Charles admonished, "Well, it's up to the gay or lesbian teacher to act like a person, and not have bizarre or flamboyant character." He went on to explain that such a "character" would be an impediment in the classroom: "It distracts from what they are trying to present and they are supposed to be presenting the subject matter, primarily, and that [would be distracting]. So nothing that distracts from the overall tone and presentation is appropriate." Charles referenced both the neutral ideal of teaching professionalism—nothing "distracting" from teaching—and the homonormative ideal. The fundamental identity of "person" is limited to those who behave in normative ways, and Charles's directive that "it's up to the gay or lesbian teacher to act like a person" is right in line with the neoliberal demand to change yourself rather than critique the institutions that demand such narrow and normative presentations.

Some teachers contrasted themselves with unacceptable gay archetypes, in comments that echoed the role model discourse described in chapter 3. Larry defined his presence as an openly gay teacher in direct contrast to the gay men and trans women he presumed his students encountered in their communities:

CC: *Do you think it's important for teachers to be out in their classrooms?*
LARRY: I think so.

CC: *Why is that?*
LARRY: It's just, um, especially in our neighborhood, a neighborhood that's 90 percent Hispanic, the only gay people they see are what the kids call the "half trannies." The really effeminate Hispanic gay men, they keep the bottom and get boobs in Mexico City, really cheap boobs. And they're hookers and prostitutes or something.... [In their communities], there's no such thing as gay. Not like, "I'm going to live with a guy, spend the rest of my life with a guy, and you know, we're going to share a life." No.

Larry juxtaposed an imagined unacceptable gay—effeminate, possibly trans-identified queer men of color who participate in sex work—against himself to shore up his identity as a potential gay role model. In this process, he drew upon the assumptions that US gay identities are more evolved than those in Mexico, positing his white, upper-middle-class presentation of gay identity as superior. In carving out a place for himself as a gay professional, Larry reinforced negative stereotypes of queer men of color, positioning whiteness as a more enlightened and progressive racial identity with respect to LGBT identity and rights.

Gay and lesbian teachers were not the only ones drawing on this idea of the unacceptable gay to legitimize their classroom presence; its specter also appeared in interviews I conducted with self-identified straight allies. Delia, a twenty-eight-year-old white straight ally and teacher, spoke of one gay colleague as a better role model than others, saying, "I think a lot of kids still feel like, oh, gay people are 'this' or 'that.' And by seeing [my coworker] and seeing, oh, this is a really intelligent person, he's very serious, he's not flamboyant, like, in the ways—or, he's not a child molester, just horrible stereotypes they have put into them from an early age are dispelled very easily being around him." Delia pitted her perceptions of the positive qualities of her coworker—intelligent, serious, conventionally gendered—against the unacceptable gay archetype, specifically referencing two of the key discursive weapons deployed by the antigay movement against gay and lesbian teachers: the pernicious influence of gender non-normative gays and the link between homosexuality and pedophilia, both, of course, alleged. Over time, these "horrible stereotypes" have a powerful symbolic link in the cultural imagination. Through their co-circulation, gender variance becomes discursively tied to child molestation, one of the most virulently maintained social taboos.[11] In attempting to defend her coworker against these coexisting stereotypes, Delia had to rely on the only progay discourse available to her: homonormativity. This process shows how the conflict between gay rights and child welfare discourses is nearly inescapable, for those who support LGBT rights as much as those who oppose them.[12]

In interviews, depictions of the unacceptable archetype mainly referenced gay men, not lesbians. The gendered dynamics of the teaching profession may be shaping this phenomenon; the stereotypes of women and men who work in feminized occupations posit the women as maternal and inherently caring, while the men are presumed to be effeminate and, often, gay.[13] Along these lines, the sociological context of predominantly female occupations could make gay men teachers more readily visible, while allowing lesbians to be overlooked. This imbalance has negative ramifications on both sides: it contributes to the invisibility of lesbians, while stigmatizing gay men.

Although gay men predominated as the imagined perpetrators of unacceptable representations, some interviewees did reference a corresponding stereotype of the bad lesbian. Christi, a thirty-year-old white lesbian, contrasted her own conventionally gendered presentation with the archetypical butch lesbian: "It sounds callous but I've said for years that the girls want to be me and the boys want to 'do' me. And that is why I get along so well with my students. I just operate on knowing that thirteen-year-old boys and thirteen-year-old girls just want attention. And between the two of them, they all want attention. I think if I were butch, it would be very difficult." Christi recognized the added burden for gender-transgressing teachers, who must "battle" to develop legitimacy in the school context. Christi herself drew on her presentation as a conventionally feminine woman to negotiate her relationship with her students, whose heterosexuality she assumed. She later acknowledged this advantage, saying, "Yeah, that heterosexual privilege? Hell yeah, I'm gonna use it." Christi's strategy underscored the limited choices gay and lesbian teachers perceived: either conform to acceptable self-presentations and find acceptance, or stand out and face possible persecution. While Christi could negotiate her professional and sexual identity through her own fairly conventional gender presentation, not all teachers had this option. Ultimately, Christi relied on the compromise at the troubling heart of homonormativity: giving up a critique of systems of privilege to secure a place in the institutions that perpetuate that privilege and its accompanying exclusions.

HOW DO THESE HOMONORMATIVE EXPECTATIONS SHAPE EXPERIENCE?

Teachers' comments about idealized performances of gay and lesbian identity in schools demonstrated the pervasive impact of homonormativity on their lives. Their ideas about good and bad representations of gay and lesbian people lined up with contemporary gay rights strategy, which emphasizes commonality with the norms of heterosexual culture, including marriage, monogamy, procreation, and productivity. This strategy is especially compatible with the teaching context, given the gender-normative, sexually neutral expectations for teachers. (Of course, as I have now demonstrated, what is coded as "sexually neutral" is in fact deeply normative and privileges heterosexual teachers.) As I have pointed out, this particular combination—the homonormative demands of gay pride and the ideal performance of professionalism—is somewhat unique to the teaching context. In contrast, Christine Williams, Patricia Giuffre, and Kirsten Dellinger find that other kinds of workplaces, like bars, bookstores, and hair salons, not only allow gender non-normative performances of sexual identity but expect it of their gay and lesbian employees.[14]

How do teachers navigate this mutually reinforcing context of homonormative expectations? Educational scholar and out gay teacher Eric Rofes has written about his experience of this process.[15] Rofes described his own performance of gay masculinity in the classroom as a perilous process: he felt pressure either to perform hegemonic masculinity (and thereby subvert gay stereotypes while upholding homophobia) or to play up gay performativity (thereby confirming the very stereotypes that deem gays and lesbians inappropriate to the school context). Similarly, gay and lesbian teachers in my sample faced a difficult (and, for many, frustrating) binary: try to limit their visibility to a narrow set of acceptable options or risk the harassment and stereotyping that come with more transgressive forms of visibility. In the remainder of this chapter, I focus on how they dealt with this binary, including the specific ways that gay and lesbian visibility did emerge in schools, namely through either partnership or gender non-normativity.

Representation through Partnership

For the teachers who managed to carve out a visible gay or lesbian identity by conforming to the homonormative ideal, a common entry point to visibility was through references to a partner. Chelsea, a twenty-eight-year-old white lesbian teacher, explained: "I would just start talking about it very casually. Like they'd ask, 'What did you do this weekend?' And I'd say, 'Oh, my girlfriend and I went to . . .' whatever. Or, 'Oh my God, last night my girlfriend and I were talking . . .' and I would just see this sort of, casual thing about it, and they got used to it." Being in a partnership with another woman gave Chelsea a casual way to perform her lesbian identity for her students that resembled the way heterosexual teachers reveal their sexuality. Amy chose a similar route to visibility: "If they asked [about my sexual identity], I told them the truth, and then I started to get bolder, I'd mention my partner and say things like that." Likewise, John explained, "Sometimes in the beginning of the week, I would talk about the weekend, and I would say 'My boyfriend . . . ' and that got some reactions too, at first. Yeah, just talking about, normal conversations with students and it would come out."

Brian, a forty-year-old white high school teacher, was the only teacher in the Texas sample who was out to his students. He explained his method of representing himself as gay:

> I don't know that I necessarily actively bring it in, but I talk openly about my husband and my family and what we do. And high school kids are so inquisitive that everything comes up. They ask every question you could think of and more. So I don't really have to put anything out there, it all comes out.... It's not an exceptional thing, it's not a special thing, and when they bring it up, fine, but I'm not going to make a big deal out of it. You know? The one thing I do if kids ask me—because they ask me about my wedding ring. And if they ask me about it, I hand it to them and let them read it. Because inside it says [my partner's name] and then the date we were married. So some of the kids sit there for a second and then they go, "Oh, okay." So that's really the only way that I really directly come out to kids. The rest of it just sort of filters out. And I think they talk about it, too. I think I'm pretty open about it.

Brian's use of his marriage and family to signify his sexual identity echoed the performance of his heterosexual colleagues. Indeed, his specific focus on of his wedding ring symbolized his commitment to the rituals, traditions, and institutions of heterosexuality. Brian approached the disclosure and performance of his gay identity through a lens of normality: as he put it, "It's not a special thing, an exceptional thing." Brian, Chelsea, Amy, and John all had fairly conventional gender presentations, which would likely lead most colleagues and students to initially assume they were straight. Referencing their partners allowed them to be visibly gay in the absence of other homosexual cues.

Héctor, the California administrator who helped organize a gay and lesbian advocacy group, also used partner cues, though his were visual: he noted, "I have pictures of my boyfriend and my family with him all over my cubicle." He also acknowledged that having a partner made it easier to come out to students, explaining, "If you have someone in your life, then it makes it easier because then you can talk about family." Like Brian, Héctor emphasized family in presentations of gay identity at work. Rufus also used pictures of his boyfriend and his boyfriend's mother, whom Rufus called his mother-in-law, to present his gay identity to new students.

Unlike Chelsea and Brian, however, Héctor and Rufus were unconventional in their gender presentations. Héctor's broad, muscular body conformed to the hegemonically masculine ideal,[16] but the way he walked, moved his hands, and talked with a theatrical flair was non-normative. Rufus moved and talked with an even stronger camp aesthetic, which suggested his gay identity. While Héctor, who worked in the LA Unified School District's central office, felt that he faced little harassment on account of his gay visibility, Rufus had a different experience working in junior high school. Héctor's distance from students afforded him more comfort in his non-normative presentation. Meanwhile, Rufus regularly faced harassing behavior from students, usually from students he didn't know but encountered in the school halls.

Rufus's and Héctor's experiences suggest that the normalizing effect of visible partnership was not guaranteed and could be mitigated by a teacher's gender expression. Nonetheless, references to partners allowed many teachers in monogamous, committed relationships to present their identities in a way that was in line with the acceptable gay archetype, emphasizing normality and corresponding to the heterosexual ideals of marriage and family. Still, not all teachers can access this domesticated presentation of a sexual self. In particular, single teachers likely struggle to articulate their gay and lesbian identities outside the context of a partnered relationship, especially in their interactions with students. This challenge draws out one of the significant limitations of using gay rights discourses of homonormativity to gain acceptance for gay and lesbian identities in schools.

Representation through Gender Performance

Chapter 4 discussed how students and coworkers read some teachers as gay or lesbian not through their words (e.g., references to partners) but through their actions. As Rufus's experiences of harassment illustrate, using a partner to signal visibility does not mean automatic acceptance. When teachers look, speak, dress, or otherwise present as gay or lesbian, their visibility does not easily conform to the ideal of teaching professionalism.

James, a young Black gay teacher in Texas, had not come out to his coworkers. Nonetheless, he said, his non-normative gender expression prompted teachers to make pointed comments that made him uncomfortable. He gave an example of what he meant: "We're doing this fitness boot camp at school. And the teachers involved in it are these older Black women and me. I was power-walking around the track during the camp, and one of them was like, 'Well, you sure swish your hips, don't you?'" James interpreted this comment as an attempt to "feel [him] out" and a reminder to monitor his own mannerisms for possible signs of homosexuality.

James's story can also help us understand how racial politics imbue the disciplining power of homonormativity, which may be experienced differently by teachers of color. Evelyn Brooks Higginbotham developed the concept of "politics of respectability" to describe how middle-class Black women have been expected to project a public image of propriety to help advance civil rights.[17] Higginbotham describes how respectability politics are reinforced by intraracial policing of behavior, which in turn can become an internalized, self-policing process. In her analysis of the impact of HIV/AIDS on African American communities in the United States, Cathy Cohen describes how the politics of respectability silenced Black gay men and lesbians attempting to educate their communities about health risks.[18] This process of secondary marginalization, Cohen argues, continues to negatively influence queer people of color.

Teachers like James must contend with accountability structures of doing gender that are inflected with the politics of respectability. James was already self-conscious about how his presentation of Black masculinity did not accord with the expectations of his students and coworkers. By joking about James's swishing hips, a quintessentially feminine bodily action, James's coworkers, who were mostly Black women, reminded him of the ways his Black masculinity was transgressive. Whether they intended to reprimand him or not, James interpreted the joke as a warning, and it reinforced his resolve to fly under the radar and do everything he could to pass as straight.

By contrast, a few teachers, like Taylor, felt empowered to play up their gender nonconformity. While Taylor was comfortable presenting as gender nonconforming in the workplace, her descriptions of her workplace interactions suggest that her coworkers and students may have had difficulty resolving her gender presentation:

> Always at the beginning of the year, there's always new ninth graders who are like, "Oh my God, man!" And I've had kids like ... walk by and then maybe a kid will bring by a friend to be like, "Look at

that weird teacher." You know? And like, point or whatever, and I get up and shut the door. My own students, though, I don't have that issue. I do think that I'm generally pretty respectful of my students and you know, treat them with respect, so then they often are pretty respectful back. I have discipline issues in general . . . but I've never really had [homophobic incidents] in any way.

Taylor felt that her rapport with her own students resolved their potential anxiety about her gender expression. Of coworkers, she said: "I don't feel like I get personally attacked, well, as far as I know—I'm sure there's a ton of comments that are said behind my back. I kind of have that feeling. But I've never had a confrontation with anyone, I've never had a problem." Though nobody explicitly confronted Taylor about her nonconforming visibility, she could tell that some teachers and students were uncomfortable with it. Still, her confidence in her self-presentation showed in the fact that she felt empowered to ignore any potentially negative reactions.

It is important to note that Taylor was in a very different structural position than James. As a white woman, she was afforded more flexibility in terms of gender presentation. She also taught in a gay-friendly school microculture in a state with multiple safeguards against discrimination and harassment on the basis of sexual identity and gender expression. While we already know that policy, culture, embodiment, and race affect teachers' experiences of coming out, Taylor and James's experiences show that they also affect a teacher's ability to resist homonormative expectations of self-presentation.

Gay and lesbian teachers must negotiate numerous factors in making their sexual identities visible or invisible on school campuses. The emphasis on homonormativity in both gay pride and teaching professionalism makes this negotiation much more than a matter of simple individual preference. While many work environments continue to suppress any expression of homosexual identity, some school contexts, particularly in California, are beginning to provide opportunities for visible gay and lesbian presentations in the classroom. Unfortunately, insofar as schools allow a space for these presentations, there is pervasive pressure to limit them to the forms of visibility that emphasize normality, productivity, gender conformity, marriage, and family. Many gay and lesbian teachers themselves bought into this vision of acceptable gay and lesbian teachers and forcefully rejected alternative possibilities. Even teachers who were troubled by its limitations were resigned to its necessity for securing gay rights in schools.

The pressures on visibly gay and lesbian teachers to appear just like their straight counterparts result in the continued marginalization of "deviant" sexualities. One key way teachers could safely enact visibility was by referring to a partner or spouse. Visibility through partnership presents a palatable version of LGBT identity that hews closely to the normative expectations of teaching professionals. However, nonpartnered and nonmonogamous teachers cannot access this self-presentation and probably struggle to find other pathways to visibility. Gender presentation also made teachers visible, some willingly, others not. Students and staff members read their gender presentation as indicative of their gay or lesbian identity and interacted with them accordingly. As seen in the prior chapter, this kind of visibility constrained and shaped the coming out process, outing some teachers against their wills. Beyond the process of coming out, gender non-normativity shaped the everyday experience of visibility. Gender-nonconforming gay and lesbian teachers experienced an additional layer of difficulty in the classroom, as they faced pressures to perform gender normativity from both the teaching profession and the mainstream discourse of gay rights.

This constrained version of gay and lesbian visibility in the classroom perpetuates homonormativity and limits the challenge to gendered and sexualized inequalities that gay and lesbian teacher visibility could achieve. Relying on such narrow representations of gay and lesbian teachers may coax key decision makers to expand gay rights in schools, but it does so at a high price, leaving behind teachers who can't (or don't want to) fit the demands of homonormativity. In this homonormative vision of "gay-friendly" schools, some LGBT teachers—namely, those with race and class privilege, those who are gender normative, and those who are married and/or monogamous—gain security, while the rest fall further behind, pushed even further away from a more just future. Before considering alternatives to this model, I turn to one more phenomenon that prevents a more expansive vision of social justice in schools: racialized discourses of homophobia.

CHAPTER SIX

Racialized Discourses of Homophobia

Using Race to Predict and Discredit Discrimination

The Gay Straight Alliance at the Woodrow High School in Austin, Texas, meets Tuesdays after school.¹ One Tuesday afternoon, early in the fall of 2008, Brian, the GSA adviser, allowed me to sit in on a meeting. About a dozen students were present that day. All of them were white, and about half were girls and half boys. Most identified as lesbian, gay, or bisexual, although three described themselves as "allies," or straight-identified supporters of LGBT rights.

That afternoon, the group was deciding on a mission statement. Justin, a gay-identified student, led the discussion. The students considered several statements, including "We aim to provide a place for anyone less than straight" and "We want to make it okay to like people different from what people expect." In the midst of the debate, Ben suddenly interjected, "What *is* our purpose anyway? I mean, in Austin, everyone's pretty much all right [with LGBT people] except the old people and their kids." Darren added, "And ghetto people." Another student seconded this, "Yeah, and ghetto people!" Staci quietly countered,

"No ... I live in one of those neighborhoods and they aren't like that."

Justin ignored this digression and announced an upcoming GSA mixer with other schools. Woodrow High School was west of a highway that ran through the center of the city, dividing it into two distinct areas: the "East Side," which was predominantly Black and Latino (although gentrification was pushing these residents even further out of town), and everything else, which was largely white. When Justin listed the East Side schools that were participating in the GSA mixer, students murmured among themselves and looked surprised. After he named one school, a student interrupted, asking incredulously, "*They* have a GSA?" Later, when Justin opened the floor for new business, Staci stood and asked if anyone was interested in asking a local graffiti art group to make a mural for the GSA, adding, "[The graffiti group] is from [an East Side school]." Cody, a fifteen-year-old gay-identified student, responded with wonder, "Gay people and the East Side, intermingling!" The other students laughed and nodded.

This discussion illustrates how homophobia, race, and class are socially defined within the school context. The students in the Woodrow GSA believed that "ghetto" Black and Latino communities were a homophobic blight on a city otherwise characterized as gay-friendly. They were surprised that progay organizations like GSAs existed in poor communities of color, revealing their privileged assumption that the opportunity to be openly LGBT in high school was restricted to schools like theirs, which was located in a mostly white, upper-middle-class neighborhood with a reputation for progressive politics. Finally, they laughed at the idea of gay, Black, and Latino students "intermingling," suggesting that they not only presumed homophobia among

Black and Latino students but also believed that identifying as Black or Latino precluded identifying as gay.

In their reactions and the assumptions they surfaced, the Woodrow GSA students were participating in a broader discourse about the relationship between race and homophobia that is predicated upon the presumption of greater homophobia among poor and working-class people of color. In this chapter, I argue that gay and lesbian teachers also draw upon this discourse to make sense of homophobia in schools. Like these students, the teachers I interviewed used race and class to anticipate homophobic responses from coworkers, parents, and students, assuming that working-class people of color were more prone to homophobia than other groups. Race often emerged in interviews as a kind of shorthand to explain fears about coming out and incorporating LGBT issues into the curriculum.

This deployment of race to conceptualize homophobia is especially relevant in the context of the ongoing culture war over marriage equality. In November 2008, as I conducted the last of my interviews, California's Proposition 8 passed by a narrow margin. Proposition 8, which invalidated legal marriages between gays and lesbians, was at the fore of the national conversation about gay rights. In its wake, some suggested that high turnout of Black and Latino voters secured the proposition's narrow victory.[2] However, while exit polls demonstrated that Black and Latino voters were more likely than white voters to vote for Proposition 8, other analyses of the voting patterns found that, after controlling for other factors, race was not an accurate predictor of voting trends.[3] Other scholars suggested that to the extent that Black voters did favor Proposition 8, their support was generated as much by ambivalence about the institutional power of marriage as by homophobia.[4]

The controversy over the role race played in passing the anti-gay legislation set off a heated debate, which has since contributed to the broader discourses about the relationship between race and homophobia. Gay and lesbian teachers conceptualize this relationship in ways that affect their individual decisions about coming out and displaying their sexual identities and ultimately reproduce racist discourses of homophobia. The significance of this use of race and class to predict homophobia is not necessarily its validity or lack thereof but rather the way it shapes social relationships with respect to race, class, and sexuality. Racist discourses of homophobia contribute to the continued invisibility of queers of color and perpetuate the discursive linking of gayness and whiteness, which in turn supports the continued enforcement of homonormativity.[5] The operation of racialized discourses of homophobia thus thwarts the possibility of intersectional political challenges that might critique racism and homophobia together.[6]

In addition to using race, class, and religion to predict homophobia, many research participants likened LGBT discrimination to racial discrimination in their attempts to make sense of their own experiences as people marginalized by sexual identity. White participants often used the metaphor of racial discrimination to explain (and discredit) homophobia in schools, particularly in describing interactions with students. While this metaphor seemed to serve teachers as a powerful tool against homophobia, mapping sexuality discrimination onto the model of racial discrimination has problematic implications, which I will consider here. Although the comparison may have the capacity to create common ground between gay and lesbian teachers and their students of color, it also contributes to discursive divisions between sexual and racial identities. This chapter demonstrates how both gay pride and teaching professionalism are imbued with whiteness, in contrast to the imagined extreme homophobia of students' home communities.

THEORIES OF RACE AND RACIALIZATION

The concept of "racialization" has been used within sociology to debunk popular biological understandings of race and instead foreground it as a socially constructed system of domination. Although the term *racialization* formally entered academic scholarship through the anticolonization work of Frantz Fanon, the roots of racialization theory can be traced back at least as far as sociologist W.E.B. Du Bois's work at the turn of the twentieth century.[7] Du Bois, Fanon, and later critical race theorists argue that race has no biological reality but is instead a historically and culturally mediated artifact of power. White and Black are relational, not actual or absolute; whiteness exists only in relationship to Blackness, and this relationship hinges on the cultural superiority of white over Black. While Black/white relations, in particular, have been central to the development of race in the US context, scientific discourses of race have imposed a variety of racial categories that further maintain a social order of white supremacy over racialized others.[8] Racialization is the practice of using these scientific explanations of racial difference to justify social hierarchies of race.[9] It is a part of what Eduardo Bonilla-Silva calls the "racial structure" of our social world, or the "totality of the social relations and practices that reinforce white privilege."[10]

Since its emergence, racialization as a concept has been expanded to refer not just to how individuals become racialized but also to how institutions and social practices are racialized.[11] Scholars of racialization now distinguish between the distinct but reinforcing processes of "practical racialization" (the process of creating racial groups) and "ideological racialization" (the discursive uses of race).[12] Racialization is a historically specific ideological process that categorizes not only people but also practices. The process of racializing discourses of homophobia is just one part of a long history of using sexuality as a key marker of racial distinction. Notions of the sexual deviance of nonwhites have been used to justify colonial practices of enslavement, dispossession, and political disenfranchisement.[13] Siobhan Somerville argues that in the United States emerging discourses of racial and sexual deviance in the late nineteenth century mutually reinforced each other.[14] The logics that justified the rigidly policed color line, as Frederick Douglass and W. E. B. Du Bois called it, gave coherence and legitimacy to the newly emerging distinction between homo- and heterosexual.

Given the centrality of sexuality to the historical process of racialization, I am interested in understanding how race and sexuality are co-constructed in the narratives of gay and lesbian teachers. In this chapter, I consider how race, gender, and sexuality inequalities are mutually constituted through shared understandings of homophobia. I am especially interested in how sexual taxonomies—heterosexual and homosexual, gay-friendly and homophobic—are racialized in a way that privileges whiteness and contributes to racial hierarchies. The teachers I interviewed drew on a social definition of homophobia that was racialized in a manner that sustained white superiority. Specifically, they relied on a discursively upheld assumption that Black and Latino communities were more homophobic, particularly in comparison to white communities. In this chapter, I show how this process of racializing discourses of homophobia sustains and reinforces race and sexuality inequality.

NARRATING HOMOPHOBIA

Bonilla-Silva defines *racial ideologies* as "racially based frameworks used by actors to explain and justify (dominant race) or challenge (subordinate race or races) the status quo."[15] Racial ideologies share common frames, rhetorical styles, and *racial stories*, the narratives people tell themselves to make sense of race and racial distinctions. Racial ideologies, when they did explicitly emerge in my interviews with gay and lesbian teachers, did so almost exclusively in the context of fears of, stories about, and metaphors for homophobia. For example, Larry, who had experienced harassment from students as an out gay teacher in a Los Angeles–area high school, talked about a perceived lack of support from Latino immigrant parents for his rigid enforcement of the school's anti–hate speech policy. He explained: "[It's hard getting parents on board], especially with our school, almost 90 percent Hispanic, first-generation immigrants, they're like, 'He called you a fag? What's your problem? You're lucky he didn't shoot you in the head or something. I don't understand what the problem is.' Because that's the way it is where they come from." When pressed for specific interactions with parents, Larry by and large described Latino parents who were contrite on behalf of their children. Yet he still drew on a racialized expectation of homophobia when describing his school community. According to Larry, these ideas were informed by how his students discussed sexuality in relation to Latino culture, explaining, "[Students] tell me there's no such thing as gay in Mexico." In relating his experience, Larry called upon stereotypes of Latino immigrants as violent, ignorant, and virulently homophobic.

Recent work on the experiences of first- and second-generation gay Latino immigrants does suggest that there is some truth to the experience Larry describes on behalf of students.[16] What is important about this racial narrative, though, is not so much its veracity as how it is being deployed—as a race story. Imani Perry argues that "the impact of such narratives as race stories is potentially quite significant beyond their perceived truth.... The problem with the narrative presented as truth is that it often turns into a deterministic and exceptionalizing account of individuals and groups."[17] In Larry's narrative, the nuances of his students' experiences are erased. Homophobia is posited as "just the way it is where they come from," in imagined contrast to the relative enlightenment of the United States.

This racialized understanding of homophobia also shaped Larry's decision to be visible to his students. He described himself as a positive gay role model who provided a contrast to the queer people they saw in their home communities, the "half-trannies" or the "really effeminate Hispanic men [who] keep the bottom and get boobs in Mexico City, really cheap boobs." Larry's self-concept as a role model was shaped by the acceptable gay archetype discussed in the prior chapter, revealed here as deeply embedded in racist, classist assumptions that posit white US gay identities as more evolved and sophisticated. This racialized narrative of gay pride concurrently reinforces homonormativity and whiteness.

Barbara, a white lesbian special education teacher in Texas, was concerned about being out to Black coworkers. She explained, "I was nervous about [coming out to a coworker], because I've had some odd reactions from African Americans. Culturally, I've noticed that they seem to have a bit of an issue with it." Barbara subsequently said that she was surprised by the relatively open-minded reaction of her African American administrator, to whom she came out after several months on the job. She said, "One of my administrators at that school was also African American, and I was worried about her reaction and hers was the funniest. She just blushed and went, 'I know nothing about that, you're going to have to teach me.'" Although her actual experiences showed no evidence of a link between race and homophobia, Barbara nonetheless drew upon discourses about African American "culture" to explain her hesitation about coming out to coworkers. In the process, she reinforced the belief that people of color, especially Black people, are inherently more homophobic than white people.

Joan, a white teacher and straight ally, wove religion together with class and race in her analysis of homophobia. She said of her school, "Well, this is a very poor community, dominated by very religious people. And you know how the Black church is about LGBT issues, there's always exceptions, but in general, they're not very welcoming." In saying, "You know how the Black church is," Joan assumed a shared understanding of homophobia embedded in assumptions about the religious traditions of US Black communities and the relationships between race, class, and religion.

Like Larry's comments, Joan's interpretation is one that finds some scholarly support;[18] for example, Elijah Ward has demonstrated how intersecting theologically informed beliefs and black nationalism do, in fact, contribute to the production of homophobia in Black churches in the United States.[19] Ward shows how the historical sexual exploitation of Black men and women and the necessity of a race survival consciousness within Black communities fostered homophobic discourses from the pulpit. While Joan may be attuned to the realities of homophobia experienced within communities of color, she misses the crux of *why* these realities exist. Rather than name the real source of such homophobia—white supremacy—her narrative fosters an essentialized understanding of "the Black church" as less evolved. In the context of the history of racialization, which has consistently deemed people of color as less than, as undercivilized, illogical, and irrational,[20] such a statement, even if intended sympathetically, has the effect of reinforcing Black communities and religious traditions as inferior. (Her narrative also ignores how homophobia is produced in white religious contexts—ironically, it would be the largely white Church of Jesus Christ of Latter-day Saints that would contribute the estimated $22 million that many believe helped secure the passage of California's Proposition 8 just three months after our interview.)[21]

Some white teachers mentioned shifting racial demographics in schools when they discussed their fears of homophobia. In Los Angeles, the racial makeup of a neighborhood can change rapidly in response to immigration and gentrification. Teachers who had worked in the same schools for years often witnessed demographic changes in their student population, which led them to make sense of changes in school microcultures by mapping them onto changing racial compositions. Larry described his school thus: "One of the things we're finding, being so close to downtown, is that Chinese, Korean, and Filipino families are displacing, because the rents are so high. And they are displacing Hispanic families, meaning that there are much smaller families coming in. And a lot of the Chinese are educated, so they have smaller families and are probably much more tolerant as far as gay people and the issues and stuff." Larry attributed a more progressive ethos to Asian immigrants, suggesting, in particular, that Chinese residents were more educated and tolerant than the neighborhood's previous Latino residents, and therefore more gay-friendly as a whole. His reference to education suggested a class difference between the Latino and Chinese immigrants, as he brought raced and classed assumptions together to construct social definitions of homophobia. Larry's comments moved beyond a white/nonwhite binary to suggest a racialized hierarchy of gay-friendliness, which ranked ethnoracial groups as more or less homophobic.

Larry was not the only teacher to allude to ethnoracially determined hierarchies of LGBT acceptance. Lisa, a retired white lesbian in California, described her experiences with homophobia similarly: "Well, when I started out at [my school] it was a totally Jewish school. But ... that changed in the '60s. But as time went on, the school became mostly African American, and among the African Americans there is a real, real dislike of homosexuality. So I didn't get much support from the parents." Lisa's comparison between Jewish and African American communities ranked Jewish parents as more enlightened on an ethnoracialized scale of homophobia. It would be easy to dismiss comments like Larry and Lisa's as racist stereotypes, but they actually represented crucial interpretive lenses by which these teachers and others drew on discourses of race, class, and homophobia to make sense of why and how they had experienced homophobia in their schools. In other words, these moments of inequality maintained by racialized interpretations of homophobia are not isolated incidents of individual bigotry but rather part of a discursively constructed belief system that affects teachers as a whole.

The hierarchy of groups from which one anticipates homophobia has implications that extend beyond teachers' experiences in the classroom. Robert, a forty-six-year-old white straight political adviser for a Texas LGBT organization, also drew on racialized discourses of homophobia to analyze the political climate his organization faced. He told me:

The acceptance of the LGBT community within [communities of color] is lower than in others. Somewhat higher in the Hispanic community if you talk about family, and supporting family members, but there has to be some crossover into the understanding that gay marriage and everything else is a civil right. And that it doesn't matter what you believe, you have to make room for other people. There's a growing Hispanic majority and a stable African American community [in Texas], which means that the African American population will be shrinking in proportion. And with a growing population of LGBTs coming out—between those three groups, there's going to be tension because of different beliefs and changing power structures. Every nonprofit, every activist, progressive group, even conservative groups, are worried about how to relate to the African American community right now, how to relate to communities of color. But it's easier to get Hispanics and Latinos active on these issues than it is African Americans.

Robert's analysis relied on an understanding of LGBT communities and communities of color as mutually exclusive political constituencies. By conflating gay interests with "whiteness" and defining Latino interests as separate, such an analysis reinforces racialized interpretations of homophobia. It also draws on hierarchical constructions of gay acceptance by arguing that the cultural importance of family in Latino communities creates a potential bridge to gay acceptance that is lacking in the Black community. This argument itself relies on familiar stereotypes: that Latino families are more family oriented, while Black families are dysfunctional and fractured.[22] In the process of arguing for gay rights, Robert reinforced the racist discourses used to legitimate racial inequalities.

These examples illustrate the difficulties individuals face in making sense of the relationship between racial and sexual marginalization. Racial and sexual identities are socially constructed as distinct—and often mutually opposed—axes of identity. Racialized discourses of homophobia are a consequence of this process, as gay and lesbian teachers draw on culturally circulating definitions of race and sexuality to anticipate and explain antigay sentiment. In her research on how white teachers make sense of race in the educational context, Brianna Picower finds that white teachers are equipped with "tools of whiteness" they use to narrate their experiences in a way that ultimately maintains and enacts racist worldviews.[23] The linking of racial marginalization and homophobia is, I would argue, one of these tools. As white teachers' narratives framed whiteness as a more enlightened and progressive racial subject position, they absolved themselves of racist intent and ascribed homophobic prejudice to communities of color, thus sustaining inequality in multiple dimensions. Applying an intersectional lens to this process, we can see that racial and sexual inequalities are not only deeply interrelated but also mutually reinforcing.

Teachers of Color and Racialized Discourses of Homophobia

Because the sexual pathologization of people of color was so central to the process of racialization, resisting and reframing these sexual distinctions became a key civil rights strategy at the turn of the twentieth century. As Higginbotham has documented, African American women reformers of the time rejected the stigmatizing framing of their sexuality by emphasizing sexual purity, propriety, and respectability.[24] This turn to respectability politics has been credited with successfully undermining the project of racialization, but at the cost of reinforcing class and status politics among African Americans.[25]

While Higginbotham uses the concept of respectability politics in a historically specific way, E. Francis White conceptualizes the politics of respectability more broadly, as an ongoing concern with propriety and reputation that has characterized African American politics and intellectual life well beyond its Progressive Era emergence.[26] As a result of these politics, the experience of being marginalized by both race and sexual identity carries with it the weight of more than a century of contestation over the presumed sexual deviance of nonwhite people.[27]

Perhaps unsurprisingly, then, I found that white teachers were not the only ones to articulate racialized understandings of homophobia; teachers of color also narrated a relationship between race and homophobia in making sense of their decisions and self-presentations. Some framed their thinking in terms of generational differences: James explained, "I'm not really out to the teachers over forty.... [They are] mostly this group of older Black women who are like, 'I ain't tryin' to hear that.'" Similarly, Kenny, another young Black gay teacher in Texas, described his coworkers as "these older Black women, who—I don't know, but I *know*—they don't play that game. Our relationship, personal and professional, would change [if they knew I was gay]." These examples suggest that racialized discourses of homophobia are constructed, in part, by ideas about generational changes in gay and lesbian acceptance within communities of color. James and Kenny were attuned to how the politics of respectability among Black professionals shaped interactions between generations.

Assumptions about the religious influences in communities of color also shaped the process of racializing homophobia for teachers of color, as it did for white teachers. Kenny explained his fears of coming out at school:

CC: *What kinds of clues give you the idea that you can't [come out] at your
school?*

KENNY: I guess just knowing the makeup of the student body. Not to
pigeonhole or stereotype or anything, but the Black community, the
very religious Texas community, is, as far as I understand, not very
open and accepting of that. And my school—the student body and
staff members are very religious.

Kenny, who was raised in the Northeast, fused religion (and
geography) into racialized predictions of homophobia. By saying that as he understood it the influence of Black religious traditions in Texas was hostile to homosexuality, Kenny referenced
a shared meaning of homophobia that he had adapted into his
understanding of race and sexuality.

When James said that he "was going to act differently than
the other Black men these kids have in their lives," positing
himself as a role model of alternative masculinity, he implicitly
referenced the social construction of Black masculinity as
hypervigilant and expressly homophobic. In his study of Black
gay and bisexual men, Wesley Crichlow traces how rejection of
homosexuality and effeminacy was central to the struggle for
Black men's self-determination.[28] As a way of responding to and
repairing from a long history racist injury, Black masculinity
was constructed as hypermasculine, tough, and aggressive, in
contrast to the projected effeminacy and weakness of white masculinity.[29] The result of this struggle was a thoroughly heteronormative conceptualization of Black masculinity, which contributed to the marginalization of same-sex-desiring Black men.

James's experiences resonate with this definition of Black
masculinity and his own distance from it. Creatively, James
turned this distance into a source of pride: because he defined

Black masculinity as homophobic, he was able to make sense of—and thereby legitimate—his own presentation as a gay, effeminate Black man in terms of a challenge to his Black and Latino school community's prevailing culture of masculinity. In other words, he repaired his "failings" of Black masculinity by positioning himself as a Black gay role model.

David drew on racialized expectations of homophobia based on his own experience growing up Latino, citing "Hispanic culture" as his reason for not coming out to students and arguing that "they are more into the male *machismo* thing, and mom's in the kitchen, barefoot and pregnant and making tortillas." His reliance on the concept of *machismo* to make sense of his decision to remain closeted racialized homophobia via the assumption that homophobia was an inevitable part of Latino masculinity, which was posited as less enlightened with respect to gender and sexual politics. Likewise, Cheryl, a Latina lesbian in California, argued: "Also, being a lesbian, it's kind of hard, because a lot of people don't understand. At this school, well, at the last school I was at, I was not out—at all. It was a very small community, very closed-minded, mostly Latinos, mostly immigrants who are not educated, who don't get diversity. So it was very, I would talk about my 'roommate' very little, and it was very 'Aren't you going to get married again? Why are you single? Don't you date?' And I'm like, 'No, I don't have time, I don't want to,' you know." Cheryl included "Latino" as part of a cluster of raced and classed stereotypes about her school community—closed-minded, immigrant, uneducated, antidiversity—that she used to anticipate homophobia and explain her decision to hide her lesbian identity. Like Kenny, James, and David, Cheryl was a member of the ethnoracial group she defined as especially homophobic. These examples illustrate the ways in

which racialized discourses of homophobia shape social definitions of race not only for white teachers but also for teachers of
color. There is, however, a crucial distinction between how
white teachers and teachers of color deploy these discourses.

When white teachers draw on racialized discourses of
homophobia, especially as a way of defining themselves as role
models, they accrue racial advantage that mitigates the potentially stigmatizing or dangerous "gay teacher" label. In fact, they
gain a kind of moral advantage that puts them into the position
of potential victimhood vis-à-vis their largely Black and Latino
school communities. When teachers of color draw on similar
discourses, they may find a way to distance themselves from
harmful exclusions of queers of color (as James does in his narrative), but they do not benefit from the same exchange of racial
capital to make up for sexuality disadvantage as white teachers.

Instead, they must contend with forces of internalized racism, since they have long been exposed to the dominant discourses that pathologize their communities and identities in
addition to internalized homophobia. In other words, although
teachers of color may also participate in racialized discourses of
homophobia, the stakes of their participation are different. To
the extent that teachers of color do experience enactments of
homophobia as unique to their racial communities, such enactments are less about innate homophobia (as white narratives
position them) and more about maintaining politics of respectability in the name of racial uplift.

The social assumption that gay equals white and well-to-do is
the other side of the coin of these racialized discourses of
homophobia.[30] White middle-class men are the face of mainstream gay politics.[31] Furthermore, the "exclusively gay issues"
taken up by the major gay and lesbian organizations in the

United States all too often ignore the interrelated social problems that uphold racism, sexism, and classism,[32] a political trend
that is further reflected in racist and racially segregated LGBT
cultures and communities. This whitening of gay identity erases
queers of color, further marginalizing them within and outside
of gay communities. The gay-equals-white assumption thus supports oppression by both race and sexual identity. This racialized understanding of gayness circulates in tandem with the discursive colonization[33] of people of color as by their very nature
homophobic, reinforcing an assumed incompatibility between
identifying as queer and identifying as a person of color. Teachers of color struggle to make sense of themselves in this no-
man's-land. They have to situationally distance themselves from
their families and communities by labeling them as "homophobic" as a way of affirming their gay and lesbian identities. When
white teachers use these labels, they do not have to worry about
the same kind of trade-off; in fact, they tacitly benefit from the
racialization of homophobia. This process illustrates the discursive difficulty of negotiating racial, familial, and sexual identifications for teachers of color.

COMPARING DISCRIMINATIONS

In addition to using race to anticipate and explain homophobic
reactions in schools, many of the teachers I interviewed used racism as a metaphor for homophobia. Specifically, they drew on discourses of racial discrimination to make sense of—and challenge—the operations of homophobia. At first glance, this seems
antithetical to how gay and lesbian teachers used race first
to explain the existence of and then to discredit homophobia.
Upon further consideration, however, the construction of racial

discrimination as comparable to sexual identity discrimination turns out to be compatible with the essentialist discourses of race and sexuality used to anticipate homophobia. Both racialized discourses lack an intersectional understanding of race and sexuality and, as such, have serious political implications.

The racial discrimination comparison frequently emerged in discussions of how gay and lesbian teachers dealt with hate speech in the classroom. Virtually every teacher reported hearing homophobic language from students on a regular basis, including individual epithets, such as *faggot*, *dyke*, and *queer*, and generalized statements like "That's so gay" and "No homo." Teachers dealt with these incidents in a variety of ways. Some reprimanded students only for targeted epithets (like *faggot*), ignoring generalized statements (like "That's so gay") because, they believed, these generalized comments didn't insult anyone directly. More often, though, gay and lesbian teachers attempted to teach their students that both directed and generalized antigay sentiments were harmful. They often did this through a comparison to racism. Larry explained that he dealt with antigay comments the same way he would address racist speech, saying, "It comes under civil rights, you know, just like an African American student being called nigger." He used this comparison to persuade students to stop using antigay speech.

This strategy deployed a parallel between racial slurs and pejorative comments about LGBT individuals and the framework of "civil rights." *Civil rights* refers to citizens' rights to be protected from discrimination; in the United States, the term *civil rights movement* has been used to describe a set of political reforms that emerged in the 1960s to prohibit racial discrimination. Since gay liberation, the movement to protect LGBT individuals has adopted this civil rights framework, arguing that

LGBTs constitute a minority group in need of civil protections.[34] Larry's reference to civil rights thus knitted together the Black civil rights movement and the civil rights discourse that has come to dominate arguments for LGBT equality. The problem with this strategy, though, is that it occludes queer people of color and reinforces homonormativity. As Siobhan Somerville writes in *Queering the Color Line,* aligning civil rights and LGBT equality "implicitly posit[s] whiteness and heterosexuality as the norm. To say gay people are 'like' Black people is to suggest that those same gay people are not Black."[35]

White gay and lesbian teachers who worked with students of color often used analogies of racism to attempt to relate their own experiences of discrimination to their students'. Amy explained:

cc: *What do you say when you hear antigay slurs in the classroom?*
AMY: Same thing I say when I hear any kind of slur, you know. "That's not acceptable, we don't talk about people that way." "Can't you find some better way to express how you're feeling?" And we'd talk about that. You know, yeah. We'd talk about it, people could call you names. "How would you feel if people talked about you?" I would make it something that we all discussed together as a class, unless I heard it in the hallway or something.... Like the kids used to call the Korean kids "Chino," which is Chinese in Spanish, and I'd say, "Where are you from?" "El Salvador." "Okay, but everybody calls you Mexican. How does that make you feel? You don't like that, right? So don't do it to others." And I say the same thing about gay slurs.

In pushing her students to avoid homophobic language, Amy drew on their own sensitivity to feeling racially harassed or misunderstood. Amy used students' experiences of feeling invisible or insulted to foster their empathy for how antigay language might hurt LGBT students and teachers. While perhaps effective, this move both conflates the experiences of racism and homophobia and inadvertently re-exposes students to psychic injury by asking them to recall experiences of racism in the name of a "teachable moment."

Brian, the out Texas high school teacher and GSA adviser, attempted to make this point in a more "humorous" manner. In explaining how he responded to antigay slurs, Brian said: "And I usually do it in a humorous way. Like last year—I had a number of Black students who would joke about 'Oh, you're not picking me because I'm Black.' And it was all in fun, and all perfectly humorous. So then when those students would say something like 'Oh, that's gay,' then I'd say, 'Better gay than Black.' And they'd look at me like, oh, that's horrible you said that! And then they'd realize, oh, that's the same thing." Brian believed that his light-hearted approach would compel his students to reconsider the homophobic implications of their words. Like Amy, he drew upon their experiences as people of color in an attempt to sensitize them to the damaging consequences of homophobia. Brian assumed that his rapport with students allowed him to make such potentially dangerous digs at their racial identifications without repercussions; in my observations of his classroom instruction, Brian did indeed seem to have an extraordinarily high level of connection with his students.

Nonetheless, Brian's joke struck me as problematic for several reasons. First, in making the statement "Better gay than Black," Brian in effect reinforced a system of social inequality that places Black identity at the bottom of a hierarchy of marginalization. Second, Brian's comment assumed that "Black" and "gay" are distinct and mutually exclusive identities, thereby perpetuating the conflation of whiteness and gayness and eliding the existence of LGBT people of color. Finally, Brian, like almost every other teacher in my study, unwittingly participated in heterosexism by assuming his students were straight unless proven otherwise. The comment "Better gay than Black" makes no sense unless he assumed the student he was talking to was Black and heterosexual. This set of assumptions reinforced both heterosexism and racialized assumptions about gay identity.

Amy's and Brian's parallels were, like racialized discourses of homophobia, not just perpetrated by individuals but institutionally upheld. Comparing racial and sexual discrimination is a staple of the diversity discourse promoted in teacher training. Rufus used a book called *Cootie Shots: Theatrical Inoculations against Bigotry for Kids, Parents, and Teachers* to teach antihomophobia to his students. He read me a poem from the book that he used on the first day of class:

Snootie Patootie

Snootie Patootie just didn't care
about other people's feelings, his nose in the air.
About other folks' feelings, he needed no reason
to start with name-calling and really mean teasing.
Snootie Patootie called fat people whales
and when they walked on by he said they broke the scales.
Snootie Patootie called Black people "nappy"
he'd say, "Scratch on a record and make me a rappy."
He called white folks honkies and Latin folks beaners
he said that poor kids eat nothing but white bread and
    wieners.
If a girl wore glasses, he'd yell out "four eyes!"
He'd call short people midgets and small fries.

If you were a boy who couldn't play tag,
He'd laugh, and he'd point, and he'd call you a "Faaaaag!"
Big Nose and Jew Boy, he named Tommy Finkle
"You're a gross lezzie!", he said to Kate Winkle.
Snootie Patootie, that big nose in the air,
Snootie Patootie, walking nightmare.
Until one day, the new kid in school, Jennie Moody
finally met up with that nasty ol' Snootie.
He took just one look and said with a snicker
that she looked like a big old nose picker!
Well, Jenny just stared with a mad look on her face
and she put Snootie right back in his place.
"You rant and you rave, and you cause so much grief,
if you'd clean up your act, we'd all get some relief.
Look if all you can see is Black, fat, or gay,
you'll find you're alone at the end of the day.
No one enjoys being called this or that.
All you do is make people feel awful and that is a fact."
"Gosh, you're right and I just want to say,
I'm terribly sorry for acting that way."
So Snootie, he took his nose down from the air
and Snootie Patootie, he learned how to care.
Thanks to Jennifer Moody he found a reason
to stop with the name-calling and really mean teasing.

The poem likens homophobia to racial discrimination, as well as discrimination on the basis of gender, class, size, and disability. Rufus read the poem to his students every fall as part of his introductory lessons about tolerance and respect, which included a lesson plan around AB 537, the antiviolence educational code that protects students and staff from harassment on the basis of actual or perceived sexual orientation and gender identity. Teachers who drew comparisons between race and sexuality did not do so in a vacuum but were immersed in curricula that used such comparative language to promote an ethos of acceptance for diversity.

What are the implications of comparing LGBT discrimination to racial discrimination? One argument in favor of the comparison is that using an established and culturally validated antidiscrimination discourse to promote tolerance and respect in classrooms gives students of color common ground with white LGBT people, which might be an effective tool for helping students reconsider the use of antigay slurs. To the extent that this strategy is successful, it has the potential both to abate homophobia in schools and to reinforce shared understandings of the pernicious nature of racialized hate speech.

However, this strategy also has negative repercussions with regard to antiracist politics. Equating discrimination against LGBT individuals and racial discrimination risks erasing the unique sociohistorical context of each form of oppression.[36] Legal scholar and queer theorist Janet Halley finds that so-called "like race" arguments have become increasingly popular in legal discourse over LGBT rights.[37] In particular, the miscegenation analogy, which draws parallels between the laws outlawing interracial marriages that were deemed unconstitutional in *Loving v. Virginia* and contemporary bans on same-sex marriage, has been enthusiastically deployed in the legal and popular rhetoric of the marriage equality movement.[38] As a rhetorical device, analogy manipulates how we understand two subjects by reducing them to their similar elements.[39] In calling the marriage equality movement "our *Loving*," LGBT activists reduce the complex dynamics of interracial intimacies to a simple victory of equality through legal recourse. They also erase the compound experience of queers of color who continue to experience legal and. extralegal violence. Likewise, when gay and lesbian teachers use racism as an analogy for homophobia, they perpetuate a discursive divide between LGBT people and people of color that ignores the experiences of queer people of color and ultimately reinforces white privilege. Discrimination on the basis of sexuality and discrimination on the basis of race are not two mutually exclusive forms of oppression that can be added or multiplied to explain the sum experience of oppression for any given individual; rather, they are mutually constituted and experienced in tandem. As women of color feminists have pointed out, comparing experiences of discrimination without paying attention to these overlapping systems either renders the experience of overlapping oppressions invisible or encourages a "ranking of oppressions" that is divisive and counterproductive to a politics of liberation.[40]

By taking an intersectional perspective on the relationship between LGBT and racial discrimination, this chapter has drawn out the problems with these comparisons in the classroom. Homophobia is not comparable to racial discrimination; rather, the two are mutually constituted through racism within the matrix of domination.[41] Attempts to challenge homophobia that do not recognize this dynamic may end up reinforcing racism within progay discourses.

This chapter has explored how gay, lesbian, and straight-ally teachers conceptualized homophobia in the context of their school workplaces. Many of the teachers I spoke with drew upon a racialized understanding of homophobia that used race to predict homophobic responses from students, coworkers, and parents. Specifically, these teachers assumed homophobia in Black and Latino students, parents, and coworkers, regardless of whether their actual experiences in schools supported this assumption. When white teachers participated in discourses of racialized homophobia, it reinforced their racial superiority, giving them a purported moral high ground over the communities of color they often worked in. Teachers of color also drew on racialized predictions of homophobia, but their narratives were informed by a different relationship to power than white teachers had. The politics of respectability and history of race survival consciousness that circulate in communities of color influenced how they approached interactions with fellow Black and Latino coworkers or anticipated reactions from students and their parents. Racialized discourses of homophobia offered teachers a bridge between pride and professionalism; by positioning themselves as positive gay/lesbian role models for students of color who otherwise lacked them, teachers were able to bring pride to bear on their professional duties. Teachers like Larry rationalized being out in the classroom as a necessary correction against the imagined homophobia of his students' families and communities. While this may ease the pride/professionalism tension for teachers, it simultaneously perpetuates the superiority of whiteness.

In addition to using race as a proxy for homophobia, the teachers I interviewed used race to discredit homophobia to their students. They paralleled LGBT discrimination to racial discrimination, often via their students' own experiences as marginalized students of color. By drawing on a common experience of oppression, these teachers found a way to transcend the perceived antagonism between racial minorities and homosexuality. At the same time, however, they participated in a larger discursive process that ignored the interlocking nature of racial and sexual oppression.

I have suggested here that this process of racializing homophobia prevents intersectional understandings of identity and inequality, thereby limiting the political potential of a multiracial antihomophobic politics. The conflation of "gayness" with "whiteness" may perpetuate a political antagonism between antiracist and antihomophobic rights-based movements. As demonstrated in the controversy over Proposition 8 voting patterns, this discursive divide leaves little room for coalition building. In contrast, queer of color scholars Grace Kyungwon Hong and Roderick Ferguson argue that nuanced analysis of racial formations reopens the possibility of coalitional politics.[42] In unpacking the process of the racialized discourses of homophobia, we can begin to envision such possibilities in the context of schools.

CHAPTER SEVEN

From Gay-Friendly to Queer-Friendly

New Possibilities for Schools

When I tell students in my undergraduate courses about my research, they collectively react with surprise, but for contradictory reasons. Many of my current students were raised in Massachusetts or other New England states with strong progay policies, and they are often taken aback at the idea that gay and lesbian teachers still face workplace discrimination. They gasp aloud when I tell them that teachers in many parts of the country can be legally fired for identifying as LGBT. But others are surprised for entirely different reasons: they have experienced firsthand how homophobic school climates can be and are amazed at the idea that there are teachers who have managed to come out as gay or lesbian to their administrators, coworkers, and students without severe retribution. This mixed reaction typifies our paradoxical historical moment with respect to LGBT rights in schools: gay and lesbian teachers face continued discrimination, but, at the same time, nonheterosexual identities and teaching can coexist.

My students come from high schools where Gay Straight Alliances and homophobic slurs and violence exist side by side, where teachers and students might openly identify as gay but remain virtually invisible in the formal curriculum. In this context, what it means to identify as a gay or lesbian teacher is shifting rapidly, often in ways that were once inconceivable to the retired teachers I interviewed. From the mass purges of suspected homosexual teachers in the McCarthy era to the ongoing legal battles over the right to teach while gay or lesbian, the classroom has been a dangerous place for gay and lesbian teachers. But suddenly, due to the efforts of the gay rights movement, things are changing. It's an uneven change, to be sure: for every teacher I met who brought a date to a faculty party or came out on the first day of class, I met another teacher who could not hold hands with her partner in public or who traveled hours to frequent gay bars without fear of workplace reprisal. It is precisely because we are in this transitional, tentative moment that we must think critically about the contours of the gay and lesbian teacher experience. What we do now—how we approach the challenge of changing schools and workplaces to be less hostile to LGBTs—will shape the future. While this book has documented some striking advances for LGBT teachers and students, it also reveals significant limitations to the way we currently pursue the "gay-friendly" classroom.

Today's gay and lesbian teachers are pinned between two competing discourses: the traditional ethic of teaching professionalism and the rhetoric of gay pride. How teachers experience this tension speaks volumes about the co-construction of professional and sexual identities; interpreting their experiences reveals how much is truly at stake when we talk about next directions for the gay rights movement. What it means to be "professional" in the teaching context is shaped by the history of teachers as moral authorities, charged with protecting the so-called innocence of children, who should be shielded from sexual knowledge. As a matter of course, teachers are expected to present sexually neutral versions of themselves in the classroom. Yet the ethic of sexual neutrality is a myth; in fact, it is safe and neutral for straight teachers to display their sexuality by talking about and displaying pictures of their partners, but when gay or lesbian teachers do the same thing, they violate that supposed ethic of neutrality. In some places, this is changing: some gay and lesbian teachers I spoke with did, indeed, reference their partners in their classrooms to minimal fanfare. But is this enough? Should this be our vision of sexual justice in schools? What avenue does this model provide unpartnered gay and lesbian (and bisexual and straight) teachers for sexual expression in the classroom? Considered this way, the ethic of sexual neutrality for teachers is not just a myth but a way of limiting the sexual self in the classroom to marriage and monogamy for queer and straight teachers alike.

While the expectations of teaching professionalism ask gay and lesbian teachers to mute their sexuality, the expectations of gay pride insist that they turn up the volume and be loud and proud about their sexual identity in all contexts. Beginning with the homophile organizations of the 1950s and gaining steam with the gay liberation movements of the 1970s, coming out has come to be defined as the quintessential LGBT political act. As gay *liberation* gave way to gay *rights*, the tactics and demands of the movement shifted, but the emphasis on coming out did not. Today, gays and lesbians face more pressure than ever to be out and proud and are shamed and even harassed by other LGBTs when they remain in the closet. The identities of "gay" and "lesbian" have been codified as distinct cultural entities with overlapping political interests and then commodified within the growing gay pride market. This increasingly homogenized ideal of gay and lesbian personhood pressures gay and lesbian teachers to role-model a one-size-fits-all mode of gay pride for their coworkers and students.

How do gay and lesbian teachers navigate these opposing expectations of gay pride and teaching professionalism? As we have seen, they have three primary options. First, teachers can choose to *split* their sexual and professional identities, drawing a hard line that separates their classroom self (professional, neutral, apolitical) from their gay or lesbian self (proud, public, political). Second, they can try to *knit* these selves together into a coherent whole by reinterpreting the ethics of teaching professionalism to include a responsibility to be "authentic" and to role-model gay and lesbian identities for their students. Each of these decisions—to split or to knit—has its costs, so some teachers choose a third option: quitting. Teachers who cannot feel comfortable with the sacrifices required by splitting or knitting may *quit* teaching (either leaving education altogether or moving into administration) to resolve their dilemma.

The importance of coming out as a political strategy for the gay rights movement keeps the metaphor of the closet alive for gay and lesbian teachers, even as sexualities scholars have begun to argue that it is anachronistic in the contemporary era of gay-friendliness. I have shown how, for teachers, coming out is shaped by three context-specific factors: legal protections or vulnerabilities, the microcultures of schools, and gendered and raced embodiment. Considerations about coming out are not simply a matter of personal preference or choice; they are also shaped by institutionalized inequalities. Place (California or Texas, urban or rural, gay-friendly or gay-hostile schools), race, and gender inform how, when, and why gay and lesbian teachers disclose their sexuality.

But coming out is only one moment (or, more accurately, a series of moments) in the experience of being a gay or lesbian teacher. Being gay or lesbian in the classroom includes not only the decision about whether to be in or out of the closet but also everyday, routine expectations about how to *be,* period. The expectations of teaching professionalism and the mainstream gay rights movement unexpectedly converge on the subject of how gays and lesbians should perform identity in the classroom. A hallmark of today's gay rights movement is the emphasis on sameness, rather than difference, between straight and LGBT people. This strategic political emphasis on commonality has had a cultural impact: LGBTs are increasingly expected to conform to a "virtually normal" presentation of self.[1] We live in the era of homonormativity, a "depoliticized gay culture anchored in domesticity and consumption."[2] As a result, the demands of gay pride facilitate the ethic of sexual normativity within teaching professionalism. Notions of how an acceptably gay or lesbian teacher sounds, looks, and acts are co-constructed by the teaching profession and the gay rights movement. Gay and lesbian teachers often feel compelled to emphasize their commonalities with straight teachers and students over and above their differences, including by stressing the importance of marriage and family when talking about their relationships and advocating for "appropriate" displays of normative masculinity and femininity. Teachers who will not—or cannot—adhere to these homonormative expressions of identity have a much more difficult time making their identities visible in ways that will not put them at risk.

The expression of sexual identities in schools is also shaped by the interconnected inequalities of race and class. First, teachers of color must negotiate their in-school identities from a location of multiple marginalities. As such, they must consciously consider race and ethnicity as they make decisions about coming out and presentations of self. Some teachers of color choose to present themselves as gay or lesbian in the classroom to challenge teachers' and students' racialized stereotypes regarding sexuality. Others try to avoid outing themselves because of the added vulnerability such disclosure might bring to them as teachers already marginalized by race and ethnicity. Either way, their perspectives on coming out and the everyday performance of sexual identity in schools are influenced by their experiences of race and racism. Likewise, white teachers experience coming out and the performance of gay and lesbian identity through the lens of white privilege.

Second, race shapes how teachers anticipate and make sense of homophobia, potential and actual. Teachers of color and white teachers alike use race and class to anticipate homophobic responses from coworkers, parents, and students. Specifically, they assume that poor people of color are more prone to homophobia than other groups. Race and ethnicity, in particular, often emerged in interviews as a kind of shorthand to explain fears about coming out and incorporating LGBT issues into the curriculum. These teachers are immersed in discourses that conflate gayness with whiteness and construct queer and racially marginalized identities as incompatible.

By taking an intersectional approach to understanding these deployments of race, I argue that racism and homophobia are mutually sustained through the process I call racializing homophobia discourse. Constrained by racist notions about how homophobia operates, gay and lesbian teachers end up drawing on racist and classist stereotypes in an attempt to protect themselves from harassment and discrimination on the basis of sexual identity. While this process helps them make sense of and feel a sense of control over their experiences, it ultimately maintains the oppression of those marginalized by race, class, gender, and sexuality.

Gay and lesbian teachers also use racism as a metaphor for making sense of homophobia. While this coping strategy challenges the pain and alienation of inequality, it simultaneously reinforces inequality by assuming that racism and homophobia are distinct yet identical experiences of inequality. Compartmentalizing discrimination in this manner thus thwarts an intersectional understanding of identity. Racial and sexual discrimination are mutually constituted and mutually reinforcing components of systems of privilege and oppression. Homophobia is socially reproduced within the context of mutually interconnected relationships among all forms of discrimination. All of these factors come into play as gay and lesbian teachers attempt to cope with homophobia in their schools.

RESEARCH IMPLICATIONS

Feminist perspectives on work suggest that inequalities are not only present in the workplace but actively *sustained* by workplace practices.[3] While much of the prior feminist research on work has explored how work reproduces inequalities of race, class, and gender, less has been said about how sexuality shapes and is shaped by work.[4] This is because both conservative and progressive political approaches tend to consider sex and sexuality a private experience, largely undetermined by social forces. The hunt for the "gay gene" and other possible biological determinants of same-sex desire, for instance, is driven by the desire to debunk earlier conceptualizations of such desire as pathological or sinful. This notion occludes discussion of how sexuality is a social experience that is shaped even by seemingly unrelated institutions such as the workplace. The gay rights movement has been especially invested in the idea of sexuality as biologically driven and separate from the social, but the insistence on the private nature of sexuality is widespread, embedded in the institutions that govern us, the worldviews we share, and our very senses of self.

This book challenges our collective reluctance to consider sexuality as a public and socially constructed experience. Specifically, I have shown that workplaces—in this case, schools—play a significant role in the construction of gay, lesbian, and straight identities. Work can have a deep, transformative effect on one's sense of sexual self. Workplaces legitimize and stigmatize expressions of sexuality in a way that doesn't just reproduce inequality but actually contributes to the production of a docile, compliant, and depoliticized sexual subject. The norms of teaching professionalism, steeped in heteronormativity and homophobia, affect how gay and lesbian teachers see themselves and act. The gender nonconformity often associated with gay and lesbian identities becomes especially suspect in schools, and teachers make concerted efforts to distance themselves from it, disciplining their own bodies—and sometimes their gay and lesbian peers—into performing more normative masculinities and femininities. The performative demands of teaching, along with the homonormative expectations of mainstream gay rights discourse, transform how gay and lesbian teachers experience their sexual identities and how they disclose and perform them.

That said, there is much more to be done to understand the experiences of queer teachers. The theoretical contributions of this book are limited by the constraints of my project sample and my methodological approach. In particular, the limited racial and ethnic diversity in the sample precluded a fuller examination of the impact of race and sexuality on the experiences of gay and lesbian teachers of color, an examination that I believe is integral to understanding inequality in schools and workplaces. Further, this project did not focus on the experiences of bisexual and transgender teachers; future research might take up their stories to explore how enactments of bisexual and transgender identities play out in the school context, and what implications these enactments have for challenging inequality. Finally, while interviews and observations are invaluable sources of data, future research might consider other approaches to understanding gay and lesbian teacher experiences, including surveying, content analysis, and a more thoroughly ethnographic account of their experiences than I could provide here.

In addition to its contributions to sociological theory, this book has implications for educational and employment policies and practices. The countervailing pressures of teaching professionalism and gay pride create a sense of forced choice for many teachers between "out and proud" and "closeted and safe." The specific tensions of our current historical moment with respect to gay rights have significant bearing on the working lives of gay and lesbian teachers. This book shows that while antidiscrimination legislation and other kinds of supportive policies do affect the experiences of gay and lesbian teachers, they are only part of the story. Occupational cultures, interpersonal interactions, racism and normative gender expectations, homonormativity, and preconceived notions of potential homophobia also contribute to their overall experiences. Thus this research shows that we cannot rely on legal interventions alone to achieve true equity for gay and lesbian teachers; we must address the sources of discrimination in the cultures of occupations and schools, as well as the intersecting inequalities of race and gender.

So what *would* make a meaningful difference in the lives of gay and lesbian teachers? How might we move beyond the standard of "gay-friendly" to a "*queer*-friendly" model that would allow for a broader range of being than the rigidly gender-conforming and homonormative standards that are currently privileged? While I have outlined the limitations of using nondiscrimination protections as the primary solution to the challenges gay and lesbian teachers face, they can provide some legal recourse and symbolic legitimacy. Extending federal nondiscrimination protections to all LGBT workers would be a good place to start. To the extent that existing nondiscrimination policies can and do contribute to an atmosphere of safety for LGBT teachers, teachers must have complete and accurate information about them, for policies are effective only if individual workers know enough about them and feel empowered to take advantage of them. Accordingly, the first step in bolstering nondiscrimination policy is extensive information campaigns within schools to ensure that teachers have adequate knowledge of their policy environments. According to legal scholar and queer activist Dean Spade, harnessing the power of nondiscrimination protections to provide the most effective aid to the broadest constituency requires four pillars of legal action: first, demystifying the legal system, as described above, then providing free or affordable legal services to those who cannot afford to take advantage of nondiscrimination protections, developing law and policy reform targets to improve existing legislation, and providing technical assistance to the advocacy organizations working on behalf of the target population.[5] Applying these principles to

LGBT nondiscrimination law and policy would go a long way toward making them more effective and accessible.

But this, of course, is not enough. As we have seen, even those who have full knowledge of the antidiscrimination policies that apply to them often face quiet bias, or subtler forms of sexual identity discrimination, due to an occupational culture that is at best oblivious and at worst hostile to homosexuality. Unlike changing policy or reinforcing knowledge of existing policy, changing occupational cultures is much less straightforward. Cultural change requires a significant shift in the ideological frameworks that individuals bring to bear on their experience. There are thus two questions we need to ask when considering how to bring about this change. First, what kinds of cultural shifts are required to challenge the kinds of workplace inequalities gay and lesbian teachers describe? Second, how do these changes come about?

I believe this book offers some answers. Although schools that I would deem "gay-friendly" are hospitable to certain ways of divulging and expressing gay and lesbian identities, this hospitality often extends only to certain gay and lesbian teachers. Specifically, these schools seem to support partnered, normatively gendered, race- and class-privileged teachers. Teachers who do not meet these standards—nonwhite, nonpartnered, non-normative queer teachers—continue to be silenced and regarded as Other. The goal of gay-friendliness simply isn't pushing far enough for a truly inclusive vision of social and sexual justice in schools.

As opposed to a gay-friendly school, a *queer*-friendly school would transform the ethic of teaching professionalism. Dismantling the hierarchies of acceptable sexualities in schools requires challenging fiercely held beliefs about childhood, sexual agency, and sexual knowledge. The notion that children must be shielded from sexuality, in particular queer sexuality, is harmful to queers and children alike. Until we undo this notion, teachers' sexuality will remain under close scrutiny and social control. Ironically, both antigay advocates and marriage equality activists have begun to stake their claims in the question of harm to children, the one claiming that gay and lesbian teachers endanger children, the other focusing on how marriage protects the children of same-sex couples.[6] What if, instead of using children to legitimate antigay and progay claims, we took more seriously the idea of children's own sexual agency and moved from a discourse of child welfare to one of child empowerment? Acknowledging childhood sexuality and stepping away from the rhetoric of adult protection of children would benefit children as well as queer adults. If children's sexual agency is taken seriously, then the desire to keep them from sexual knowledge is recognized as misplaced. When we acknowledge that children have a right to the world of sexuality, then we no longer have to worry about hiding same-sex desire and gender non-normativity from them. Teaching professionalism no longer requires sexual neutrality, and, even more importantly, the pedagogical mission of teaching is transformed to allow for a more expansive vision of sexual and social justice.

A queered pedagogical approach would purposefully disrupt the narrative of child protectionism. Key tenets of queer pedagogy include bringing marginalized knowledge to the center, critiquing heteronormativity and homophobia as part of the formal curriculum, and committing to deconstructing and challenging hegemonic ways of knowing.[7] Education scholars have discussed the role of coming out in the practice of queer pedagogy, at once acknowledging the radical potential of visibility and noting the failures and limitations of "coming out" as a political strategy.[8] A queer-friendly school would move beyond the reliance on coming out as the key strategy of queering the classroom. Instead, it would focus on deconstructing and decolonizing heteronormative and homophobic discourse through the formal and informal curriculum. It also would not limit itself to a single-oppression model of social change but would, as Cathy Cohen once suggested, take on "a politics where the non-normative and marginal position of punks, bulldaggers, and welfare queens, for example, is the basis for progressive transformative coalition work."[9] A queer-friendly school would acknowledge how race, class, gender, and other systems of privilege and oppression inform sexual inequality and would give students the tools necessary to challenge these systems.

This vision may seem lofty or unrealistic, but if we truly want to dismantle sexual inequalities in schools, nothing short of it will do. We are at a crossroads, turning from the ghosts of the teacher purges and Briggs Amendments of the past and moving toward the possibility of a new future for nonheterosexual, non-normative teachers. To create security for some of those teachers—the race, class, and gender privileged, the partnered, the *normal*—at the expense of others is not an acceptable compromise. If gay rights advocacy continues on its current path of homonormativity, we will lose much potential for change. Let us dream bigger, hope for more, and expand our vision of justice, for the sake of our own futures and generations of queer teachers to come.

METHODOLOGY

Although I did not embark on my research until 2008, this book project really began in the summer of 2006 during a conversation with my younger sister, Emily. That conversation, seemingly inconsequential in the moment, would change the course of my future as a scholar of sexualities. Emily was at that time a graduate student in teacher education at UCLA's Center X. Founded in 1992, Center X's mission is to transform teaching into a social justice practice. Center X prides itself on providing teachers with training in antiracist, antisexist, anticlassist, and antihomophobic pedagogy, which is reflected in its course listings, including a number of required courses that draw on feminist, queer, and critical race theories to inform students' understandings of education as an institution. During her studies there, my sister became devoted to critical pedagogy, the practice of constructing a formal and informal curriculum to help students develop what philosopher Georg Hegel once called a consciousness of freedom. This consciousness is, according to critical pedagogy advocates, necessarily rooted in an awareness of the injustices of race, class, gender, and sexual hierarchies.

When she began classroom instruction under the guidance of Center X, Emily saw how her training in critical pedagogy positively affected the lives of her students, transforming the oppressive belief systems that were already deeply rooted by the time they reached her sixth-grade class. In 2006, I visited her in Los Angeles during her last semester under supervision, and we began discussing the relationship between her training and practice. As a fellow graduate student and an instructor specializing in gender and sexualities, I was particularly curious to know if Center X had given her antihomophobic teaching strategies and how she, in turn, enacted these strategies in the classroom. I was excited to hear how the program instructed future teachers about addressing homophobia and heterosexism in schools, and proud of her successes bringing those lessons to bear on her classroom.

At some point in this discussion, Emily paused and said, "You know, it's weird, though, that some of my classmates who are gay themselves find it hard to bring these lessons into the classroom." Intrigued, I asked her to tell me more. She described a gay classmate who was passionate about teaching to subvert the oppression of LGBTs but was nervous and hesitant about including such lessons into his curriculum. "What does he have to be worried about?" I asked, perhaps naïvely. "It sounds like your grad program is the perfect place to try this out!" My sister, already an astute observer of the very phenomenon that would launch and guide my future research, replied, "With an engagement ring on my finger, I can say whatever I want about supporting gay rights, and even if my students don't end up agreeing with me, they also don't think that I'm secretly a lesbian and therefore have an agenda. Wearing a ring and talking about [my male fiancé] neutralizes the threat." She explained that supporting gay rights in the classroom wasn't as easy for her friend and other gay and lesbian classmates. They worried that if they brought up gay issues in the classroom their students would out them and parents would worry about their inappropriate influence.

I pressed a little further. It seemed to me that gay and lesbian teachers in her program had many avenues of recourse if issues arose: the school district had antidiscrimination legislation, the teachers' union was vocal in its support for gay rights, the school sounded progressive, and it seemed as if the field supervisors from UCLA would be staunch defenders, if it came to that. Emily answered, "I would hope that all that would protect them, but they don't want to have to find out. Even if the school and the program protected them, it would damage their classroom environment. Then their students might not trust the other things they are teaching them, like the antiracist and antisexist stuff. I guess it's just a risk they don't want to take right now."

This conversation got me thinking. How was it that, under the best possible circumstances, a gay teacher might still feel afraid to teach antihomophobia in the classroom? What did this mean about the profession of teaching? How could LGBT teachers ever expect to feel comfortable in the classroom if even an extensive safety net of policy and training didn't do enough? These questions would eventually form the basis of my dissertation and, later, this book, an exploration of the experiences of gay and lesbian teachers, not only in California, where Emily taught, but also in Texas.

EPISTEMOLOGY AND METHOD

Critical sociology seeks to privilege people's accounts and experiences while using their narratives to demystify and dismantle the inner workings of inequality.[1] This research was conducted according to this goal and was further shaped by the epistemological influences of symbolic interactionism, feminist theory, and queer theory. In accordance with symbolic interactionist tradition, this project assumes that meaning is produced and reproduced through social interaction and that it is therefore important to closely examine the day-to-day experiences of individuals in their social context.[2] Feminist sociology challenges researchers to take power and domination into account. I take as a starting assumption the feminist principle that each individual in society is positioned within a matrix of domination based on gender, race, class, sexuality, and various other identity groupings.[3] Further, this project assumes that this system of privilege and oppression affects every aspect of our lives, from the structural to the individual. The goal of feminist sociology is to identify the dynamics of this process in order to ascertain ways it might be challenged.

Queer theory offered a further epistemological foundation. Deconstructing the impact of discourses on self and society is central to queer theory.[4] Accordingly, rather than taking gay rights and child welfare claims as incontrovertible truths, I sought to understand their role in constructing the work experiences of LGBT-identified teachers. Queer theory is deeply suspicious of binaries, which, it claims, serve the interests of power. The social context of this project is rife with binary constructions, including adult/child, teacher/student, heterosexual/homosexual, in the closet/out of the closet, pure/corrupting, private/public, individual rights/public harm, and so on. A preliminary review of the relevant research made it clear how these binaries serve to maintain systems of power built upon race, gender, age, class, and sexual identity.[5] Accordingly, I sought out and paid attention to binaries as they appeared in the research field.

RESEARCH DESIGN

Feminism not only informs this project epistemologically but also guided its methodological direction. Feminist methodology is defined by three elements: a commitment to bringing the perspectives of women and marginalized Others into social science research, an intent to minimize harm to research participants and beneficiaries, and an interest in doing research that is of value to women and ameliorates inequality.[6] Accordingly, this research project used the experiences of marginalized gay and lesbian teachers to produce knowledge that might be used to improve their working conditions and challenge the production of inequality in workplaces and schools.

Considering the perspectives of gay and lesbian teachers is also useful for theorizing the larger experience of sexuality and work. Their social distance from the taken-for-granted heterosexuality that infuses our daily lives makes LGBT research subjects key to understanding the mechanisms of sexuality construction. For example, in her research, Kristen Schilt drew upon the experiences of transgender men as gender "outsiders-within" to unveil the gendered expectations of men and women workers.[7] Similarly, this study uses the perspectives of gay and lesbian teachers to reveal the sexualized expectations for education workers.

Teachers are often taught to use the "pedagogy of the personal" when interacting with students, which means to use examples from their own lives, families, and experiences to make their lessons more relatable for students.[8] However, gay and lesbian teachers are simultaneously encouraged to leave their personal lives *out* of the classroom.[9] As a result, straight teachers are able to use personal examples more effectively than gay and lesbian teachers. More importantly, these conflicting imperatives allow heteronormativity to predominate in classroom narratives, since heterosexual personal examples are acceptable and homosexual examples are not. Because gay and lesbian teachers have to navigate these moments of disclosure by weighing pedagogical effectiveness against job security, they have a heightened awareness of the role of sex and sexuality in constructing the teaching experience.

RESEARCH SAMPLES

I began my research in California in the summer of 2008, while I lived for three months with my sister and her husband in a town about an hour from Los Angeles. My sister put me in contact with some of her former classmates and professors from her graduate teaching program. Ultimately, I was able to secure two interviews from these initial contacts. One of these participants subsequently referred me to a colleague, who in turn referred me to friends. Simultaneously, I reached out to area acquaintances for referrals, contacted faculty advisers for Gay Straight Alliances, posted on websites, forums, and message boards, and reached out to LA Unified School District employees who worked in LGBT student affairs. In the end, my contact with district employees was the most helpful avenue. One district administrator agreed to send my recruitment statement to an e-mail listserv for teachers and administrators interested in LGBT issues, which generated a number of interviews. From these and a few other interviews that I managed to secure, I snowball-sampled to find teachers who were less directly involved in educational activism around LGBT issues.

The sample that emerged from these recruitment techniques included teachers who were directly involved in LGBT activism (including GSA advisers, members of an advocacy/support group for

LGBT teachers and administrators, and district administrators working on LGBT curriculum and school safety committees), teachers who were tangentially involved (by marching in a Pride parade or receiving e-mails from the e-mail list), and teachers with no involvement in LGBT educational issues. The sample was fairly balanced with respect to age and gender and somewhat less balanced with respect to teaching position, with roughly equal numbers of elementary school teachers, middle school teachers, and administrators, but a slight overrepresentation of high school teachers.

I made a concerted recruitment attempt at overrepresentation of teachers of color, knowing that social science research is hindered by the exclusion of people of color's experiences. Despite this effort, the majority of interviewees were white. This significantly limited the project's findings by making it difficult to get sufficient data on teacher experiences of multiple marginality. To help counteract this limitation, I have tried, when possible, to privilege the voices and experiences of teachers of color in the presentation of the data. It was difficult to apply an intersectional perspective to my research questions, which I knew was a crucial lens for the project, when my sample construction and interview guide did not facilitate the gathering of that kind of data. This was certainly a lesson learned for future work: it's not enough to be intersectional in your theoretical orientation; intersectionality must also be a methodological orientation that goes beyond trying (and failing) to recruit more participants of color.

In addition to the in-depth interviews, I engaged in participant observation in both states, tapping several "key informants" from the in-depth interview sample and following this smaller cohort through their school days and after-school activities. The resulting "thick description" provided an important complement to the broader range of experiences represented in the in-depth interviews.[10] In California, I attended the West Hollywood Pride Parade with a contingent of LGBT teachers and students, observed four teachers in their classrooms (two gay men, one lesbian, and one straight), attended meetings of the LAUSD's Gay and Lesbian Allied Administrators (GALAA) group, and observed a mandatory professional development training about LGBT issues for teachers in a Southern California high school.

These observations generated important insights into the everyday experience of teaching. Engaging with teachers' environments—from the classroom to the Pride parade—helped me understand the dual identity expectations they face.

The majority of California teachers I interviewed and observed lived and worked in Southern California, and a significant proportion of those worked in the LAUSD. This meant that many of the teachers I interviewed enjoyed an extra layer of resources and protections, since the district has programs and support groups aimed at protecting LGBT students and staff. However, as chapter 4 demonstrates, the visibility and accessibility of such protections can vary widely from school to school. In addition, because it is the second-biggest school district in the nation, its resources are diffuse and spread thin, which affects access to and knowledge of such protections across the district. I also interviewed teachers in surrounding school districts, which provided additional diversity of experience vis-à-vis administrative conditions.

Just as most of my California interviews were conducted in Southern California, most of my Texas interviews and observations were located in central Texas. As in California, regional proximity did not mean regional uniformity. I interviewed teachers working in major metropolitan areas, tiny rural communities, and growing suburban enclaves. The Texas sample was also balanced with respect to age and gender, and more balanced than the California sample in terms of classroom level (elementary, middle school, and high school teachers). Where the California sample included six administrators, the Texas sample included only one. This discrepancy is due at least in part to differences in how the samples were generated. When I left California to conduct the Texas comparison, I began my recruitment efforts in much the same way I had begun them in California, with personal contacts, Web forums, and e-mails to administrative and advocacy contacts. Unlike the LAUSD, Texas districts do not have administrators dedicated to LGBT issues, which made the administration route less fruitful. After a slow start, I contacted the Texas chapter of the Gay, Lesbian, Straight Education Network (GLSEN), where I found a contact who was able to facilitate my

networking as my California contact had. This person sent my recruitment statement out to the GLSEN Texas e-mail list, which generated
a number of interviews. As in California, I snowballed from this wave
of participants to find other teachers who were less actively involved
in LGBT educational politics.

Teachers were more reluctant to allow classroom observation in
Texas than in California, perhaps because only one was out to his students and my presence might have been hard to explain. I did conduct
classroom observations with two teachers, one in a middle school and
one in a high school; I also observed a Gay Straight Alliance (GSA) in
a central Texas high school. These observations were, once again,
crucial for interpreting and analyzing the experience of my sample.
The middle school classroom observations alerted me to the significance of gender performativity in the classroom, as I watched students
interact with their closeted yet gender nonconforming science teacher.
The GSA observations were also formative for understanding the
tensions between racial and sexual politics in LGBT community
organizing.

REFLEXIVE RESEARCH AND INTERVIEW
RAPPORT

When conducting in-depth interviews, a qualitative researcher must
carefully consider the effect on data quality of rapport, impression
management, and face-to-face discussions of sensitive topics.[11] In this
study, interview rapport was established in two ways. First, my snow-
ball-sampling method meant that most respondents met me through
personal networks. As a result, I believe that most respondents came to
the interview with a certain amount of preestablished trust and confidence. Second, I was upfront with respondents about my own positionality as a queer educator, as well as my epistemological stance,
which included an interest in improving their working conditions
through this study. I believe that this added assurance helped establish
a trust with teachers that encouraged them to be more forthcoming in
their responses. While interview rapport cannot entirely guard
against the limitations of impression management in discussions of

TABLE A.1
Summary of Research Participants

State	Pseudonym	Age	Gender	Sexual Identity	Race/Ethnicity	Education	Occupation
CA	Alfred	27	Man	Gay	Latino	MA	Elementary teacher
CA	Amy	48	Woman	Bisexual	White	BA	High school teacher
CA	Charles	77	Man	Gay	White	MA	High school teacher (retired)
CA	Chelsea	28	Woman	Lesbian	White	MA	Middle school teacher
CA	Cheryl	37	Woman	Lesbian	Latina	MA	Elementary teacher
CA	Dale	72	Man	Gay	White	BS	High school teacher (retired)
CA	Delia	28	Woman	Straight	White	MA	High school teacher
CA	Héctor	35	Man	Gay	Latino	MA	Administrator
CA	Joan	62	Woman	Straight	White	MA	High school teacher
CA	Jody	60	Woman	Lesbian	White	BA	High school teacher
CA	John	24	Man	Gay	Asian	MA	High school teacher
CA	José	43	Man	Gay	Latino	EdD	Elementary teacher
CA	June	51	Woman	Lesbian	White	MA	High school teacher
CA	Karen	34	Woman	Lesbian	White	MA	High school teacher
CA	Larry	42	Man	Gay	White	MA	High school teacher
CA	Lisa	74	Woman	Lesbian	White	PhD	High school teacher (retired)

(continued)

TABLE A.I (continued)

State	Pseudonym	Age	Gender	Sexual Identity	Race/ Ethnicity	Education	Occupation
CA	Mark	45	Man	Gay	Latino	MA	Administrator
CA	Mary	60	Woman	Lesbian	White	MS	High school teacher (retired)
CA	Mike	47	Man	Gay	White	MA	Administrator
CA	Peter	60	Man	Gay	Asian	EdD	Administrator
CA	Ruben	60	Man	Gay	Latino	BA	Administrator
CA	Rufus	31	Man	Gay	White	MA	Middle school teacher
CA	Stanley	37	Man	Gay	White	MA	Middle school teacher
CA	Susan	54	Woman	Lesbian	White	PhD	Administrator
CA	Taylor	30	Woman	Lesbian	White	BA	High school teacher
CA	Wilson	34	Man	Gay	Biracial	BA	Elementary teacher
TX	Barbara	44	Woman	Lesbian	White	MA	Middle school teacher
TX	Brian	40	Man	Gay	White	BA	High school teacher
TX	Christi	30	Woman	Lesbian	White	MA	Middle school teacher
TX	Darlene	47	Woman	Lesbian	White	PhD	Administrator
TX	David	43	Man	Gay	Latino	BA	Elementary teacher
TX	Debbie	52	Woman	Lesbian	White	MA	Elementary teacher
TX	Elizabeth	30	Woman	Lesbian	White	MA	High school teacher
TX	Harry	55	Man	Gay	White	BA	Elementary teacher

State	Name	Age	Gender	Sexuality	Race	Education	Occupation
TX	Hugh	37	Man	Gay	Latino	MA	High school teacher
TX	Ian	61	Man	Gay	White	PhD	High school teacher (retired)
TX	James	23	Man	Gay	Black	BA	Middle school teacher
TX	Jenna	34	Woman	Straight	White	BA	Middle school teacher
TX	Joe	31	Man	Gay	White	MA	Middle school teacher
TX	Kenny	24	Man	Gay	Black	BA	Elementary teacher
TX	Kevin	30	Man	Gay	White	MA	Educational advocate
TX	Kyle	47	Man	Straight	White	MA	Union president
TX	Leon	46	Man	Straight	Black	BA	Educational advocate
TX	Linda	45	Woman	Lesbian	White	BA	Middle school teacher
TX	Liza	51	Woman	Lesbian	White	BS	Elementary teacher
TX	Marsha	37	Woman	Lesbian	White	BA	Elementary teacher
TX	Mauricio	40	Man	Gay	Latino	MA	Middle school teacher
TX	Melissa	44	Woman	Lesbian	White	MA	High school teacher
TX	Phillip	34	Man	Gay	White	BA	Elementary teacher
TX	Robert	46	Man	Straight	White	JD	Gay rights lobbyist
TX	Tabitha	37	Woman	Lesbian	White	BS	Elementary teacher

sensitive topics, establishing such rapport does, to some degree, mediate these limitations.[12]

Of course, the dynamics of rapport depended on more than my shared insider positionality as a queer educator.[13] In any given interview, my whiteness, femaleness, normative gender presentation, affiliation with a PhD program at a large, prestigious research university, and any number of other characteristics marked me as in or out with regard to possible shared identifications and positions of privilege or oppression. Although I spent my adolescence in California and lived at the time in Texas, both groups perceived me as a geographic outsider. To California teachers, I was a Texan visiting for the summer, learning the progressive ways of the West. Even after years of living in Austin, to Texas teachers, I was still a Californian who might judge them unfairly. As Lyle Lovett croons in "That's Right (You're Not from Texas)," it's hard to earn insider status with Texans, but thankfully, "[They] still love you anyway."

To remain aware of how my own subjectivity affected the research experience and to consider how these various insider/outsider perceptions might affect my research, I kept track of my thoughts and feelings with a field journal. I kept records of my own responses to interviews and observations, including empathy, anger, fatigue, confusion, and more. I even kept track of my moods as I entered interviews: Was I exhausted from doing too many interviews in one day? Was I nervous about meeting an interviewee face to face for the first time? These kinds of notes not only helped me be mindful in the moment but also provided much-needed context when I was interpreting interview and observation data. In addition to tracking my emotional responses, I used the journal to reflect on issues such as my fears about the research process, my preconceived notions of what gay and lesbian teachers *should* do, and my ongoing insights into possible research conclusions. Overall, this journaling endeavor taught me about effective research strategies (for example, I should never try to do more than two interviews in one day!) but also about how to turn unfavorable reactions (for example, toward teachers who made what I interpreted as racist and sexist remarks) into opportunities for insight and reflection. Interrogating my own responses to the research participants turned up as many theoretical insights as coding the "real" data of interview transcripts and field notes.

Speaking of coding, all data were coded line by line and focus-coded using the qualitative analysis program Atlas.ti.[14] Initially, I coded transcripts line by line to create an extensive taxonomy of the analytical material. I then used focused coding to develop a sense of overall trends and emergent themes, which were sorted into code families and code networks. I organized focused codes by major and minor thematic categories, cross-listing quotations and codes that were appropriate to more than one thematic family. During coding, I again kept a journal of patterns, connections, useful anecdotes, themes, and possible theoretical directions to guide further analysis. After coding the data for my dissertation work, I conducted a full recode before embarking on the book project. A two-day Atlas.ti advanced training taught me new ways to organize the data. Armed with this additional training as well as the distance of one year away, I combed through all the transcripts and field notes with fresh eyes. This new analysis both confirmed the results of my initial coding output and generated new insights.

ETHICAL CONSIDERATIONS

Ethical considerations are always an integral part of the research design and process, but they were especially relevant to this project. Some of the teachers I interviewed and observed were not out in their workplaces. Even those who were out were sometimes still subject to harassment or at risk of termination because of their sexual identity, especially in Texas, where no state laws protected them. Confidentiality and prudence in the field were thus of the utmost importance. Because of these cautions, I ended up with less ethnographic data than I would have ideally liked, but it was important to me that my research process not put participants at risk. I observed IRB protocols of confidentiality, including protecting written and verbal records with identifying information, concealing interviewee identity in any published work, and respecting participants' parameters in terms of the interview process. This respect included allowing them to choose the location of the interview and deciding whether the interview could be tape-recorded. I also briefed my research participants on their rights in the research process and explained the terms of consent before any interview.

Even with all these protections in place, it would be a mistake to claim that I left the research field—and the research participants— exactly as I found them. A month or so after our interview, one teacher sent me an e-mail to inform me that our discussion had inspired her to come out not only to her coworkers but also to her twelve-year-old daughter. When I read her words, my stomach dropped. Was this happening for other participants? Was it causing possible harm to them? This teacher spoke in glowing terms, saying she felt more comfortable and connected now that this secret was no longer in the way of her relationships with her coworkers and family. Still, it made me realize researchers' enormous responsibility to be sensitive to the possibility that their research could directly affect—and possibly harm— research participants. In the future, I will be more mindful of how this possibility complicates questions of research ethics when studying sexuality.

While confidentiality and minimal interference were my key ethical concerns for this project, I considered other ethical questions as well. At one point, a dissertation committee member asked if I was prepared for the possibility of encountering knowledge of intimacies between teachers and students that went beyond the "acceptable" parameters of the teacher-student relationship. I certainly was not, so I spent some time thinking about how I might handle such information and considering my own assumptions about teacher-student relationships. As it turned out, I did not encounter any such information; nonetheless, preparing for this possibility was an important part of my reflexive process as a researcher. I was also concerned about how my analysis (and the publication of this book) might affect participants. Would research participants reading this recognize themselves, and would they be hurt by how I described them or analyzed their responses? *Can* there be a feminist ethnography, or in this case, a feminist interview study, if the research process exposes marginalized participants to the possibility of further exploitation, betrayal, and pain?[15]

Like Judith Stacey in her groundbreaking article on the (im)possibility of feminist ethnography, I have had to grapple with the reality that perhaps there can be only partial and humble attempts to provide benefits that outweigh this moral cost. I hope that my interactions with research participants provided some measure of comfort and support, and perhaps even positive outcome, as in the case of the participant who was so happy to have come out to her daughter and coworkers.

I also hope that my research will more broadly benefit the larger constituency of gay and lesbian teachers (and perhaps, even more broadly, queer workers of all kinds). In the actual writing of this book, I have pushed myself not just to speak to fellow academics but to write for anyone and everyone who has a stake in the future of sexuality in workplaces and schools. I worried about the consequences of exposing how gay and lesbian teachers themselves participate in the racist, sexist, classist and homophobic discourses that maintain systems of inequality. I worried about asking "too much" from them, being too critical of gay rights activism, and inadvertently making it harder for gay and lesbian teachers to withstand critique. In these kinds of methodological concerns I am not alone; for example, Orit Avishai, Lynne Gerber, and Jennifer Randles have written of the anxiety that some feminist researchers experience when the reality of their data is not easily reconciled with orthodox feminist principles.[16] In a reflection on her own research in schools, Jessica Fields grapples with the political consequences of being critical of the feminist sex education advocates she studied. Fields suggests that feminist ethnographers adapt a position of "ambivalent observance" vis-à-vis our work and "resist the pull to reconcile our political and intellectual agendas and realities."[17] These kinds of methodological reflections helped me deal with my own impulse to minimize the uncomfortable tensions that emerged in this research.

Some might argue that these kinds of worries give too much credit to the influence of sociology, but recent events regarding sociological research and LGBT political rights are a warning that sociologists need to ask such questions of the impact of their work. In 2012, sociologist Mark Regnerus published research purporting to demonstrate that children with gay or lesbian parents fare worse than children of what he called intact biological families (married hetero-sexuals with biologically related children). While this research has been roundly dismissed by sociologists for its methodological flaws, antigay activists have nevertheless deployed it in political battles.[18] Although Regnerus is virtually the only sociologist to suggest that gay and lesbian parenting is harmful, Supreme Court justice Antonin Scalia used his work, in Supreme Court hearings on the constitutionality of California Proposition 8, to declare that "there is considerable dis-agreement amongst sociologists as to what the consequences of raising a child in a single-sex family, whether that is harmful to the child or not." The study was also used in Russia to push passage of a law against exposing "propaganda of nontraditional sexual relations" to minors and, as of 2014, continues to be used in similar efforts in the United States and internationally. The fact that these examples are about child protectionism suggests that the use of child welfare discourse is far from over in contemporary gay rights struggles, and sociologists must consider the risk of being pulled into this discourse. The Regn-erus study continues to pop up with alarming and increasing fre-quency in battles over gay rights across the globe.

The example of Regnerus's work demonstrates the very real power that sociological research *can* have on the bigger political stage. It is thus imperative that sociologists think about the political impact of their work, and sociologists who care about sexual justice must be especially mindful. This book takes a critical look at the gay rights movement and its impact in the daily lives of gay and lesbian teachers. Ultimately, it does not shy away from dealing with the ugly realities of issues like racism and internalized homonormativity among LGBTs. But I fervently believe that this honesty is a necessary step in moving forward to a more just future, in schools, workplaces, and communi-ties, and for that reason my feminist research ethics compel me to share these stories in the hope that they may make a difference.

INTERVIEW SCHEDULE FOR
TEACHERS

I. BACKGROUND

1. Describe your teaching experience. Where have you taught? What subjects? How long?
2. How did you become interested in teaching? Did you have any family/friends in the profession? Were you especially inspired by any of your own teachers to go into education?
3. What was your undergraduate major? Did this prepare you for your teaching career? Did you attend a master's-level teacher education program? What did this program entail? Tell me about your preservice teaching experiences [if applicable].

II. CURRENT (OR MOST RECENT) TEACHING EXPERIENCES

1. Where do you currently teach? What grade(s), subject(s)? How long have you been there? Do you supervise, coach, or participate in any extracurricular activities at the school?
2. Tell me about your teaching duties. Describe a typical day at school. What work do you need to do to prepare for school (curriculum prep, grading, etc.)?

3. What are your relationships with your coworkers like? Fellow teachers, administrators, school staff? How have these relationships impacted your teaching experience?

4. What are your relationships with your students like? How have these relationships impacted your teaching experience?

5. How do you feel about teaching? Are you happy, satisfied with your job? Why or why not?

6. Are you "out" as LGBT to your co-workers? To students? To others outside school? How did you come to your decision to disclose/ not disclose your sexual identity at school?

7. Does your city/county/state have any policies protecting you from discrimination on the basis of sexual identity or gender expression? Does your school have a policy? Have you or any other teachers you know taken advantage of these policies? What was your/ his/her experience like?

8. Do you think it is important to be an "out" teacher? Why or why not?

9. How does being LGBT impact your teaching? Do you try to incorporate "gay-friendly" aspects into your teaching (lesson plans, language, classroom décor, examples)?

10. Do you have or have you had LGBT students in your classroom? What was your relationship with those students?

III. FUTURE PLANS

1. Where do you see yourself in five years? Would you like to continue teaching this grade? This subject? At this school? Do you have any interest in moving into school administration? Why or why not?

2. What do you like best about teaching? What aspects do you like the least?

3. How do you think your school could improve? How could it do better with respect to LGBT issues? Describe your vision of the "perfect" school.

NOTES

I. PRIDE AND PROFESSIONALISM

1. *LGBT* stands for "lesbian, gay, bisexual, and transgender." When talking about current events and research, I use *LGBT*, the most common contemporary term (along with *GLBT*) for referring to nonheterosexual and transgender people as a group.

2. All names of research participants are pseudonyms, unless otherwise indicated.

3. The euphemism "the love that dare not speak its name" for homosexuality, which comes from a poem by Lord Alfred Douglas (1894), was famously referenced during Oscar Wilde's trial for sodomy and gross indecency in 1895.

4. While I am aware of the limitations of the concept of homophobia as overly psychological and reductionist (Bryant and Vidal-Ortiz 2008 and Redman 2000), I use it throughout because it reflects the way my research participants talk about antigay bias.

5. McIntosh 1968.

6. Gagnon and Simon 1973; see also Longmore 1998.

7. Plummer 1994.

8. Stein 1989. McIntosh's 1968 homosexual role concept is an exception in this regard; her claim that the role was a modern invention

used to leverage social control presaged Foucault's similar but more widely recognized claims in *The History of Sexuality* (1976).

9. For a review of queer theory's central tenets and its applications within sociology, see Gamson and Moon 2004. While *queer* intentionally resists definition, it broadly refers to the rejection of the static sexual identity politics of "gay" or "lesbian" in favor of a more inclusive, explicitly radical, and antiassimilationist politics of sexuality.

10. Rubin 1984.

11. A theory of sexuality popularized by the work of Sigmund Freud, among others.

12. Sedgwick 1990 argues that modernity hinges on a chronic homo/hetero binary and that this binary affects all aspects of life, including art, science, and commerce.

13. See Brekhus 2003; Gamson 1998; Hennen 2008; Stein 1997; Walters 2001.

14. Epstein 1999.

15. See Jurik and Siemsen 2009.

16. West and Zimmerman 1987.

17. Risman 2009.

18. Deutsch 2007.

19. Lorber 2000.

20. *Transgender* refers to a mismatch between gender identity or sex category with birth-assigned sex. *Intersex* is a variation in sex characteristics that makes it difficult to assign the binary categories of "male" or "female" to a particular person. *Genderqueer* refers to an alternative gender identity from the binary categories of "man" and "woman" (sometimes also used to denote the practice of "queering" or transgressing gender norms). For analyses of the political potential of trans people to "undo" gender, see Butler 2004; C. Connell 2010.

21. West and Zimmerman 2009.

22. Butler 1990.

23. See Weeks 1979 for a history of homosexuality, including its emergence as a medical/psychiatric category.

24. Sedgwick 1990.

25. Collins 1990; Crenshaw 1989.

26. Alexander 2006; Collins 1990; Spelman 1988.

27. See Zinn and Dill 1996; Collins 1990; Crenshaw 1989.

28. Collins 1990.

29. Collins 1990, p. 225.

30. Crenshaw 1989.

31. Moraga and Anzaldúa 1981. See also the Combahee River Collective Statement, and work by Audre Lorde and Merle Woo.

32. On the hypersexualization of Black women's bodies, see Collins 1990; on the racialized politics of prostitution, pornography, and rape, see Collins 2004.

33. On how race, class, and gender shape of sexual desire, see, for example, J. Ward 2008 and Wilkins 2012. On their shaping of communities, see Carrillo 2002; C. Cohen 1997; Decena 2001. On their shaping of identities, see Battle and Linville 2006; Bettie 2003; Cantú, Naples, and Vidal-Ortiz 2009; Choo and Feree 2010; Collins 2004; Moore 2011.

34. R. Ferguson 2003.

35. R. Ferguson 2003; Somerville 2000.

36. R. Ferguson 2003.

37. See Reddy 2011a; Hong and Ferguson 2011.

38. A. Ferguson 2001.

39. Bettie 2003.

40. McCready 2010.

41. On the politics of respectability, see Higginbotham 1993.

42. The study of work, occupations, and organizations began with Marx and Engels's critique of gender and sexuality. They argued that in capitalist economies, the sexual division of labor in the family exists to serve the interests of capitalism and the reproduction of workers (see Tucker 1978). Gendered and sexual distinctions and divisions are influenced not only by reproductive and physical differences but also by the material conditions of a society. This insight was all but abandoned in subsequent sociological analyses of work until Marxist feminists revisited the materialist analysis of gender and sexuality in the 1960s and '70s. See Donovan 2000.

43. Acker 1990, 2006.

44. On work as raced, see, for example, Moss and Tilly 2006; Wilson 1997; Wingfield 2009. On work as classed, see, for example, Damaske 2011; Villarreal 2010; Williams and Connell 2010.

45. Acker 2006, p. 443.

46. Hearn and Parkin 1987 first noted the dearth of research on sexuality in organizations, but even as recently as 2008, Britton and Logan argued in a review of the gendered organization literature that analysis of sexuality continues to be absent from the field.

47. See Williams and Giuffre 2011 for a review of the emerging "sexualities in organizations" perspective.

48. For examples of this kind of work, see Bernstein 2008; Frank 2002; Price 2008; Trautner 2005.

49. See Berebitsky 2012; Dellinger and Williams 2002; Giuffre and Williams 1994; McLaughlin, Uggen, and Blackstone 2012; Saguy 2003.

50. See, for example, Badgett et al. 1992; Badgett et al. 2007; Berg and Lien 2002; Tilcsik 2011.

51. See J. Ward 2004, 2008.

52. Woods and Lucas 1993.

53. Williams, Giuffre, and Dellinger 2009.

54. Rumens and Kerfoot 2009.

55. Irwin 2002.

56. Harbeck 1997.

57. Thorne and Luria 1986, p. 188.

58. Pascoe 2007.

59. Bettie 2003, p. 59.

60. P. Jackson 1968; Fields 2008, pp. 72. 96–97.

61. For a full review of the formal and informal sexual education students receive, see Connell and Elliot 2009.

62. Evans 2002; Khayatt 1992; Kissen 1996; Jennings 1994; S. Woods and Harbeck 1992. Evans 2002 refers to the process of fitting gay and lesbian identity into the teaching context as a "negotiation of the self."

63. Evans 2002, p. 176.

64. For more on the concept of emotional labor, see Hochschild 1983.

65. S. Woods and Harbeck 1992.

66. Khayatt 1992; Sanlo 1999.

67. Goffman 1986 uses the concept "impression management" to refer to the ways that individuals attempt to control and influence public perceptions of themselves.

68. Evans 2002; J. Jackson 2007. Dellinger and Williams 1997 developed the concept of workplace appearance rules in their analysis of women's use of makeup at work.

69. Rofes 2000.

70. Britt and Heise 2000.

71. Stonewall was actually not the first riot of its kind. See Stryker 2008 for the history of a similar riot in San Francisco at Gene Compton's Cafeteria that occurred several years earlier. Moreover, the symbolic importance of Stonewall downplays the unique histories of gay liberation internationally. See Manalansan 1995.

72. Shilts 1988.

73. For further critiques of the notion of gay pride, see Halberstam 2005; O'Brien 2008; Vidal-Ortiz 2008.

74. Love 2009.

75. Halperin and Traub 2009, p. 359.

76. See Charmaz 2006.

77. Esterberg 2002, p. 85.

78. See Hochschild 2003, p. 16. See also Pugh 2013 for a rich discussion of how well-executed interpretive interviewing can access multiple levels of the interplay between the individual and culture.

79. Following Esterberg (2002), I use the term *participant observation,* rather than other terms like *field observations,* to emphasize the active role the observer inevitably takes in shaping the social space she is observing. While I did not participate by becoming a teacher in the schools I observed, I did participate in other ways. In classroom observations, I often helped teachers with small tasks or chatted with students. In extracurricular observations, like GALAA meetings, GSA meetings, or the West Hollywood Pride Parade, I took an even more active role in the process, offering comments and suggestions, helping with poster making, passing out literature, and marching alongside teachers in the parade. In my analysis of these field experiences, I consciously analyzed my "self as instrument" (Esterberg 2002, p. 61) and reflected on how my participation, experiences, interpretations, and political and ethical concerns shaped the data I gathered.

80. Zussman 2004, p. 354.

81. Only one respondent identified as bisexual, and she was somewhat unsure about using the label, after having been in a relationship with a woman for over a decade. To avoid the mischaracterization of the sample as at all substantively inclusive of the unique experiences of bisexual teachers, I generally refer to my sample as gay and lesbian.

82. Again, with the exception of one respondent.

83. C. Connell 2010.

84. US Census 2012. According to recent projections, California's demographics have shifted to equal numbers of white and Latino residents. At the time of my research, however, there were more white than Latino residents, according to census data.

85. California Student Safety and Violence Prevention Act, S. 2001, California Assembly Bill 537 (2000).

86. GLBTQ Encyclopedia 2009; Harbeck 1997.

87. On the closet's decreasing power as a metaphor, see Seidman 2002.

88. Acker 2006.

89. Duggan 2002.

90. Sullivan 1996.

2. "LIKE A FOX GUARDING THE HENHOUSE"

1. The real name of this research participant is being used with her permission. Since Virginia's involvement in founding Project 10 is public knowledge, using a pseudonym did not make sense in this instance.

2. In Lortie 1975.

3. On teaching becoming a woman's profession, see Harbeck 1997. On its loss of status, see Hearn 1992; Williams 1995.

4. Harbeck 1997.

5. On the history of homosexual identity, see Foucault 1976. On homosexual behavior as a sin and a crime, see Harbeck 1997.

6. Thorne and Luria 1986, p. 177. See Aries 1962 for the history of the Western transformation of children from "little adults" to vulnerable innocents.

7. Graves 2009.

8. See Abbott 1998 for a sociological account of the professionalization process.

9. For a fuller discussion of men in "women's professions," see Williams 1995.

10. Dillabough 1999.

11. Williams 1992; 2013.

12. Fairclough 2007.

13. Roberts and Andrews 2013.

14. Roberts and Andrews 2013.

15. See Blount 2006 for an account of how the invention of heterosexuality coincided with the preference for heterosexual teachers.

16. Blount 2006.

17. Graves 2009.

18. Woods 2004.

19. See Graves 2009 for discussion of the decision.

20. Davis 1972.

21. Graves 2009.

22. Although *transgender* is now the preferred term for many, it was not yet in commonplace circulation at the time of Stonewall. Accordingly, I here use the more common nomenclature of the time.

23. Scagliotti 1999.

24. Morrison v. State Board of Education, 1 Cal.3d 214 L.A. No. 29632 (1969).

25. Harbeck 1997.

26. Significantly, this same claim to privacy would be used to overturn sodomy laws in *Lawrence v. Texas,* another landmark LGBT legal victory.

27. Epstein 1999; Vaid 1996.

28. Don't Ask, Don't Tell Act, 10 U.S.C. § 654 (1993).

29. See McCreery 1999 for a critique of the legal framing of nondiscrimination protections.

30. Quoted in Fetner 2001, p. 411.

31. From a *Washington Star* news article quoted in Harbeck 1997.

32. Harbeck 1997.

33. See McCreery 2008.

34. Quoted in Shilts 1988, pp. 230–31.

35. Shilts 1988.
36. Harbeck 1997.
37. Decision quoted in Harbeck 1997, p. 91.
38. Shilts 1988.
39. Buchanan quoted in Shilts 1987.
40. For a history of state (non)response to the AIDS crisis, see Shilts 1987.
41. Biegel 2010.
42. In Harbeck 1997.
43. ENDA legislation proposals have since been expanded to include transgender employees but continue to be otherwise limited in scope. As of 2014, no version of ENDA has passed, despite decades of attempts.
44. Glover v. Williamsburg Local School Dist., 20 F. Supp. 2d 1160 (S.D. Ohio 1998). The Equal Protection Clause had been invoked in previous gay and lesbian teacher cases in the 1970s and 80s, but was not used successfully until the 1990s.
45. Weaver v. Nebo School District 29 F. Supp.2d 1279 (D. Utah 1998). See Clark 1998.
46. Biegel 2010.
47. Schroeder v. Hamilton School District, 282 F.3d 946 (7th Cir. 2002). For a detailed summary of the *Schroeder* case, see Biegel 2010.
48. *Lawrence v. Texas,* 539 U.S. 558 (2003).
49. Yes on 8 commercial, accessible at https://www.youtube.com/watch?v=l61Pd5_jHQw.
50. Fischer 2011.
51. Quoted in Deflem 2013. For the antigay research Scalia cited, see Regnerus 2012.
52. McCreery 2008, p. 187.

3. SPLITTERS, KNITTERS, AND QUITTERS

1. For historical accounts of the evolving social construction of childhood, see Aries 1962; Mintz 2006; Zelizer 1994.
2. Aries 1962.
3. Kincaid 1992/1994.
4. Angelides 2004.

5. See Cavanagh 2007 for more on sex scandals featuring women teachers.

6. Martin and Luke 2010.

7. Angelides 2004.

8. Angelides 2004, p. 142.

9. Fields 2008; Irvine 2002.

10. Fields 2008; Irvine 2002; Luker 2007.

11. Weeks 1981; Lancaster 2011.

12. S. Cohen 1972.

13. Lancaster 2011, p. 2.

14. Lancaster 2011.

15. Lewin 2005.

16. Cavanagh 2007.

17. Angelides 2004, 2013.

18. Levine 2002.

19. Hollibaugh 2000, p. 43.

20. Stein 2001.

21. Mayo 2007.

22. For an autoethnographic account of these tensions, see Rofes 2005.

23. On expectations of "how to be gay," see Halperin 2012.

24. Acker 1990.

25. Rumens and Kerfoot 2009.

26. Merton 1957; see also Holton 2004 for a discussion of Merton's many conceptual contributions, including the concept of role modeling.

27. See Pascoe 2007. Since the 1990s, sociologists have increasingly moved away from the language of roles because of its static and predetermined character. Instead, they now tend to use concepts like performances or social expectations. I chose to use *role* here to extend Merton's concept of role modeling to gay and lesbian teachers' experiences.

28. Navratilova 2013.

29. Respondents brought it up so often in my early interviews that I eventually began asking about it in later interviews, which accounts for the twelve occasions where I mention role modeling first.

30. J. Jackson 2007.

31. Sedgwick 1990.

32. Chase 1995.

33. For examples, see Kanter 1977; Pierce 1995; Roth 2006.

34. Pierce 1995.

35. See Budig and England 2001; Correll, Benard, and Paik 2007.

36. Vidal-Ortiz 2008, p. 488.

37. An important methodological note is warranted here concerning the limitations of my research sample. By virtue of focusing on current teachers in my research design and data collection, I missed much of this crucial voice in the conversation. However, I did speak to a number of teachers who were retired/retiring or had moved into administration, and these interviews alerted me to this third alternative.

38. Williams 1995, 2013.

39. On the stresses of the splitting strategy, see Day and Schoenrade 2000; Evans 2002; Riggle, Rostosky, and Horne 2010.

40. Harbeck 1997.

4. DANGEROUS DISCLOSURES

1. Chauncey 1994.

2. Seidman 2002.

3. Herdt 1992; Langridge 2008; Rust 1993.

4. Morris 1997.

5. See Phelan 1993.

6. Freire 1970.

7. See hooks 1994 for a discussion of the importance of attending to power imbalances in the classroom.

8. Khayatt 1997; Krywanczyk 2007.

9. Silin 1999, p. 99.

10. See Silin 1999; Rofes 2005.

11. Khayatt 1997.

12. Rasmussen 2004.

13. Spade 2011.

14. Freeman 1996.

15. Crenshaw 1989.

16. On the limits of nondiscrimination law in protecting the sexual rights of workers, see McCreery 1999. On its limits in protecting freedom of gender expression, see Spade 2011.

17. Quoted in McCreery 1999, pp. 40–41.

18. May 2006.

19. Rostosky and Riggle 2002.

20. See Burgess 1997 for evidence of the relationship between policy protections and coming out. See Day and Schoenrade 2000 for how this affects job satisfaction.

21. Riggle, Rostosky, and Horne 2010.

22. Schneider 1986.

23. Riggle, Rostosky, and Horne 2010.

24. California Student Safety and Violence Prevention Act, S. 2001, California Assembly Bill 537 (2000).

25. For examples of scholarship documenting the history of LGBT people, see Faderman 1991; Halperin 1990; Katz 1976; Newton 1979, 1993; Smith-Rosenberg 1975.

26. Butler 1993.

27. Bourdieu 1977.

28. Halperin 2012.

29. Podesva 2011.

30. J. Jackson 2007.

31. R. Connell 1995.

32. de Beauvoir 1949.

33. Cantú, Naples, and Vidal Ortiz 2009; Carrillo 2002; C. Cohen 1996; Díaz 1997; Fung 2005; Han 2007; Manalansan 2003; Moore 2011; Vidal-Ortiz 2008.

34. Eng 2001; Espiritu 1997; Hamamoto 1994.

35. For example, Donadey 2002; Kohli 2009; TuSmith 2002; Quaye and Harper 2007.

36. Anderson and Tomaskovic-Devey 1995; Britton 2003; Hall 1993; Pierce 1995; Wharton 1993.

37. Acker 2006.

5. "A BIZARRE OR FLAMBOYANT CHARACTER"

1. Duggan 2002.

2. Sycamore 2004; Muñoz 2009; Spade 2011; Vaid 1996.

3. R. Connell 1992.

4. Stryker 2008.

5. C. Cohen 1997, p. 438.

6. For an excellent legal critique of the limitations of turning to the state to redress sexuality inequity, see Spade's *Normal Life: Administrative Violence, Critical Trans Politics, and the Limits of the Law* (2011).

7. R. Ferguson 2008.

8. Murphy 2010.

9. Sullivan 1996.

10. Seidman 2002, p. 126.

11. Angelides 2004.

12. For more on how straight friends and family reinforce homonormativity in their allyship, see Fields's 2001 case study of a support group for parents and friends of lesbians and gays.

13. Williams 1995.

14. Williams, Giuffre, and Dellinger 2009.

15. Rofes 2000.

16. R. Connell 1995.

17. Higginbotham 1993.

18. C. Cohen 1999. See also Moore 2011 for an analysis of how the politics of respectability shapes the experience of Black lesbians/gay women.

6. RACIALIZED DISCOURSES OF HOMOPHOBIA

1. The high school name here is a pseudonym.

2. Wetzstein and Harper 2008.

3. Egan and Sherrill 2009.

4. Hunter 2013.

5. Bérubé 2003; R. Ferguson 2003; Somerville 2000.

6. For more on the possibility of coalition building in lieu of identity politics, see C. Cohen 1997 and Hong and Ferguson 2011.

7. Du Bois 1903; Fanon 1952.

8. Smedley 2007.

9. Banton 1977, 1988/1997; Fanon 1952; Miles 1982, 1993; Miles and Brown 2003.

10. Bonilla-Silva 2003, p. 9.

11. Omi and Winant 1994; Reeves 1983.

12. Reeves 1983.

13. R. Ferguson 2003; Mercer and Julien 1988; Somerville 2000; Smith 1994; Stoler 1995.

14. Somerville 2000.

15. Bonilla-Silva 2003, p. 9.

16. Cantu, Naples, and Vidal-Ortiz 2009; Ocampo 2013.

17. Perry 2011, p. 58.

18. Douglas 1999; Moore 2011; E. Ward 2005.

19. E. Ward 2005.

20. Ferreira da Silva 2007.

21. Reported by McKinley and Johnson 2008.

22. For examples of how such depictions of African American families became popularized, see the works of Moynihan 1965; Murray 1994; Niskanen 1998.

23. Picower 2009.

24. Higginbotham 1993.

25. Harris 2003.

26. White 2001.

27. Cantú, Naples, and Vidal-Ortiz 2009; C. Cohen 1999; Moore 2011; E. Ward 2005; White 2001.

28. Crichlow 2004.

29. See Majors and Bilson 1992 for an analysis of how this version of masculinity, exemplified in what they call the "cool pose," is constructed as resistance to white dominance; see also Ward 2005 for a discussion of how this then contributes to homophobia in Black communities.

30. Bérubé 2003; Han 2007.

31. Halperin and Traub 2009; Han 2007.

32. J. Ward 2008. On gay and lesbian organizations' focus on "exclusively gay issues," see Bérubé 2003, p. 254.

33. For more on discursive colonization, see Mohanty 1991.

34. Epstein 1999.

35. Somerville 2000, p. 37.

36. Kerchis and Young 1995.

37. Halley 2000.

38. Somerville 2005.
39. Reddy 2011b.
40. On rendering overlapping oppressions invisible, see Spelman 1988; on ranking oppressions, see Collins 2000.
41. Collins 1990.
42. Hong and Ferguson 2011.

7. FROM GAY-FRIENDLY TO QUEER-FRIENDLY

1. Sullivan 1996.
2. Duggan 2002, p. 179.
3. Britton 2003; Britton and Logan 2008; Acker 1990, 2006; Williams 1995.
4. Britton and Logan 2008.
5. Spade 2011.
6. McCreery 2008.
7. Britzman 1994; Bryson and de Castell 1993; Khayatt 1997; Krywanczyk 2007; Luhmann 1998; Sumara and Dennis 1999.
8. Khayatt 1997; Seidman 1994.
9. C. Cohen 1997, p. 438.

APPENDIX A

1. Bourdieu 1977.
2. Blumer 1969.
3. Collins 1990.
4. Valocchi 2005.
5. Seidman 1994a; Valocchi 2005.
6. DeVault 1996; Naples 2003.
7. Schilt 2010. For more on "outsiders-within," see Collins 1990.
8. Evans 2002.
9. Evans 2002; Harbeck 1997; J. Jackson 2007; Khayatt 1997; Sanlo 1999.
10. On "thick description," see Geertz 1973.
11. Esterberg 2002.
12. Esterberg 2002.

13. See Merton 1972 on the insider/outsider vantage points on the production of knowledge.

14. See Charmaz 2006 for definitions of line-by-line and focused coding.

15. On feminist ethnography, see Stacey 1988.

16. Avishai, Gerber, and Randles 2013.

17. Fields 2013.

18. For a good example of this critique, see Perrin, Cohen, and Caren 2013.

REFERENCES

Abbott, Andrew. 1998. *The System of Professions: An Essay on the Division of Expert Labor.* Chicago: University of Chicago Press.

Acker, Joan. 1990. "Hierarchies, Jobs, Bodies: A Theory of Gendered Organizations." *Gender and Society* 4: 139–58.

———. 2006. "Inequality Regimes: Gender, Class, and Race in Organizations." *Gender and Society* 20: 441–64.

Alexander, M. Jacqui. 2006. *Pedagogies of Crossing: Meditations of Feminism, Sexual Politics, Memory, and the Sacred.* Durham, NC: Duke University Press.

Anderson, Cynthia D., and Donald Tomaskovic-Devey. 1995. "Patriarchal Pressures: An Exploration of Organizational Processes That Exacerbate and Erode Gender Earnings Inequality." *Work and Occupations* 22: 328–56.

Angelides, Steven. 2004. "Feminism, Child Sexual Abuse, and the Erasure of Child Sexuality." *GLQ: A Journal of Lesbian and Gay Studies* 10: 141–77.

———. 2013. "Technology, Hormones, and Stupidity: The Affective Politics of Teenage Sexting." *Sexualities* 16: 665–89.

Aries, Philippe. 1962. *Centuries of Childhood.* New York: Vintage Books.

Avishai, Orit, Lynne Gerber, and Jennifer Randles. 2013. "The Feminist Ethnographer's Dilemma: Reconciling Progressive Research

Agendas with Fieldwork Realities." *Journal of Contemporary Ethnography* 42: 394–426.

Badgett, M.V. Lee, Holning Lau, Colleen Donnelly, and Jennifer Kibbe. 1992. *Pervasive Patterns of Discrimination against Lesbians and Gay Men: Evidence from Surveys across the United States.* Washington, DC: National Gay and Lesbian Task Force Policy Institute.

Badgett, M.V. Lee, Holning Lau, Brad Sears, and Deborah Ho. 2007. *Bias in the Workplace: Consistent Evidence of Sexual Orientation and Gender Identity Discrimination.* Los Angeles: Williams Institute, UCLA School of Law.

Banton, Michael. 1977. *The Idea of Race.* London: Tavistock.

———. 1988/1997. *Ethnic and Racial Consciousness.* London: Longman.

Battle, Juan, and Darla Linville. 2006. "Race, Sexuality and Schools: A Quantitative Assessment of Intersectionality." *Race, Gender and Class* 13: 180–90.

Berebitsky, Julie. 2012. *Sex and the Office: A History of Gender, Power, and Desire.* New Haven, CT: Yale University Press.

Berg, Nathan, and Donald Lien. 2002. "Measuring the Effect of Sexual Orientation on Income: Evidence of Discrimination?" *Contemporary Economic Policy* 20: 394–414.

Bernstein, Elizabeth. 2008. *Temporarily Yours: Intimacy, Authenticity, and the Commerce of Sex.* Berkeley: University of California Press.

Bérubé, Allan. 2003. "How Gay Stays White and What Kind of White It Stays." In *Privilege: A Reader,* edited by Michael S. Kimmel and Abby Ferber, 253–86. Cambridge, MA: Westview Press.

Bettie, Julie. 2003. *Women without Class: Girls, Race, and Identity.* Berkeley: University of California Press.

Biegel, Stuart. 2010. *The Right to Be Out: Sexual Orientation and Gender Expression in America's Public Schools.* Minneapolis: University of Minnesota Press.

Blount, Jackie M. 2006. *Fit to Teach: Same-Sex Desire, Gender, and School Work in the Twentieth Century.* Albany: State University of New York Press.

Blumer, Herbert. 1969. "The Methodological Position of Symbolic Interactionism." In *Symbolic Interactionism,* edited by Herbert Blumer, 1–60. Englewood Cliffs, NJ: Prentice-Hall.

Bonilla-Silva, Eduardo. 2003. *Racism without Racists: Color-Blind Racism and the Persistence of Racial Inequality in the United States.* Lanham, MD: Rowman and Littlefield.

Bourdieu, Pierre. 1977. *Outline of a Theory of Practice.* Cambridge: Cambridge University Press.

Brekhus, Wayne. 2003. *Peacocks, Chameleons, Centaurs: Gay Suburbia and the Grammar of Social Identity.* Chicago: University of Chicago Press.

Britt, Lori, and David Heise. 2000. "From Shame to Pride In Identity Politics." In *Self, Identity, and Social Movements,* edited by Sheldon Stryker, Timothy Owens, and Robert White, 252–68. Minneapolis: University of Minnesota Press.

Britton, Dana. 2003. *At Work in the Iron Cage: The Prison as Gendered Organization.* New York: NYU Press.

Britton, Dana, and Laura Logan. 2008. "Gendered Organizations: Progress and Prospects." *Sociological Compass* 2: 107–21.

Britzman, Deborah P. 1994. "Is There a Queer Pedagogy? Or, Stop Reading Straight." *Educational Theory* 45: 151–65.

Bryant, Karl, and Salvador Vidal-Ortiz. 2008. "Introduction to Retheorizing Homophobias." *Sexualities* 11: 387–96.

Bryson, Mary, and Suzanne de Castell. 1993. "Queer Pedagogy: Praxis Makes Im/Perfect." *Canadian Journal of Education* 18: 285–305.

Budig, Michelle, and Paula England. 2001. "The Wage Penalty for Motherhood." *American Sociological Review* 66: 204–25.

Burgess, Carole A. 1997. "The Impact of Lesbian/Gay Sensitive Policies on the Behavior and Health of Lesbians in the Workplace." In *Gay/Lesbian/Bisexual/Transgender Public Policy Issues,* edited by Wallace K. Swan, 35–48. London: Hayworth Press.

Butler, Judith. 1990. *Gender Trouble: Feminism and the Subversion of Identity.* New York: Routledge.

———. 1993. *Bodies That Matter: The Discursive Limits of Sex.* New York: Routledge.

———. 2004. *Undoing Gender.* New York: Routledge.

Cantú, Lionel, Nancy Naples, and Salvador Vidal-Ortiz. 2009. *The Sexuality of Migration: Border Crossings and Mexican Immigrant Men.* New York: NYU Press.

Carrillo, Héctor. 2002. *The Night Is Young: Sexuality in Mexico in the Time of AIDS*. Chicago: University of Chicago Press.

Cavanagh, Sheila. 2007. *Sexing the Teacher: School Sex Scandals and Queer Pedagogies*. Vancouver: University of British Columbia Press.

Charmaz, Kathy. 2006. *Constructing Grounded Theory: A Practical Guide through Qualitative Analysis*. Newbury Park, CA: Sage Publications.

Chase, Susan. 1995. *Ambiguous Empowerment: The Work Narratives of Women School Superintendents*. Amherst: University of Massachusetts Press.

Chauncey, George. 1994. *Gay New York*. Chicago: University of Chicago Press.

Choo, Hae Yeon, and Myra Max Ferree. 2010. "Practicing Intersectionality in Sociological Research." *Sociological Theory* 28: 129–49.

Clark, S. 1998. "Case Profile: Citizens of Nebo School District for Moral and Legal Values, et al. v. Utah State Board of Education, et al." American Civil Liberties Union Archive. www.acluutah.org/98sum.htm#nebo.

Cohen, Cathy J. 1996. "Contested Membership: Black Gay Identities and the Politics of AIDS." In *Queer Theory/Sociology,* edited by Steven Seidman, 362–94. Oxford: Blackwell.

———. 1997. "Punks, Bulldaggers, and Welfare Queens: The Radical Potential of Queer Politics." *GLQ: A Journal of Lesbian and Gay Studies* 3: 437–65.

———. 1999. *The Boundaries of Blackness: AIDS and the Breakdown of Black Politics*. Chicago: University of Chicago Press.

Cohen, Stanley. 1972. *Folk Devils and Moral Panics*. London: MacGibbon and Kee.

Collins, Patricia Hill. 1990. *Black Feminist Thought: Knowledge, Consciousness, and the Politics of Empowerment*. New York: Routledge.

———. 2004. *Black Sexual Politics: African Americans, Gender, and the New Racism*. New York: Routledge.

Connell, Catherine. 2010. "Doing, Undoing, or Redoing Gender? Learning from the Workplace Experiences of Transpeople." *Gender and Society* 24: 31–55.

Connell, Catherine, and Sinikka Elliot. 2009. "Beyond the Birds and the Bees: Learning Inequality through Sexuality Education." *American Journal of Sexuality Education* 4: 83–102.

Connell, R. W. 1992. "A Very Straight Gay: Masculinity, Homosexual Experience and the Dynamics of Gender." *American Sociological Review* 57: 735–51.

———. 1995. *Masculinities: Knowledge, Power, and Social Change.* Oxford: Polity Press.

Correll, Shelley, Stephen Benard, and In Paik. 2007. "Getting a Job: Is There a Motherhood Penalty?" *American Journal of Sociology* 112: 1297–1339.

Crenshaw, Kimberlé. 1989. "Demarginalizing the Intersection of Race and Sex: A Black Feminist Critique of Antidiscrimination Doctrine, Feminist Theory and Antiracist Politics." *University of Chicago Legal Forum* 140: 139–68.

Crichlow, Wesley. 2004. *Buller Men and Batty Bwoys: Hidden Men in Toronto and Halifax Black Communities.* Toronto: University of Toronto Press.

Damaske, Sarah. 2011. *For The Family? How Class and Gender Shape Women's Work.* New York: Oxford University Press.

Davis, John C. 1972. "Teacher Dismissal on Ground of Immorality." *Clearing House* 46: 418–23.

Day, Nancy E., and Patricia Schoenrade. 2000. "The Relationship among Reported Disclosure of Sexual Orientation, Anti-discrimination Polices, Top Management Support and Work Attitudes of Gay and Lesbian Employees." *Personnel Review* 29: 346–63.

De Beauvoir, Simone. 1949. *The Second Sex.* New York: Vintage.

Decena, Carlos. 2011. *Tacit Subjects: Belonging and Same-Sex Desire among Dominican Immigrant Men.* Durham, NC: Duke University Press.

Deflem, Mathieu. 2013. "Sociologists and Same-Sex Marriage: Politics of Truth." *ASA Footnotes* 41: 13.

Dellinger, Kirsten, and Christine L. Williams. 1997. "Makeup at Work: Negotiating Appearance Rules in the Workplace." *Gender and Society* 11: 151–77.

———. 2002. "The Locker Room and the Dorm Room: Workplace Norms and the Boundaries of Sexual Harassment in Magazine Editing." *Social Problems* 49: 242–57.

Deutsch, Francine. 2007. "Undoing Gender." *Gender and Society* 21: 106–27.

DeVault, Marjorie. 1996. "Talking Back to Sociology: Distinctive Contributions of Feminist Methodology." *Annual Review of Sociology* 22: 29–50.

Díaz, Rafael M. 1997. *Latino Gay Men and HIV: Culture, Sexuality, and Risk Behavior.* New York: Routledge.

Dillabough, Jo-Anne. 1999. "Gender Politics and Conceptions of the Modern Teacher: Women, Identity and Professionalism." *British Journal of Sociology of Education* 20: 373–94.

Donadey, Anne. 2002. "Negotiating Tensions: Teaching about Race Issues in Graduate Feminist Classrooms." *National Women's Studies Association Journal* 14: 82–102.

Donovan, Josephine. 2000. *Feminist Theory: The Intellectual Traditions of American Feminism.* London: Continuum.

Douglas, Kelly Brown. 1999. *Sexuality and the Black Church: A Womanist Perspective.* Maryknoll, NY: Orbis Books.

Du Bois, W. E. B. 1903. *The Souls of Black Folk.* Chicago: A. C. McClurg.

Duggan, Lisa. 2002. "The New Homonormativity: The Sexual Politics of Neoliberalism." In *Materializing Democracy,* edited by Russ Castronovo and Dana D. Nelson, 175–94. Durham, NC: Duke University Press.

Egan, Patrick J., and Kenneth Sherrill. 2009. "California's Proposition 8: What Happened, and What Does the Future Hold?" National Gay and Lesbian Task Force, www.ngltf.org/reports_and_research/prop8_analysis.

Eng, David. 2001. *Racial Castration: Managing Masculinity in Asian America.* Durham, NC: Duke University Press.

Epstein, Steven. 1999. "Gay and Lesbian Movements in the United States: Dilemmas of Identity, Diversity, and Political Strategy." In *The Global Emergence of Gay and Lesbian Politics,* edited by Barry D. Adam, Jan Duyvendak, and Andre Krouwel, 30–90. Philadelphia: Temple University Press.

Espiritu, Yen Le. 1997. *Asian American Women and Men: Labor, Laws, and Love.* Lanham, MD: Rowman and Littlefield.

Esterberg, Kristin. 2002. *Qualitative Methods in Social Research.* New York: McGraw-Hill.

Evans, Kate. 2002. *Negotiating the Self: Identity, Sexuality, and Emotion in Learning to Teach.* New York: Routledge.

Faderman, Lillian. 1991. *Odd Girls and Twilight Lovers: A History of Lesbian Life in Twentieth Century America*. New York: Penguin.

Fairclough, Adam. 2007. *A Class of Their Own: Black Teachers in the Segregated South*. Cambridge, MA: Belknap Press.

Fanon, Frantz. 1952. *Black Skin, White Masks*. London: Pluto Press.

Ferguson, Ann Arnett. 2001. *Bad Boys: Public Schools and the Making of Black Masculinity*. Ann Arbor: University of Michigan Press.

Ferguson, Roderick A. 2003. *Aberrations in Black: Toward a Queer of Color Critique*. Minneapolis: University of Minnesota Press.

———. 2008. "Administering Sexuality; Or, the Will to Institutionality." *Radical History Review* 100: 158–69.

Ferreira da Silva, Denise. 2007. *Toward a Global Idea of Race*. Minneapolis: University of Minnesota Press.

Fetner, Tina. 2001. "Working Anita Bryant: The Impact of Christian Anti-gay Activism on Lesbian and Gay Movement Claims." *Social Problems* 48: 411–28.

Fields, Jessica. 2001. "Normal Queers: Straight Parents Respond to Their Children's Coming Out." *Symbolic Interaction* 24: 165–87.

———. 2008. *Risky Lessons: Sex Education and Social Inequality*. New Brunswick, NJ: Rutgers University Press.

———. 2013. "Feminist Ethnography: Critique, Conflict, and Ambivalent Observance." *Journal of Contemporary Ethnography* 42: 492–500.

Fischer, Bryan. 2011. "Implementation of LGBT Law in Military Will Be a Confused Snarl." *Rightly Concerned*, April 26, 2011. www.afa.net/Blogs/BlogPost.aspx?id=2147505152.

Foucault, Michel. 1976. *The History of Sexuality*. New York: Vintage Books.

Frank, Katherine. 2002. *G-Strings and Sympathy: Strip Club Regulars and Male Desire*. Durham, NC: Duke University Press.

Freeman, Alan David. 1996. "Legitimizing Racial Discrimination through Anti-Discrimination Law: A Critical Review of Supreme Court Doctrine." In *Critical Race Studies: The Key Writings That Formed the Movement*, edited by Kimberlé Crenshaw, Neil Gotanda, Garry Peller, and Kendal Tomas, 29–45. New York: New Press.

Freire, Paulo. 1970. *Pedagogy of the Oppressed*. New York: Herder and Herder.

Fung, Richard. 2005. "Looking for My Penis: The Eroticized Asian in Gay Video Porn." In *A Companion to Asian American Studies*, edited by Kent Ono and Richard Fung, 235–53. Malden, MA: Blackwell.

Gagnon, John H., and William Simon. 1973. *Sexual Conduct: The Social Sources of Human Sexuality.* Chicago: Aldine.

Gamson, Joshua. 1998. *Freaks Talk Back: Tabloid Talk Shows and Sexual Nonconformity.* Chicago: University of Chicago Press.

Gamson, Joshua, and Dawne Moon. 2004. "The Sociology of Sexualities: Queer and Beyond." *Annual Review of Sociology* 30: 47–64.

Geertz, Clifford. 1973. *The Interpretation of Culture.* New York: Basic Books.

Giuffre, Patti, and Christine L. Williams. 1994. "Boundary Lines: Labeling Sexual Harassment in Restaurants." *Gender and Society* 8: 378–401.

GLBTQ Encyclopedia. 2009. "Teachers." www.glbtq.com/social-sciences/teachers,6.html.

Goffman, Erving. 1986. *Stigma: Notes on the Management of Spoiled Identity.* New York: Simon and Schuster.

Graves, Karen. 2009. *And They Were Wonderful Teachers: Florida's Purge of Gay and Lesbian Teachers.* Chicago: University of Illinois Press.

Halberstam, Judith. 2005. "Shame and White Gay Masculinity." *Social Text* 23: 219–33.

Hall, Elaine J. 1993. "Smiling, Deferring, and Flirting: Doing Gender by Giving 'Good Service.'" *Work and Occupations* 20: 452–71.

Halley, Janet. 2000. "Like-Race Arguments." In *What's Left of Theory*, edited by Judith Butler, John Guillory, and Thomas Kendall, 40–74. New York: Routledge.

Halperin, David M. 1990. *One Hundred Years of Homosexuality.* New York: Routledge.

———. 2012. *How to Be Gay.* Cambridge, MA: Belknap Press.

Halperin, David, and Valerie Traub, eds. 2009. *Gay Shame.* Chicago: University of Chicago Press.

Hamamoto, Darrell. 1994. *Monitored Peril: Asian Americans and the Politics of Representation.* Minneapolis: University of Minnesota Press.

Han, Chong-Suk. 2007. "'They Don't Want To Cruise Your Type': Gay Men of Color and the Racial Politics of Exclusion." *Social Identities* 13: 51–67.

Harbeck, Karen M. 1997. *Gay and Lesbian Educators: Personal Freedoms, Public Constraints*. Malden, MA: Amethyst Press and Productions.

Harris, Paisley. 2003. "Gatekeeping and Remaking: The Politics of Respectability in African American Women's History and Black Feminism." *Journal of Women's History* 15 (1): 212–20.

Hearn, Jeff. 1992. "Notes on Patriarchy: Professionalization and the Semi-professions." *Sociology* 16: 184–202.

Hearn, Jeff, and Wendy Parkin. 1987. *"Sex" at "Work": The Power and Paradox of Organization Sexuality*. New York: St. Martin's Press.

Hennen, Peter. *Faeries, Bears, and Leathermen: Men in Community Queering the Masculine*. Chicago: University of Chicago Press.

Herdt, Gilbert. 1992. "'Coming Out' as a Rite of Passage: A Chicago Study." In *Gay Culture in America*, edited by Gilbert Herdt, 29–67. Boston: Beacon Press.

Higginbotham, Evelyn Brooks. 1993. *Righteous Discontent: The Women's Movement in the Black Baptist Church, 1880–1920*. Cambridge, MA: Harvard University Press.

Hochschild, Arlie. 1983. *The Managed Heart: The Commercialization of Human Feelings*. Berkeley: University of California Press.

———. 2003. *The Commercialization of Intimate Life: Notes from Home and Work*. Berkeley: University of California Press.

Hollibaugh, Amber. 2000. *My Dangerous Desires: A Queer Girl Dreaming Her Way Home*. Durham, NC: Duke University Press.

Holton, Gerald. 2004. "Robert K. Merton." *Proceedings of the American Philosophical Association* 148: 506–17.

Hong, Grace Kyungwon, and Roderick A. Ferguson, eds. 2011. *Strange Affinities: The Gender and Sexual Politics of Comparative Racialization*. Durham, NC: Duke University Press.

hooks, bell. 1994. *Teaching to Transgress: Education as a Practice of Freedom*. New York: Routledge.

Hunter, Marcus Anthony. 2013. "Race and the Same-Sex Marriage Divide." *Contexts* 12: 74–76.

Irvine, Janice. 2002. *Talk about Sex: The Battles over Sex Education in the United States*. Berkeley: University of California Press.

Irwin, Jude. 2002. "Discrimination against Gay Men, Lesbians, and Transgender People Working in Education." *Journal of Gay and Lesbian Social Services* 14: 65–77.

Jackson, Janna M. 2007. *Unmasking Identities: An Exploration of the Lives of Gay and Lesbian Teachers*. Lanham, MD: Lexington Books.

Jackson, Phillip W. 1968. *Life in Classrooms*. New York: Holt, Reinhart, and Winston.

Jennings, Kevin. 1994. *One Teacher in 10: Gay and Lesbian Educators Tell Their Stories*. Boston: Alyson Publications.

Jurik, Nancy, and Cynthia Siemsen. 2009. "'Doing Gender' as Canon or Agenda: A Symposium on West and Zimmerman." *Gender and Society* 23: 72–75.

Kanter, Rosabeth. 1977. *Men and Women of the Corporation*. New York: Basic Books.

Katz, Jonathan Ned. 1976. *Gay American History: Lesbians and Gay Men in the U.S.A.* New York: Harper and Row.

Kerchis, Carla Zarlenga, and Iris Marion Young. 1995. "Social Movements and the Politics of Difference." In *Multiculturalism from the Margins: Non-dominant Voices on Difference and Diversity*, edited by Dean A. Harris, 156–91. New York: Bergin and Garvey.

Khayatt, Didi. 1992. *Lesbian Teachers: An Invisible Presence*. Albany: State University of New York Press.

———. 1997. "Sex and the Teacher: Should We Come Out in Class?" *Harvard Educational Review* 67: 126–43.

Kincaid, James. 1992/1994. *Child-Loving: The Erotic Child and Victorian Culture*. New York: Routledge.

Kissen, Rita M. 1996. *The Last Closet: The Real Lives of Lesbian and Gay Teachers*. Portsmouth, NH: Heinemann.

Kohli, Rita. 2009. "Critical Race Reflections: Valuing the Experiences of Teachers of Color in Teacher Education." *Race, Ethnicity, and Education* 12: 235–51.

Krywanczyk, Loren. 2007. "Queering Public School Pedagogy as a First-Year Teacher." *Radical Teacher* 79: 27–34.

Lancaster, Roger. 2011. *Sex Panic and the Punitive State*. Berkeley: University of California Press.

Langridge, Dorothy. 2008. "Are You Angry or Are You Heterosexual? A Queer Critique of Lesbian and Gay Models of Identity Development." In *Feeling Queer or Queer Feelings? Radical Approaches to Counselling Sex, Sexualities and Genders*, edited by Lyndsey Moon, 23–35. London: Routledge.

Levine, Judith. 2002. *Harmful to Minors: The Perils of Protecting Children from Sex*. Minneapolis: University of Minnesota Press.

Lewin, Tamar. 2005. "Are These Parties for Real?" *New York Times*, June 30. http://www.nytimes.com/2005/06/30/fashion/thursdaystyles/30rainbow.html?pagewanted=print&_r=0.

Longmore, Monica A. 1998. "Symbolic Interaction and the Study of Sexuality." *Journal of Sex Research* 35: 44–57.

Lorber, Judith. 2000. "Using Gender to Undo Gender: A Feminist Degendering Movement." *Feminist Theory* 1: 79–95.

Lortie, Dan C. 1975. *Schoolteacher*. Chicago: University of Chicago Press.

Love, Heather. 2009. *Feeling Backward: Loss and the Politics of Queer History*. Cambridge, MA: Harvard University Press.

Luhmann, Susanne. 1998. "Queering/Querying Pedagogy? Or, Pedagogy Is a Pretty Queer Thing." In *Queer Theory In Education*, edited by William F. Pinar, 141–56. Mahwah, NJ: Erlbaum.

Luker, Kristin. 2007. *When Sex Goes to School: Warring Views on Sex—and Sex Education—since the Sixties*. New York: Norton.

Majors, Richard, and Janet M. Bilson. 1992. *Cool Pose: The Dilemmas of Black Manhood in America*. New York: Lexington.

Manalansan, Martin. 1995. "In the Shadows of Stonewall: Examining Gay Transnational Politics and the Diasporic Dilemma." *GLQ: A Journal of Lesbian and Gay Studies* 2: 425–38.

———. 2003. *Global Divas: Filipino Gay Men in the Diaspora*. Durham, NC: Duke University Press.

Martin, Karin, and Katherine Luke. 2010. "Gender Differences in the ABC's of the Birds and the Bees: What Mothers Teach Young Children about Sexuality and Reproduction." *Sex Roles* 62: 151–91.

May, Michael. 2006. "Hoover: Caught in the Flash." *Austin Chronicle*, June 23, 2006. www.austinchronicle.com/news/2006-06-23/378611/.

Mayo, Cris. 2007. *Disputing the Subject of Sex: Sexuality and Public School Controversies.* New York: Rowman and Littlefield.

McCready, Lance T. 2010. *Making Space for Diverse Masculinities: Adolescent Cultures, School, and Society.* New York: Peter Lang.

McCreery, Patrick. 1999. "Beyond Gay: 'Deviant' Sex and the Politics of the ENDA Workplace." *Social Text* 17: 39–58.

————. 2008. "Save Our Children/Let Us Marry: Gay Activists Appropriate the Rhetoric of Child Protectionism." *Radical History Review* 100: 186–207.

McIntosh, Mary. 1968. "The Homosexual Role." *Social Problems* 16: 182–92.

McKinley, Jesse, and Kirk Johnson. 2008. "Mormons Tipped the Scale in Ban on Gay Marriage." *New York Times*, November 14. www.nytimes.com/2008/11/15/us/politics/15marriage.html?_r=2&pagewanted=1&hp&oref=slogin.

McLaughlin, Heather, Christopher Uggen, and Amy Blackstone. 2012. "Sexual Harassment, Workplace Authority, and the Paradox of Power." *American Sociological Review* 77: 625–47.

Mercer, Kobena, and Isaac Julien. 1988. "Race, Sexual Politics, and Black Masculinity: A Dossier." In *Male Order: Unwrapping Masculinity*, edited by Rowena Chapman and Jonathan Rutherford, 97–164. London: Lawrence and Wishart.

Merton, Robert K. 1957. *Social Theory and Social Structure.* Glencoe, IL: Free Press.

————. 1972. "Insiders and Outsiders: A Chapter on the Sociology of Knowledge." *American Journal of Sociology* 78: 9–47.

Miles, Robert. 1982. *Racism and Migrant Labour.* London: Routledge.

————. 1993. *Race after Race Relations.* London: Routledge.

Miles, Robert, and Malcolm Brown, eds. 2003. *Racism.* London: Routledge.

Mintz, Steven. 2006. *Huck's Raft: A History of American Childhood.* Cambridge, MA: Belknap Press.

Mohanty, Chandra Talpade. 1991. "Under Western Eyes." In *Third World Women and the Politics of Feminism*, edited by Chandra Talpade Mohanty, Ann Russo, and Lourdes Torres, 51–80. Bloomington: University of Indiana Press.

Moore, Mignon. 2011. *Invisible Families: Gay Identities, Relationships, and Motherhood among Black Women.* Berkeley: University of California Press.

Moraga, Cherríe, and Gloria Anzaldúa. 1981. *This Bridge Called My Back: Writings by Radical Women of Color.* New York: Kitchen Table/Women of Color Press.

Morris, Jessica F. 1997. "Lesbian Coming Out as a Multidimensional Process." *Journal of Homosexuality* 33: 1–22.

Moss, Philip, and Chris Tilly. "Stories Employers Tell: Employer Perceptions of Race and Skill." In *Working in America: Continuity, Conflict, and Change,* 3rd ed., edited by Amy Wharton, 235–60. New York: McGraw-Hill.

Moynihan, Daniel P. 1965. *The Negro Family: The Case for National Action.* Washington, DC: US Department of Labor, Office of Policy Planning and Research.

Muñoz, José Esteban. 2009. *Cruising Utopia: The Then and There of Queer Futurity.* New York: NYU Press.

Murphy, Kevin. 2010. "Gay Was Good: Progress, Homonormativity, and Oral History." In *Queer Twin Cities,* edited by Kevin Murphy, Jennifer Pierce, and Larry Knop, 305–18. Minneapolis: University of Minnesota Press.

Murray, Charles. 1994. *Losing Ground: American Social Policy, 1950–1980.* New York: Basic Books.

Naples, Nancy. 2002. *Feminism and Method: Ethnography, Discourse Analysis, and Activist Research.* New York: Routledge.

Navratilova, Martina. 2013. "Jason Collins a 'Game Changer.'" *Sports Illustrated,* April 23. http://sportsillustrated.cnn.com/magazine/news/20130429/martina-navratilova-jason-collins-reaction/#ixzz2RxUQ75vk.

Newton, Esther. 1979. *Mother Camp: Female Impersonators in America.* Chicago: University of Chicago Press.

———. 1993. *Cherry Grove, Fire Island: Sixty Years in America's First Gay and Lesbian Town.* Boston: Beacon Press.

Niskanen, William. 1998. *Policy Analysis and Public Choice: Selected Papers by William A. Niskanen.* Northampton, MA: Edward Elgar.

O'Brien, Jodi. 2008. "Afterward: Complicating Homophobia." *Sexualities* 11: 496–512.

Ocampo, Anthony. 2013. "The Gay Second Generation: Sexual Identity and Family Relations of Filipino Gay Men." *Journal of Ethnic and Migration Studies* 40 (1), DOI: 10.1080/1369183X.2013.849567.

Omi, Michael, and Howard Winant. 1994. *Racial Formation in the United States: From the 1960s to the 1990s*. New York: Routledge.

Pascoe, C.J. 2007. *Dude, You're a Fag": Masculinity and Sexuality in High School*. Berkeley: University of California Press.

Perrin, Andrew, Philip Cohen, and Neil Caren. 2013. "Are Children of Parents Who Had Same-Sex Relationships Disadvantaged? A Scientific Evaluation of the No-Differences Hypothesis." *Journal of Gay and Lesbian Mental Health* 17: 327–36.

Perry, Imani. 2011. *More Beautiful and More Terrible: The Embrace and Transcendence of Racial Inequality in the United States*. New York: NYU Press.

Phelan, Shane. 1993. "(Be)coming Out: Lesbian Identity and Politics." *Signs: Journal of Women in Culture and Society* 18: 765–90.

Picower, Brianna. 2009. "The Unexamined Whiteness of Teaching: How White Teachers Maintain and Enact Dominant Racial Ideologies." *Race, Ethnicity, and Education* 12: 197–215.

Pierce, Jennifer. 1995. *Gender Trials: Emotional Lives in Contemporary Law Firms*. Berkeley: University of California Press.

Plummer, Kenneth. 1994. *Telling Sexual Stories*. New York: Routledge.

Podesva, Robert. 2011. "The California Vowel Shift and Gay Identity." *American Speech* 86: 32–51.

Price, Kim. 2008. "'Keeping the Dancers in Check': The Gendered Organization of Stripping Work at the Lion's Den." *Gender and Society* 22: 367–89.

Pugh, Allison. 2013. "What Good Are Interviews for Thinking about Culture? Demystifying Interpretive Analysis." *American Journal of Cultural Sociology* 1: 42–68.

Quaye, Stephen J., and Sean R. Harper. 2007. "Shifting the Onus from Racial/Ethnic Minority Students to Faculty: Accountability for Culturally Inclusive Pedagogy and Curricula." *Liberal Education* 92: 19–24.

Rasmussen, Mary Lou. 2004. "The Problem of Coming Out." *Theory into Practice* 43: 144–50.

Reddy, Chandan. 2011a. *Freedom with Violence: Race, Sexuality, and the US State.* Durham, NC: Duke University Press.

———. 2011b. "Time for Rights? Loving, Gay Marriage, and the Limits of Comparative Legal Justice." In *Strange Affinities: The Gender and Sexual Politics of Comparative Racialization,* edited by Grace Kyungwon Hong and Roderick Ferguson, 148–74. Durham, NC: Duke University Press.

Redman, Peter. 2000. "'Tarred with the Same Brush': 'Homophobia' and the Role of the Unconscious in School-Based Cultures of Masculinity." *Sexualities* 3: 483–99.6Reeves, Frank. 1983. *British Racial Discourse: A Study of British Political Discourse About Race and Race Relations.* London: Cambridge University Press.

Regnerus, Mark. 2012. "How Different Are the Adult Children of Parents Who Have Same-Sex Relationships? Findings from the New Family Structures Survey." *Social Science Research* 41: 752–70.

Riggle, Ellen, Sharon Rostosky, and Sharon Horne. 2010. "Does It Matter Where You Live? State Non-discrimination Laws and the Perceptions of LGB Residents." *Sexuality Research and Social Policy* 7: 168–72.

Risman, Barbara. 2009. "From Doing to Undoing: Gender as We Know It." *Gender and Society* 23: 81–84.

Roberts, Tuesda, and Dorinda J. Carter Andrews. 2013. "A Critical Race Analysis of the Gaslighting of African American Teachers; Considerations for Recruitment on Retention." In *Contesting the Myth of a "Post-racial" Era: The Continued Significance of Race in U.S. Education,* edited by Dorinda Carter Williams and Franklin Tuitt, 69–95. New York: Peter Lang.

Rofes, Eric. 2000. "Bound and Gagged: Sexual Silences, Gender Conformity, and the Gay Male Teacher." *Sexualities* 3: 439–62.

———. 2005. *A Radical Rethinking of Sexuality and Schooling: Status Quo or Status Queer?* Lanham, MD: Rowman and Littlefield.

Rostosky, Sharon, and Ellen Riggle. 2002. "'Out' at Work: The Relation of Actor and Worker Workplace Policy and Internalized Homophobia to Disclosure Status." *Journal of Counseling Psychology* 49: 411–19.

Roth, Louise Marie. 2006. *Selling Women Short: Gender and Money on Wall Street.* Princeton, NJ: Princeton University Press.

Rubin, Gayle. 1984. "Thinking Sex: Notes for a Radical Theory of the Politics of Sexuality." In *Pleasure and Danger: Exploring Female Sexuality*, edited by Carol Vance, 267–319. New York: Routledge.

Rumens, Nick, and Deborah Kerfoot. 2009. "Gay Men at Work: (Re) constructing the Self as Professional." *Human Relations* 62: 763–86.

Rust, Paula. 1993. "Coming Out in the Age of Social Constructionism." *Gender and Society* 7: 50–77.

Saguy, Abigail. 2003. *What Is Sexual Harassment? From Capital Hill to the Sorbonne*. Berkeley: University of California Press.

Sanlo, Ronni. 1999. *Unheard Voices: The Effects of Silence on Lesbian and Gay Educators*. Westport, CT: Bergin and Garvey.

Scagliotti, John, dir. 1999. *After Stonewall*. DVD. New York: First Run Features.

Schilt, Kristen. 2010. *Just One of the Guys? Transgender Men and the Persistence of Gender Inequality*. Chicago: University of Chicago Press.

Schneider, Beth. 1986. "Coming Out at Work: Bridging the Private/ Public Gap." *Work and Occupations* 13: 463–87.

Sedgwick, Eve Kosofsky. 1990. *Epistemology of the Closet*. Berkeley: University of California Press.

Seidman, Steven, ed. 1994. "Queer Theory." Special issue. *Sociological Theory*, 4.

———. 2002. *Beyond the Closet? The Transformation of Gay and Lesbian Life*. New York: Routledge.

Shilts, Randy. 1987. *And The Band Played On: Politics, People, and the AIDS Epidemic*. New York: St. Martin's Press.

———. 1988. *The Mayor of Castro Street: The Life and Times of Harvey Milk*. New York: St. Martin's Griffin.

Silin, Jonathan. 1999. "Teaching as a Gay Man: Pedagogical Resistance or Public Spectacle?" *GLQ: A Journal of Lesbian and Gay Studies* 5: 95–106.

Smedley, Audrey. 2007. *Race in North America: Origin and Evolution of a Worldview*. Boulder, CO: Westview Press.

Smith, Anne-Marie. 1994. *New Right Discourses on Race and Sexuality*. Cambridge: Cambridge University Press.

Smith-Rosenberg, Carroll. 1975. "The Female World of Love and Ritual: Relations between Women in Nineteenth-Century America." *Signs: Journal of Women in Culture and Society* 1: 1–29.

Somerville, Siobhan. 2000. *Queering the Color Line: Race and the Invention of Homosexuality in American Culture*. Durham, NC: Duke University Press.

———. 2005. "Queer *Loving*." *GLQ: A Journal of Lesbian and Gay Studies* 11: 335–70.

Spade, Dean. 2011. *Normal Life: Administrative Violence, Critical Trans Politics, and the Limits of Law*. Cambridge, MA: South End Press.

Spelman, Elizabeth. 1988. *Inessential Woman: Problems of Exclusion in Feminist Thought*. Boston: Beacon Press.

Stacey, Judith. 1998. "Can There Be a Feminist Ethnography?" *Women's Studies International* 11: 21–27.

Stein, Arlene. 1989. "Three Models of Sexuality: Drives, Identities, Practices." *Sociological Theory* 7: 1–13.

———. 1997. *Sex and Sensibility: Stories of a Lesbian Generation*. Berkeley: University of California Press.

———. 2001. *The Stranger Next Door: The Story of a Small Community's Battle over Sex, Faith, and Civil Rights*. Boston: Beacon Press.

Stoler, Ann. 1995. *Race and the Education of Desire: Foucault's History of Sexuality and the Colonial Order of Things*. Durham, NC: Duke University Press.

Stryker, Susan. 2008. "Transgender History, Homonormativity, and Disciplinarity." *Radical History Review* 100: 145–57.

Sullivan, Andrew. 1996. *Virtually Normal*. New York: Vintage.

Sumara, Dennis, and Brent Davis. 1999. "Interrupting Heteronormativity: Toward a Queer Curriculum Theory." *Curriculum Inquiry* 29: 191–208.

Sycamore, Matt Bernstein. 2004. *That's Revolting! Queer Strategies for Resisting Assimilation*. Berkeley, CA: Soft Skull Press.

Thorne, Barrie, and Zella Luria. 1986. "Sexuality and Gender in Children's Daily Worlds." *Social Problems* 33: 176–90.

Tilcsik, András. 2011. "Pride and Prejudice: Employment Discrimination against Openly Gay Men in the United States." *American Journal of Sociology* 117: 586–626.

Trautner, Mary Nell. 2005. "Doing Gender, Doing Class: The Performance of Sexuality in Exotic Dance Clubs." *Gender and Society* 19: 771–88.

Tucker, Robert S. 1978. *The Marx-Engels Reader*. New York: Norton.

TuSmith, Bonnie. 2002. *Race in the College Classroom.* New Brunswick, NJ: Rutgers University Press.

US Census. 2012. "State and Country Quick Facts." http://quickfacts .census.gov/qfd/index.html (accessed August 9, 2012).

Vaid, Urvashi. 1996. *Virtual Equality: The Mainstreaming of Gay and Lesbian Liberation.* New York: Anchor Books.

Valocchi, Stephen. 2005. "Not Quite Queer Enough: The Lessons of Queer Theory for the Sociology of Gender and Sexuality." *Gender and Society* 19: 750–70.

Vidal-Ortiz, Salvador. 2008. "'The Puerto Rican Way Is More Tolerant': Constructions and Uses of 'Homophobia' among Santeria Practitioners Across Ethno-Racial and National Identification." *Sexualities* 11: 476–95.

Villarreal, Ana. 2010. "The Bus Owner, the Bus Driver, and His Lover: Gendered Class Struggle in the Service Work Triangle." *Work and Occupations* 37: 272–94.

Walters, Suzanna Danuta. 2001. *All The Rage: The Story of Gay Visibility in America.* Chicago: University of Chicago Press.

Ward, Elijah. 2005. "Homophobia, Hypermasculinity, and the US Black Church." *Culture, Health, and Sexuality* 7 (5): 493–504.

Ward, Jane. 2004. "'Not All Differences Are Created Equal': Multiple Jeopardy in a Gendered Organization." *Gender and Society* 18: 82–102.

———. 2008. *Respectably Queer: Diversity Culture in LGBT Activist Organizations.* Nashville, TN: Vanderbilt Press.

Weeks, Jeffrey. 1979. *Coming Out: Homosexual Politics in Britain from the Nineteenth Century to the Present.* London: Quartet Books.

———. 1981. *Sex, Politics and Society: The Regulation of Sexuality since 1800.* New York: Longman.

West, Candace, and Don H. Zimmerman. 1987. "Doing Gender." *Gender and Society* 1: 125–51.

———. 2009. "Accounting for Doing Gender." *Gender and Society* 23: 112–22.

Wetzstein, Cheryl, and Jennifer Harper. 2008. "Blacks, Hispanics Nixed Gay Marriage." *Washington Times*, November 8. www .washingtontimes.com/news/2008/nov/08/Blacks-hispanics-nixed-gay-marriage/.

Wharton, Amy. 1993. "The Affective Consequences of Service Work: Managing Emotions on the Job." *Work and Occupations* 20: 205–32.

White, E. Francis. 2001. *Dark Continent of Our Bodies: Black Feminism and the Politics of Respectability.* Philadelphia: Temple University Press.

Wilkins, Amy. 2012. "Stigma and Status: Interracial Intimacy and Intersectional Identities among Black College Men." *Gender and Society* 26: 165–89.

Williams, Christine L. 1992. "The Glass Escalator: Hidden Advantages for Men in the 'Female' Professions." *Social Problems* 39: 253–65.

———. 1995. *Still a Man's World.* Berkeley: University of California Press.

———. 2013. "The Glass Escalator Revisited: Gender Inequality in Neoliberal Times." *Gender and Society* 27: 609–29.

Williams, Christine L., and Catherine Connell. 2010. "'Looking Good and Sounding Right': Aesthetic Labor and Social Inequality in the Retail Industry." *Work and Occupations* 37: 349–77.

Williams, Christine L., and Patti Giuffre. 2011. "From Organizational Sexuality to Queer Organizations: Research on Homosexuality and the Workplace." *Sociological Compass* 5: 551–63.

Williams, Christine L., Patricia Giuffre, and Kirsten Dellinger. 2009. "The Gay-Friendly Closet." *Sexuality Research and Social Policy* 6: 29–45.

Wilson, William Julius. 1997. *When Work Disappears: The World of the New Urban Poor.* New York: Vintage.

Wingfield, Adia Harvey. 2009. "Racializing the Glass Escalator: Reconsidering Men's Experiences with Women's Work." *Gender and Society* 23: 5–26.

Woods, James D., and Jay H. Lucas. 1993. *The Corporate Closet: The Professional Lives of Gay Men in America.* Mankato, MN: Free Press.

Woods, Jeff. 2004. *Black Struggle, Red Scare: Segregation and Anti-communism in the South, 1948–1968.* Baton Rouge: Louisiana State University Press.

Woods, Sherry E., and Karen M. Harbeck. 1992. "Living in Two Worlds: The Identity Management Strategies Used by Lesbian Physical Educators." In *Coming Out of the Classroom Closet: Gay and*

Lesbian Students, Teachers, and Curriculum, edited by Karen M. Harbeck, 141–66. New York: Haworth Press.

Zelizer, Viviana A. 1994. *Pricing the Priceless Child: The Changing Social Value of Childhood.* Princeton, NJ: Princeton University Press.

Zinn, Maxine Baca, and Bonnie Thornton Dill. 1996. "Theorizing Difference from Multiracial Feminism." *Feminist Studies* 22: 321–31.

Zussman, Robert. 2004. "People in Places." *Qualitative Sociology* 27: 351–63.

INDEX